CRANFORD PUBLIC LIBRARY N.J.
3 9520 00152 9009

THE SEEKERS

A BOUNTY HUNTER'S STORY

THE SEEKERS

A BOUNTY HUNTER'S STORY

FINDING FELONS AND GUIDING MEN

JOSHUA ARMSTRONG

WITH

ANTHONY BRUNO

HarperCollins*Publishers*

HarperCollins books may be purchased for educational, business, or sales promotional use. For information please write: Special Markets Department, HarperCollins Publishers Inc., 10 East 53rd Street, New York, NY 10022.

FIRST EDITION

Designed by Philip Mazzone

Library of Congress Cataloging-in-Publication Data

ISBN 0–06–019343–3

00 01 02 03 04 10 9 8 7 6 5 4 3 2 1

For my beloved sons, Joshua Thomas Armstrong and Solomon Jon Armstrong. You two guys have motivated me to be the best I can be. I love you so much. And for Queen Mother Cindy Larraine Mills for the blessing you bestowed upon me. I could never repay you for them. All my love to the original protectors of my earliest evolution, Ms. Lulu B. Armstrong and Mr. Johnnie Lee Thomas. I owe it to all of you.

Our scientific power has outrun our spiritual power. We have guided missiles and misguided men.

—Martin Luther King, Jr.

Desiderata

Go placidly amid the noise and haste, and remember what peace there may be in silence.

As far as possible, without surrender, be on good terms with all persons.

Speak your truth quietly and clearly; and listen to others, even to the dull and ignorant; they too have their story.

Avoid loud and aggressive persons; they are vexatious to the spirit.

If you compare yourself with others, you may become bitter or vain, for always there will be greater and lesser persons than yourself.

Enjoy your achievements as well as your plans.

Keep interested in your career, however humble; it is a real possession in the changing fortunes of time.

Exercise caution in your business affairs, for the world is full of trickery.

But let this not blind you to what virtue there is; many persons strive for high ideals; and everywhere life is full of heroism.

Be yourself.

Especially do not feign affection.

Neither be cynical about love; for in the face of all aridity and disenchantment it is as perennial as grass.

Take kindly the counsel of the years, gracefully surrendering the things of youth.

Nurture strength of spirit to shield you in sudden misfortune. But do not distress yourself with imaginings. Many fears are born of fatigue and loneliness. Beyond a wholesome discipline, be gentle with yourself.

You are a child of the universe no less than the trees and stars; you have a right to be here. And whether or not it is clear to you, no doubt all things unfold as they should.

Therefore, be at peace with God, whatever you conceive Him to be, and whatever your labors and aspirations, in the noisy confusion of life, keep peace with your soul. With all its sham, drudgery, and broken dreams, it is still a beautiful world.

Be careful.

Strive to be happy.

—Anonymous

Contents

Acknowledgments

There's not enough room on one page to put all the people who guided my footsteps. I will thank all those who added to my evolution because if you know me personally, you know that in some way large or small you have added to my being the man that I am now.

To the Rokins family, the Whitfield family, the Dawkins family, the Seger family, Guy Steward, Richard Rodbart, Henry Yeager, Ace Conrad, Chief Brennan, Judge Triarsi, Judge Alley, Luke, Colt, Max, Isiah, Big Mike, Hawk, Ice Stone, Easy, Ram, 187, Films for the Grass Roots, Preston Whitmore, Wesley Snipes (Amen-Ra Films), Peter Chernin (20th Century Fox), Joe Roth, Mark Mayhew, Kimiko Jackson Fox, Wayne Slappy, Pattie Mills, Pete Mills, Michael George, Johnny McPherson, Mr. Mack (Mack's Bonding), Terry Foy, David and Debbie Gaestel, Mark Burg, Annie Carril Grumberg, Terrie Williams, the Hudlin Brothers, Monica Breckridge, the Harper family, Juanita Hadley, the Thomas Family, Beverly Muse, Ms. Dorothy Sellers, Lashawn, Walter Williams, Michael Hill, Richard E. Miller, Kanya V. McGee, James Holloway, Brother Winfred, Calvin Blue (Blue), Kalief Blue, Jane E.D.P., Dan Shannon, David and Hester Scott, Janet Laurel, Richard Smith, the Kemper family, the Derby Crew, Sarah S. Shelton, Jose and family, the

Crawford family, the Pridgen family, Ray Murphy, Ms. Lori Laken, Bill Duke, Planet Earth, D.L. Hughley, the Grant family, the Cox family, the Mills family, Solomon, Job, Jedidiah, Rock, Jeremiah, and Zora. To the good, the bad, and the misguided.

Hotep-Maat.

—Joshua Armstrong

Introduction

Bounty hunting, which is also commonly known as skip tracing, is the most misunderstood profession in America. Contrary to what most people think, bounty hunting is not illegal. In fact, bounty hunters provide a necessary service, often going into neighborhoods and situations that the police would never dream of entering. Bail enforcement agents (the high-class term for bounty hunters) are a vital link in the American system of justice. When persons accused of a crime violate the terms of their bail by fleeing, it's the bounty hunter who brings them back into the jurisdiction of the court.

The rights of bounty hunters, as agents of the bail bondsman, were defined in 1873 by the Supreme Court decision in the case of *Taylor* v. *Taintor:*

> When the bail is given, the principal is regarded as delivered to the custody of his sureties. Their domain is a continuance of the original imprisonment. Whenever they choose to do so, they may seize him and deliver him up to their discharge; and if it cannot be done at once, they may imprison him until it can be done. They may exercise their rights in person *or by agent* [italics added]. They may pursue him into another state; may arrest him on the Sab-

bath; and if necessary, may break and enter his house for that purpose. The seizure is not made by virtue of due process. None is needed. It is likened to the rearrest by the Sheriff of an escaping prisoner.

The Seekers are an association of spiritual researchers who fund their research through bounty hunting. We are unlike any other bounty hunters working today. We are dedicated professionals governed by self-discipline and self-awareness and guided by principles of conduct established thousands of years ago, which I adopted when I started to think about forming the Seekers in 1984. Admittedly my approach to bounty hunting is unusual. I believe in being prepared and doing my homework. I also believe that all fugitives have a better nature and that if I can reach out to a person's better nature, blood does not have to be shed. I don't believe in meeting force with force. I take an ancient Egyptian approach to my work based on my study of ancient Egyptian philosophy. Simply put, my beliefs come down to one basic concept: If you treat a man like a man, he will respond in a manly way; if you treat him like a beast, he will respond like a beast. In other words, you get what you give.

I don't consider all criminals victims of their circumstances, nor do I consider them deviants who should be locked away to prevent them from harming the rest of society. Except for the truly insane, criminals are people who have been thrust into a reality that they don't understand, and this lack of understanding has kept them from becoming responsible members of society; that is, men. (When I use the word *men* in this context, it transcends gender. A *man* is a person who has evolved to a point where he can receive wisdom. A person who has not reached this state cannot comprehend wisdom, let alone benefit from it. I don't use this word as a slight against women, but since the overwhelming majority of criminals are in fact male, I think it's appropriate that I address the problems of males who have not become *men*.)

The Seekers never break the law when looking for a fugitive. In most cases I use the services of an information analyst, a retired FBI agent who legitimately sells information culled from all kinds of data bases. If my information analyst can get me an address, I can then go into what I call "street mode."

Typically I'll stake out the address to see if the fugitive is living there. If after a day or two I don't see him going in or coming out, I'll check the mailbox to see if mail is being delivered to him. If it's an apartment building, I'll look for his last name on the buzzer grid. If someone other than the fugitive is living at the address, I'll pay for a toll trace on the phone to see if there's a calling pattern. For instance, if I'm checking out an apartment in Brooklyn where a woman is apparently living alone, and I see that she's receiving calls from phone booths in the Dublin, Georgia, area every other day, then I have good reason to suspect that my fugitive may be in Dublin, Georgia. I'll then use my contacts in Georgia to see if the fugitive is down there.

Bounty hunting the way we do it takes patience. Obtaining vital information isn't like ordering a Big Mac at the drive-through counter. It must be slowly pried out of those who have it. For example, if I'm looking for someone who lives in or frequents a drug-infested area of the inner city, I'll go to the address I have and look for the closest drug fiend I can find. I'll strike up a conversation, ask him about things I'm not really interested in, then give him five or ten dollars before I leave. A few days later I'll come back, find that person, and do the same thing again. This junkie won't trust me any more than he did the first day, but now he sees me as a ready source of cash. The next time I come, I'll show him a few hundred dollars and ask him for the information I'm really seeking. In most cases the junkie will tell me what he knows.

Without a doubt, nothing pries open tight lips better than money, but sometimes the money I spend for information goes to good use. Male fugitives often leave their women in dire straits when they take off. If I can locate a fugitive's wife or live-in girlfriend, and I see that she's struggling to feed her kids, I'll take her out and buy groceries for them. I'll give her rent money. I'll play with the kids and show her pictures of my own two sons to convince her that I understand what it's like to be a parent. Sometimes I can reason with the woman, prove to her that her life isn't going to get any better by helping her man stay in the wind. But sometimes a woman's loyalty to her man can't be broken, so in those cases I have to be stealthy. If she lets me into her home, I'll wait until she's out of the room, then look for a phone bill, an address book, letters, anything that will give me another nugget of information I can build on.

If the woman has no children and I sense that she's the type who won't listen to reason, I'll engage her in conversation and maybe tell her that I have a good deal or a job for her man, anything that will gain her trust and get me closer to my target. But for better or worse, money makes the world go round, and when I dangle it in front of someone who needs it, she'll generally tell me just about anything.

The mothers of fugitives are another good source of information. This may seem surprising until you think about it. These women care about their sons. They're often afraid that if their boys are caught by the police, they'll be beaten and possibly killed. A bounty hunter may rough up a fugitive, but to get paid, he has to "bring 'em back alive." Also, if a fugitive is on drugs, his mother doesn't want him out on the streets stealing and shooting up. Better for her son to be in prison than in an AIDS ward or on a slab at the morgue.

In our community in New Jersey, the Seekers have a reputation for finding fugitives and treating them fairly. We have never beaten a fugitive gratuitously; we only use as much force as is necessary to subdue and restrain. For this reason many mothers of fugitives have come to us and asked that we find their sons.

The essence of our philosophy is contained in the Seeker insignia—a caduceus inside a triangle and a circle. The triangle represents the pyramid; its three planes stand for wisdom, knowledge, and understanding as well as the mental, physical, and spiritual realms. The circle represents completion. The two snakes of the caduceus represent the balance of the head and the heart, thinking and feeling. The snakes are entwined around the staff of life. The wings symbolize self-mastery. When a person is admitted to the Seekers, the insignia serves as a constant reminder that his or her life must be guided by these principles. Each one of us wears it proudly.

Whenever we go out on a mission, our goal is to apprehend the fugitive, not punish him. Retribution is not our job. Our shotguns are always initially loaded with Blammo Ammo, rubber cartridges that do not penetrate flesh. We also use incendiary rounds that shoot out fireballs, which will scare a target more than harm him. The first rounds in our handguns are always Glaser Safety Slugs, bullets that do not ricochet, thus minimizing the chances of hitting innocent bystanders. But in

almost twenty years as a bounty hunter, I have only had to fire my gun once during a capture. The Seekers have never been sued, and we've never picked up the wrong person. In fact, many of our former targets speak very highly of us, particularly those who have been picked up previously by other bounty hunters. A few have even recommended us to the families of other fugitives: "Have the Seekers find your son," these people say. "The Seekers will treat him right."

But does our method of bounty hunting work?

Currently the Seekers have an 85 percent capture rate. The industry standard is under 50 percent. The only fugitives who have ever eluded us are the ones who left the country—except, of course, for the ones who ran to countries where we have contacts and assists: Canada, Mexico, Puerto Rico, and the Dominican Republic.

Enlightenment is vital to becoming a Seeker. If your mind is not prepared to receive knowledge, you are not ready to become a Seeker.

It should not be assumed that everyone possesses a mind, because you're not born with one the way you're born with a brain. A mind must be acquired and cultivated. People commonly say that someone has lost his or her mind. But you can't lose your mind if you've never found it. To evolve, you have to find your mind.

Those who haven't found their minds are subject to all kinds of influences—good, bad, and just plain wasteful. To cultivate a mind properly, a person must be plugged into a constant flow of new information and challenging ideas. It only stands to reason that if you keep recycling the same old materials, your mind will not develop and you will not evolve. To get a dial tone on a telephone, you have to plug it into the jack. It's the same thing with the mind.

Reading is an excellent way to get a dial tone for the mind. It lets information in and makes the individual decide what's worthwhile and what isn't. Television, on the other hand, does little to stimulate the mind. It's a medium designed for passive absorption. Most of the time it just shoots out rapid-fire images, providing no opportunity for critical evaluation. Television is an all-or-nothing proposition, take it or leave it. It's like trying to get a drink of water from a fire hose going full blast. You end up all wet but still thirsty.

The best way to develop the mind is by cultivating the spirit. Regrettably, many people turn to organized religion for the care and feeding of their spiritual lives when in fact organized religion is often more interested in emotionalism than spirituality. Going to church on Sunday can be like being in a bar fight where fists are flying, glass is breaking, and bodies are falling. With all the singing, preaching, and hallelujahs, the service becomes a blinding emotional whirlwind. The spirit is a delicate plant; it cannot thrive under the tumultuous conditions presented in that kind of church service. Myths, parables, swelling music, testimonials, hysteria—none of this helps the spirit develop. True spirituality comes through lessons that are applicable to everyday life. This was the way ancient Egyptian spirituality was taught—through the here and now, the chores and choices we have before us in this world, not through fantastic tales of what will be in a place no living person has ever seen.

The answers we seek are not inside a church or on an altar or on the lips of a preacher. They are within us. If, through the pursuit of the spirit, we can connect with our own minds, the answers will be there. We will choose our own destinies. We will not be subject to random influences. We will have our minds and never lose them.

Before I will even consider a prospective candidate for the Seekers, he or she must read seven books. The list changes from time to time, but most often it includes some or all of the following: *At the Feet of the Master* by Alcyone; *The Kybalion* by the Three Initiates Staff; *The Secret Science, The Science of Love,* and *The Stellar Man,* all by John Baines; *The Code of the Samurai* by A. L. Sadler from the original text by Daidoji Yuzan; *The Art of War* by Sun Tzu; and *The Tactical Edge* by Charles Remsbert.

The Code of the Samurai teaches the importance of self-discipline when you are a member of a team. *The Art of War* deals with the wisdom of strategy and tactics when trying to achieve an objective. *The Tactical Edge* is a nuts-and-bolts textbook on street survival.

At the Feet of the Master, The Kybalion, The Secret Science, The Science of Love, and *The Stellar Man* are all works of ancient Egyptian philosophy. They deal with the individual's place in the universe and how all people can evolve and raise themselves to higher states. These works are not easily digested in one reading, and I always recommend that they be revisited every so often to discover new layers of meaning.

For day-to-day guidance, I always recommend *To Heal a People* by

Erriel Kufi Addae. It's a short book, but it's direct, full of solid advice and essential wisdom for living successfully within a society. If I am ever in doubt about how I should conduct myself in a given situation, *To Heal a People* will usually point me in the right direction.

After prospective Seeker candidates have read the books, they must then complete a thirteen-page, seventy-seven-question test that I have put together. The questions deal with attitudes about people as well as methods of bounty hunting. Those who are accepted into the Seekers must also read at least one book a month and discuss it with their fellow Seekers. Street smarts alone will not get you in.

Whenever a new person is accepted, we always have an initiation ceremony, a trial by fire, if you will. The initiate is taken blindfolded to the top floor of a high-rise project in one of the roughest sections of Newark, New York City, or Philadelphia, whichever place is most unfamiliar to the initiate. This ceremony always takes place on a Saturday after midnight. After counting to a hunded, the initiate is allowed to remove the blindfold. To complete the test, all he or she has to do is walk down the twenty-five or so flights of steps to the ground floor. All alone. A few of us may stay inside out of sight just in case, but basically it's a test of the person's will and composure. A person who shows no fear and betrays no feelings of superiority should be able to go anywhere unscathed. The people who encounter trouble are the ones whose faces reveal inner doubts and prejudices. So far none of our chosen candidates have failed the test. The ceremony then continues at our rural West Virginia compound for three days of intense study and self-reflection.

To remain in the Seekers, rigorous physical training at least four times a week is mandatory. Our regimen includes running (road and obstacle course), weight lifting, boxing, small-circle jujitsu, and weapons training. A fugitive will do anything to keep his freedom, and in most cases these people are young, strong, and agile. If you can't keep up with them, you don't belong in the chase. Fugitives from the law also tend to be armed, so besides marksmanship, we practice "sleight of hand," the art of drawing handguns from all possible angles and positions.

All Seekers must sign a performance contract stipulating that they will do a specified amount of work, training, and reading. If a member fails to perform his obligations, he's out, and over the years I've had to ask a few members to leave. Each Seeker also owns stock in the company and has one vote when major decisions have to be made.

For anonymity, each Seeker takes on a Seeker name, which we use whenever we're on a mission. If a fugitive were to overhear our real names, he might possibly track us down later and try to get payback. Occasionally that has happened despite all our precautions; still, we do whatever we can to minimize the danger. (To protect the Seekers' identities, I will limit my descriptions of them, omitting most physical and facial details.)

"Jedidiah" is known for his uncanny undercover techniques. I often take him as my partner when a job presents unusual obstacles. He joined the Seekers in 1987.

As his Seeker name implies, "Rock" is the muscle of the team as well as our electronics specialist. He came on board in 1989.

"Job," who started in 1990, is the oldest member of the Seekers. He's also my cousin. His specialties are backup and close-encounter takedowns.

"Zora," who is Hispanic, was admitted in 1991 and is currently our only female Seeker, though in the past there have been others. Her specialties are undercover surveillance and entrapment. To lure a cunning man, a woman is often the best bait available.

"Jeremiah" became a Seeker in 1994. He's a former pro football player and the only white member of the Seekers. His areas of expertise are communications, physical fitness, and police science.

"Solomon" is our most recent recruit.

Though not formally a Seeker, "Rick" is an invaluable associate. He's the gunsmith who customizes our weapons and makes all of our ammunition by hand. He also keeps us up to date with the latest in weapons and surveillance technology.

The Seekers never work on a single case as a group. Usually we work in pairs, sometimes trios. However, I make sure each member is apprised of all the cases the Seekers are working on so that we can pool information. What may seem like an irrelevant tidbit to one Seeker may be a vital lead to another. Without a steady flow of accurate information, we wouldn't be half as effective as we are.

Most of the initial information we get about a fugitive comes from the bail bondsman who hires us. In general, bounty hunters work for bondsmen, not for the police or the courts (although in a few special cases the Seekers have been asked by judges or police officials to assist in bringing in particularly difficult individuals). Bounty hunters primarily deal with fugitives who have violated the terms of their release on bail. Typically when a suspect is arrested and bail is set, that person will go to a bondsman to make the bail. Naturally the bondsman doesn't dig into his own pocket for the cash. Instead, he secures a bond from an insurance company, which guarantees that the court will be paid the full amount of bail if the accused fails to make his or her court dates. To obtain a bond, the bondsman pays 3 percent of the total amount of bail. The bondsman then charges the defendant a nonrefundable fee, which is usually 10 percent of the bail, and demands collateral worth at least as much as the bail amount, which can be seized if the defendant absconds. If the defendant fails to make the mandatory court dates and cannot be found, the bondsman is obligated to pay the court in full. The insurance company that wrote the bond actually pays the money to the court and initiates foreclosure on the collateral property. But foreclosures can take a lot of time, and like anyone else, these companies would prefer to get paid sooner rather than later, so if the bondsman wants to continue working with that insurer, he had better do his best to find the absconder as soon as possible. And to do that, the bondsman will often hire a freelance bounty hunter.

Bounty hunters typically charge 10 percent of the outstanding bail plus expenses to bring in a bail jumper. For out-of-state pickups we charge a flat 20 percent. Since the jumper is a fugitive from justice, the rules of due process do not apply. A search warrant is not necessary to enter his residence or any other location where he's believed to be. The bounty hunter needs only a copy of the "bail piece" (the paperwork relevant to that person's fugitive status) and in most states, a private detective's license, which all the Seekers have. Some states also require a certified copy of the bond.

Unfortunately, most of the bounty hunters working today are wannabe cops. They're usually armed to the teeth when they go out to make an arrest, and they have flashing lights and sirens installed on their vehicles. A badass attack dog is another typical accessory. Their operating procedure is very simple: meet force with even more force.

In 1997 the profession suffered an unneeded black eye when a band of five so-called bounty hunters broke into a home in Phoenix, Arizona, and touched off a firefight with a young man who was in bed with his girlfriend. Two of the intruders were wounded by the young man before he and his girlfriend were finally shot to death. As a result of this incident, bounty hunters around the country were vilified in the press, and politicians demanded a thorough investigation of the entire industry. But what was not widely reported in the press were the findings of the subsequent police investigation. The men in question were in fact not bounty hunters at all; they were burglars. They had told the arresting officers they were bounty hunters, hoping to escape prosecution. It is truly regrettable that the standards in this profession have sunk so low that petty thieves think they can protect themselves from prosecution by pretending to be one of us.

The Seekers are not wanna-be cops, and we will never be confused with criminals. I believe that many—if not most—of the bounty hunters working today abuse the position by having no training or self-discipline. Bounty hunting is not about guns and gear and breaking heads; it's about dealing with people. Unfortunately, many bounty hunters don't understand this. What's worse, they often start to feel they're above the law and don't have to answer to any authority.

Because the Seekers must answer to a higher spiritual authority, we don't step over the bounds. Though we don't subscribe to any formal religion, we recognize the power of a Supreme Being and the order that the Supreme Being imposed upon the world. We believe in treating people like "hue-man" beings because all persons—regardless of what side of the law they are on—are valuable for the unique color they bring to the spectrum of life.

As it says in the "Desiderata," "all things unfold as they should." This is the Seekers' motto. Things happen because they are meant to happen. If we capture a fugitive, it was meant to be; if we *fail* to capture a fugitive, that was also meant to be. It's not our job to alter events and force change. We are simply the instruments of the Supreme Being.

—Joshua Armstrong

Dedication to Dimitrius

Seven candles burn bright against the darkness. Suddenly, without warning, one is snuffed out by a stealthy force. The others must burn brighter, hoping to expose the source of their brother's untimely demise.

On February 14, 1998, one of our members died at the age of thirty, leaving a wife and five children. His Seeker name was Dimitrius, which also happened to be his real middle name. Our Seeker names tend to describe us better than our given names. Dimitrius selected a name that reflected his extraordinary strength and determination. He had been a Marine, and his military training brought a sense of protocol to the Seekers. He also possessed a special gift for getting right to the point, and he had moved up swiftly through our ranks.

In the weeks before Dimitrius died, he had been collecting intelligence, cruising the local bars in and around Elizabeth, New Jersey, which is one of our local bases, talking to people, asking questions, greasing palms, picking up tidbits about fugitives we had been hired to find. Though he didn't drink alcohol, he must have ordered at least one soft drink in every bar he'd gone to, and these were the kind of raucous joints the police normally won't even go into, the kind of places where patrons are frisked at the door and weapons are checked with the bouncer. When I learned of his death, my first thought was that he had been poisoned, that someone had put something in his drink. Perhaps he had asked too many questions or asked the wrong questions or just gotten to the point a little too quickly for somebody's comfort.

An autopsy was performed on his body, but the results were inconclusive. Toxicology tests were performed, but no toxins were found. More tests were performed, but still the state medical examiner's office could not say for sure why he died. Another battery of tests was conducted, and those results were also inconclusive.

One doctor suggested that a tiny screen that had been placed in a large artery in his leg the year before had come loose and caused a fatal blockage in the flow of blood to his heart. The screen had been installed to prevent clotting after Dimitrius suffered a rifle wound as a result of walking in on an armed robbery that went bad at a local bar. Dimitrius had not been a good patient, and I felt he hadn't given himself enough time to recover. Whenever I suggested that he take it easy for a while, he'd just smile and insist that he *was* taking it easy. He'd joke about his injury and say it was nothing. But it wasn't "nothing." The gunshot had left a hole in his leg so big he could stick his thumb through it.

Dimitrius's good humor had carried us through many tense situations. He knew how to handle himself with power and compassion in equal measure. He was a big man, capable of subduing people much larger than himself, but he never abused his power; it merely enhanced his being. Like all the Seekers, he was not defined by the job of bounty hunting. According to ancient Egyptian philosophy, a stellar man is not defined by what he does. He makes his vocation; it doesn't make him. He makes the job more than it was before he got there. Dimitrius was undeniably a stellar man. He was the living embodiment of the Seekers' code.

We will not rest until we learn the exact cause of his death, and we are still conducting our own investigation into the matter. He has been replaced in our ranks by his first cousin Solomon, but we will never forget him. Seven candles burn bright, seeking truths, in memory of our fallen brother.

Author's Note

This is a book about evolution—my personal evolution and the evolution of the Seekers, the organization I formed for the purpose of apprehending fugitives while researching the mental, physical, and spiritual sciences. My story unfolds more or less chronologically, as it actually happened, through my eyes and my experiences.

The Seekers are an ever-changing group; some members, like Job and Jedidiah, have been with me almost from the beginning, while others are more recent inductees. As you will see, the narrative reflects the individual members' tenure. Those who have worked closest and longest with me naturally appear more often in the book, while mention of the newer members reflects their level of experience. I haven't deliberately overlooked anyone or unjustly favored anyone. We are all equal within the Seekers. It is simply a matter of evolution. In time, every Seeker will have his or her own wealth of stories to tell.

Every person who appears in this book is real. I have changed the names of the fugitives whose captures are portrayed in these pages, as well as the names of their friends, associates, and loved ones. I have also changed some of the locations. I believe that a person's past should not poison his or her future. What's done is done. Leave it in the past. Everyone has the choice to stay the same or evolve. If a person chooses to remain stagnant and make the same mistakes over and over again, so be it. But it's not my job to brand that person. He brands himself.

THE SEEKERS

A BOUNTY HUNTER'S STORY

1 Seeking Truth

It's Christmas morning, 1998, and the sun isn't even up yet. Most people are still in bed. But I'm not concerned about Christmas or presents or any of that because I'm here on business. Right now I have to put all extraneous thoughts out of my head and focus on what has to be done. If I don't, my two sons may never see their daddy alive again.

I'm walking down the sidewalk with two of my fellow Seekers, Job and Rock, in this poor but respectable neighborhood of detached wood-frame one- and two-family houses in Jersey City, New Jersey. The Seekers are an elite team of bail enforcement officers, more commonly known as bounty hunters. We are here this morning "seeking" a young man named Ray-Ray.

Ray-Ray is a fugitive from justice. Two months ago he was scheduled to face drug charges in Newark, but he skipped out on his bail. He's living in Gainesville, Florida, now, getting ready to set up shop down there, but he's back home to visit his mom for the holidays. (This is the most common mistake fugitives make: going home for the holidays. Christmas, Thanksgiving, and Mother's Day are the busiest days of the year for a bounty hunter.) Ray-Ray intends to leave for Florida tonight right after dinner. I know all this because I talked to his mother earlier this week. She's worried sick about her son, afraid of what might happen to him if the police catch him or what he might do to others. She'd heard about the Seekers and our reputation for taking people in with minimal violence. That's why she called me and asked if we'd take her boy in before someone else did.

As we walk along the cold pavement, Job, Rock, and I are silent. The thin layer of snow that fell two days ago melted yesterday and refroze overnight, forming a crust on the ground that amplifies our footsteps as we approach the gray two-family house that we've been scouting all week. As we enter through the driveway and go to the rear of the house, I don't have to tell either man what to do. They know the plan. Rock will wait downstairs and cover the back door. Job and I will go inside.

Quietly I open the screen door, then turn the knob on the inner door. It's unlocked, which is just what I expect. Ray-Ray's mother agreed to leave it unlocked for us. She also let me know that Ray-Ray is an early riser who likes to start the day with a long hot shower.

As we enter the house, Job—broad-shouldered and in his fifties—takes out his gun, a Glock 9mm semi-automatic. I pull out my identical Glock. Rock is also carrying a Glock. We always carry the same weapons when we make an arrest, just in case. If one of us runs out of ammo, either of the other two can throw him a spare clip.

Inside, Job and I mount the wooden stairs that lead up to the first-floor apartment. We take each step carefully to minimize the squeaks. We're both wearing identical black parkas and black Polartec masks that cover the lower halves of our faces. Our insignia is on the breast pockets of our parkas, a caduceus inside a triangle and a circle.

Job and I enter through the back door of Ray-Ray's mother's apartment, the kitchen door. The room is warm, and the smells of home cooking just about break my heart. There's a ham in the oven—I can smell it—and a sweet-potato casserole on top of the stove, waiting to go in. A coconut layer cake is on the counter, a plate of butter cookies on the table. I know how hard it must be for this woman to turn her son in.

The apartment is quiet except for the sound of the running shower. Job and I move from the kitchen to the parlor. A small artificial Christmas tree is sitting on top of the television. A few wrapped presents are on the floor under the window. *Presents the woman has bought for her son?* I wonder. Suddenly I think of my own sons.

Job moves down the hallway toward the front of the house while I cover the bathroom door. He checks all the rooms to make sure no one is home, even though I'd instructed Ray-Ray's mother to clear out of the place if she could. She'd told me her son had a gun, but I would have assumed that even if she hadn't told me.

Through the door, I can hear Ray-Ray moving around in the shower. I imagine him washing his hair, rinsing out the shampoo, thinking he's got it made, thinking he's going to score big when he gets back to Gainesville and starts selling weed and blow to all the college kids once they get back from Christmas break. The world is his oyster. I'm sure he isn't thinking about the court date he missed or the bail bondsman who's now responsible for paying his $75,000 bond to the court. That's what *I'm* thinking about.

Job returns and gives me a nod. The woman has left; no one else is around. We exchange glances, my hand on the doorknob. Both our guns are pointed up. The shower is still running. I turn the knob carefully and open the door. We slip in quietly, and Job shuts the door behind him, leaving it open just a crack.

The small room is steamy, the mirror fogged over. Job and I take our positions, shoulder-to-shoulder, just on the other side of the mint-green plastic shower curtain, our masks still on. We wait for Ray-Ray to finish his shower.

I concentrate on my breathing, willing myself to stay calm and loose. I've been in this position countless times, but you only have to be careless once to regret it. I'm here to take away a man's freedom. A man will fight to the death for that; I've seen it happen many times before. Ray-Ray may be naked and he may be vulnerable, but I can't fool myself. He's still dangerous.

Thoughts swirl through my mind, interfering with my focus. *Is this really Ray-Ray?* I wonder. *Could it be his mother or some other relative who's in there? Is this even the right house?*

But I quickly dispel these doubts. The Seekers always do their homework. In twelve years we've made over two thousand apprehensions, and in that time we've never taken the wrong person or gone into the wrong house.

After a few minutes Ray-Ray finally turns off the water and whips the shower curtain open. I exhale slowly, widening the scope of my gaze so that I can see his whole body, not just his face or hands. Blindly he reaches for a towel, but his hand bumps into the body armor encasing my chest. Ray-Ray's eyes shoot open.

He's just twenty-six years old, but his baby face has been hardened by the streets. He immediately looks for a way out, his eyes quickly shifting from me to Job, then ricocheting to the toilet. The lid is down, a pair of jeans piled on top. Ray-Ray suddenly reaches down for the jeans, but I snatch his wrist and hold it. Job grabs the jeans and searches the pockets. He finds a small silver-plated .25 automatic, a typical weapon for a player like Ray-Ray.

Ray-Ray tries to pull away from my grip. "What the fuck you doin'? Let go of my hand."

I don't let go, and I don't speak until he looks me in the eye. "You screwed up, Ray-Ray," I say, keeping my voice even and nonjudgmental. "It's time to settle up."

"What're you talking about? Get the hell out of here before I call the cops on you." He struggles to get free, but he can't break my grip.

Again I wait for him to look me in the eye. "You're the one who brought us here, Ray-Ray. You know that."

He's confused, not sure who we are. Are we cops or thugs? I can see from his face that his mind is racing. *What do they want?* he's wondering. *Who sent them?* He's looking down, looking up, not looking at us.

Job reaches in to grab his other wrist. "Come on. Get out of the tub," he says.

But Ray-Ray recoils from him and glances at the window next to the sink.

I yank him forward to get his attention and just shake my head no. Ray-Ray stares at me, but he doesn't move. It's not unusual for a man in his position to leap through a window, but at least Ray-Ray has the sense to realize that we're probably not alone and someone must be covering the outside of the house. Ray-Ray's self-esteem has already taken a heavy hit. Lying naked face down in the snow with Rock on top of him won't improve it.

Ray-Ray's legs are shaking now. They're not holding him up, so he squats down before he collapses. "Oh, man," he whimpers, clutching his knees. "Fuckin' bounty hunters. That's what you are." He's staring up at our masks and matching jackets.

No doubt Ray-Ray has heard stories about bounty hunters, and he knows how cruel and vicious they can be. "Don't take me like this," he pleads. "Please, man. Lemme at least have my pants. I don't want my mother seeing you take me like this."

"Get dressed," I tell him. Job hands him his jeans.

But Ray-Ray just looks up at me, giving me a suspicious squint. He expects us to be the kind of kick-ass bounty hunters he's seen on TV. He assumes we're going to treat him like a mad dog.

I toss him a towel. "Hurry up and get dressed so you can say good-bye to your mom and wish her a Merry Christmas." I assume she hasn't gone far.

But Ray-Ray just squints at me. He doesn't get it. He thinks we should be beating him.

Slowly he stands up and starts to dry himself. "How'd you find me?" he mumbles.

"Never mind about that," I tell him. "You've got other things to worry about." He doesn't need to know that it was his mother who turned him in.

Job and I escort him to a bedroom where he finishes dressing. There are two twin beds in the room and a big poster of the singing group En Vogue on the wall. Ray-Ray is calm now, and he's cooperating. If he stays this way, I won't cuff him until we get into the car. There's no reason to humiliate him in front of his neighbors unless he forces the issue.

Silently Job and I watch him get dressed. I'm thinking about his mother and his little brother who's in the sixth grade. In my pocket I've got a copy of "Desiderata," a seventeenth-century prayer. It says in part:

> *You are a child of the universe no less than the trees and stars; you have a right to be here. And whether or not it is clear to you, no doubt all things unfold as they should.*

. . . With all its sham, drudgery, and broken dreams, it is still a beautiful world.

Be careful.

Strive to be happy.

Whenever I take a man from his home, I leave a copy of this poem for his family. On the way out I'll leave this copy on the kitchen table next to the plate of Christmas cookies. Most likely there will be a lot of crying and fretting over Ray-Ray today, but my concern is for his little brother. The boy should understand that he's not tainted by his big brother's fate. Bad things happen because of man's interference with God's plan. Still people should have hope, and they should learn how to activate it. Yes, there is nastiness and brutality all around us, but it is still a beautiful world. I want Ray-Ray's brother to understand that.

We go out through the kitchen. Job stays close to Ray-Ray, ready to tackle him if he tries to bolt, but I have a feeling Ray-Ray isn't that foolish. I glance up at the clock on the wall over the stove. It's a little after 7 a.m. We have to get Ray-Ray squared away, then get moving. I'm hoping to make five more pickups before the day is through. This won't be a Merry Christmas for everybody.

I watch Ray-Ray's face as we go down the back stairs. He's scared and disgusted, upset that his plans have been changed for him. I wonder where he went wrong, what influence in his young life sent him down the wrong path. Unfortunately, Ray-Ray's story is not unique. It happens to far too many young men. I see it every day.

As Job and I escort Ray-Ray out the back door of his mother's house, he grumbles and curses under his breath, indicating that he could have made it back to Florida if someone hadn't "ratted" on him. In fact, he didn't stand a chance of escaping from the Seekers. If we hadn't caught him today, we would have caught up with him later, wherever he was. But Job and I decline to debate the issue with Ray-Ray. He's miserable enough and needs to be alone with his thoughts now.

Every fugitive I've ever encountered is running from the same thing—the truth. My job is to find fugitives and present them with the truth, the truth of their own situations. Locating a person on the run is never easy. Information must be obtained, sources have to be worked, informants have to be paid. Occasionally I get lucky and a hunch will pay off, but that doesn't make the truth any easier to stomach, either for the fugitive or for me.

In the winter of 1996 I was asked to find a young man whose truth was pretty hard to take. I was hired by his grandmother, an elderly white woman from the suburbs whose house was about to be seized by a bail bondsman. She had put up her home as collateral to secure a $100,000 bond for her twenty-four-year-old grandson who was wanted on a variety of drug and firearms charges, including possession of a "defaced weapon"—in other words, a sawed-off shotgun. The grandson, whose name was David, had missed several court dates, and the court was demanding that the bondsman pay the bail. The bondsman had already initiated proceedings against the grandmother, which is exactly how the system works. If the person who put up the collateral knows where the fugitive is, threat of foreclosure usually gets that person to give up the fugitive. But in this case the grandmother genuinely didn't know where David was, and she was on the verge of losing everything she had.

I got David's file from the bondsman, but it was pretty thin. David had a monster drug habit. He once told the police on the record that he didn't have a monkey on his back, he had a gorilla—a four-bag-a-day heroin habit. He had never held down a regular job in his life and didn't have a regular address. He supported his habit by stealing whatever he could get his hands on. From the time David had dropped out of high school, he'd sponged off other people, crashing with various friends and fellow drug fiends until he inevitably wore out his welcome and had to move on. I tried processing his Social Security number to get a lead on his whereabouts, but that netted me zero. This was the kind of job that was going to have to be done with sweet talk and shoe leather.

I found out from one of the police reports in David's file that he had turned his high school sweetheart on to dope. The girl had kicked at one time, but David drew her back in. Now she was feeding a pretty serious habit of her own. But in spite of all that, she remained loyal to David. It was a true junkie love story.

The girlfriend's name was Lori, and the report listed her last known address as her parents' house. I went to pay a visit and wasn't surprised to find that Lori hadn't lived there in quite some time. The parents were too angry with their daughter's behavior to talk about it, but Lori's sister Megan agreed to meet me at a coffee shop.

Megan told me that she tried to stay in touch with her sister as much as possible, but it was getting more and more difficult. Lori didn't want anything to do with her parents or her old life, and recently that blanket rejection had started to include Megan. She told me that she thought Lori might stand a better chance of kicking her habit if she could get away from David. Putting David away for a couple of years might do wonders for both of them, Megan felt. I asked her what she could tell me about David and Lori's current location, and she told me that as far as she knew, they moved around a lot but mainly stayed at crummy motels on Routes 1 and 9 between Newark and Woodbridge.

I knew the area and the establishments she was talking about very well. One and Nine are truck routes that pass through Newark Airport and the oil refineries in Linden, the industrial area that most out-of-staters think of when they think of New Jersey. That stretch of highway has dozens of seedy motels that are havens for hookers and drug fiends.

I asked Megan if there was anything else she could tell me.

Megan sighed into her coffee cup. Her expression had gone from hopeful to near hopeless in the short time we had talked. Laying out all the details of a bad situation in one big heap can do that to a person. "The last time I saw Lori," Megan said, "she was driving a beat-up Ford Escort. It was either black or dark blue. I only saw it at night."

"Do you know the plate number?" I asked.

She shook her head.

I thanked her for her help, but I didn't hold out any promises. David and Lori were swimming down at the deep end. For all anyone knew, they could be in a morgue somewhere, piled up with all the other bodies that come in without identification.

But I did have the make and model of their vehicle and a place to start looking, so it wasn't totally hopeless. That evening I called my cousin Job and asked him to start checking the motels on the south-bound side of 1 and 9 for a dark-colored Escort driven by a young couple with a nasty smack habit. I told him I'd take the northbound side of the highway. If one of us found anything promising, we'd call the other for backup before making an approach.

After searching for five hours, we both came up empty. We met up at an all-night diner on the highway at around 1 a.m.

"Not too many dark-colored Escorts out there," Job said. He was sitting on the other side of a booth from me. His face never betrayed his feelings, but I could tell that he had his doubts about this job. Our waitress came by and brought two cups of tea.

I stifled a yawn. I was tired, but I was more annoyed that we hadn't found David or Lori, and I was worried about David's grandmother losing her house. "I have a feeling they're out here someplace," I said.

"Well, they're not here tonight." Job stirred honey into his tea.

We sipped our tea quietly, then started mapping out a strategy for finding the couple. We agreed to start again first thing the next day.

After we paid the bill, Job got into his car and headed for home. I did the same. But as I drove toward Elizabeth on 1 and 9, I kept thinking about David and his grandmother. I had a hunch he was here and that somehow we had just managed to miss him. Impulsively I pulled off at a jug-handle U-turn and headed back toward the motel district. I wanted to check the parking lots one more time.

Twenty minutes later I was pulling into the parking lot of a place called the Amboy Motel, and immediately I spotted a black Escort with filthy windows and a bashed-in rear panel. It was parked out front. I drove over to the front office and parked there, then went inside to see the manager, a pear-shaped Indian man who was wearing a pastel blue dress shirt open at the collar.

"I'm looking for some friends of mine," I said. "They're supposed to be staying here." I described David and Lori, and the manager told me that they were in Room 1.

I headed over to Room 1 and noticed that the door to Room 2 was wide open. The twenty-inch television on top of the dresser was on, and a pair of legs dangled off the bed. I couldn't see the face in the shadows, but I wondered what this person's story was. Had he just passed out like that? Or was he waiting for someone to come by?

I knocked on the door to Room 1.

No one answered.

I kept knocking. "Hey, David," I said. "You in there, man?"

"He ain't here," a woman's voice came back. She sounded hoarse and sleepy.

"Don't mess with me, woman. I need to talk to David."

"Go away. He ain't here."

I tried the door, but it was locked, so I went back to see the manager. I pulled out my bail enforcement agent's badge and held it in front of his face. "Three seconds," I said. "Either you open up Room 1 for me or I break it down."

"No, no, no, no, no!" the manager said, coming around the desk, his hands fluttering. "I will open it! I will open it! I do not want damage."

I followed him back to Room 1, where he used his passkey to open the door.

"Stand back," I said, moving him aside before he threw the door open.

"Fine," he said and scurried back to the front office.

I pulled out my gun and opened the door. What I found shocked even me.

Splayed out on the bed was David in his undershorts with Lori in a dirty T-shirt curled up next to him. She was a mess, but he was beyond belief. The man had so many holes in him he was literally oozing all over the place. The bed cover was splotched yellow with his puss. He had shot dope into every conceivable part of his body. He looked like a one-man plague. I was hesitant even to get near him.

Fortunately, I had a pair of surgical gloves in my pocket, which I always carry when I'm out looking for drug fiends.

"Stay where you are," I said as I pulled on the gloves.

Lori was sitting up now. "Who the fuck're you?"

I trained the gun on David, who only lifted his head and squinted at me.

"Put your hands on your head," I said to Lori. "Do it." When she finally realized that I had a gun, she did what I said, pressing her back against the wall.

"Get up, David," I said. "Come on. We have to go someplace."

"Where?" He groaned.

"Let me worry about that." I found his pants on a chair and threw them to him. "Get dressed."

"Fuck you, man," he mumbled.

"No, no, no, let me enlighten you," I said firmly. "I'll drag your sorry ass out of here and throw you in the trunk of my car naked if I have to. Your grandma's not gonna lose her house on account of you."

"What're you talking about? What do you know about my grandma?"

"Your bail, son, your bail. You skipped out, and now she's gonna have to pay up if you don't show. You remember that?"

He rubbed his nose with the back of his hand. "Yeah, yeah, I know."

"So get dressed and hurry up."

Lori was scowling at me. "You a cop or what?"

"I'm your savior, that's what I am."

"Huh?"

David sat up and started to pull on his pants.

"Lay back," I said, tipping him over with the barrel of my gun against his forehead.

"What the fuck?" he said as he drifted backward.

"Just be quiet."

I had come prepared with leg shackles and a restraining belt. I got the shackles on first, then the belt. Finally I cuffed his wrists to the belt.

"Can I go to the bathroom?" he asked. "I gotta pee."

"No," I said.

"Come on, man. Please?"

"No."

"I'm gonna pee in your fuckin' car then."

I had no doubt that he would. "Don't move," I warned him. I went around to the other side of the bed and handcuffed Lori to the frame to keep her still. Then I took David into the bathroom. The first thing I spotted was their works spread out on the sink and the top of the toilet. But something else was on the toilet, balanced on top of a roll of toilet paper: a .38 Derringer. I shook my head. Boys and their toys.

"What's this?" I said, picking up the little gun and dangling it between my thumb and index finger.

"I dunno," David said. "I didn't know that was in there." He looked at Lori through the doorway. She just shrugged and pouted.

"Please," I said. "Save the bullshit for someone who might buy it."

"Hey, I swear, man."

I didn't want to hear about it. I unlocked one of his cuffs. "Do your business," I said.

When he was through peeing, I recuffed him, led him out of the bathroom, and told him to put his shoes on.

He did as I asked, stepping into a scuffed pair of sneakers without bothering with the laces, but I was wondering how I was gonna get him into my car. He was oozing like crazy. Then I noticed a long gray tweed coat draped over the back of the only chair in the room.

"Here," I said, tossing him the coat. "Put this on."

"Hey," Lori protested, "that's mine."

"You can pick it up tomorrow at the Middlesex County jail."

"Yeah, like I'm gonna go there," she said.

David was making faces, hunching his shoulders and rolling his head.

"What's the problem?" I asked.

"I'm not gonna make it, man. I can't do it. If they lock me up, I'll die." He was sobbing like a little kid, wiping the tears away with his forearms. Lori was rubbing his back with her free hand. "Let me have a fix before we go," David pleaded. "It'll hold me till Monday. Please?"

I looked at the two of them. They were truly pathetic, especially him. His eyes were begging me. I had no doubt that he was going to suffer badly if he didn't get another fix, and I realized that it wasn't my job to punish him. I was here to make him live up to his responsibilities, that's all. One more high wouldn't hurt him any more than he'd already hurt himself. And it would probably make transporting him a lot easier for all of us.

"OK," I finally said. I pulled out my keys and unlocked Lori's handcuffs. "Fix him a needle," I said to her.

She got off the bed and went into the bathroom. I repositioned myself so that I could keep my eye on both of them. She worked fast, cooking a spoonful of white powder over a candle and filling a syringe. It always amazes me how skillful and efficient even the most strung-out junkie can be when it comes to preparing a needle.

She came back out and bounced onto the bed, handing the needle to David. He had enough play in the cuffs to be able to reach his own forearm. He flexed his arm until he found a vein, then without any hesitation he stuck himself. But instead of injecting the heroin directly, he drew out some of his own blood, which swirled into the chamber of clear liquid. He pulled out the needle and shook it until the fluids were mixed, then stuck himself again and gave himself the bloody cocktail. He squeezed his eyes closed and lay back, waiting for it to kick in. This method of shooting up was new to me, but when I asked him about it, David didn't answer me. He was already too high to respond. Lori lovingly removed the needle from his arm and set it aside on the night table.

After a minute or two, he opened his eyes and flashed a vague grin. I wondered if he remembered that I was there. "Come on, David," I said. "Up." I got him to his feet and threw the coat over his shoulders.

Lori was sulking on the bed. "You taking me in, too."

I looked at her, waiting for her to make eye contact with me. I didn't have a warrant on her, and even if I did, this girl didn't need another go-round with the police. That would only harden her further and undoubtedly deepen her addiction. What she needed was some compassion. "Call your sister," I told her. "Megan's worried about you."

Lori didn't respond, and I didn't pursue it. No amount of harping from me was going to make her call Megan. She had to make that decision herself. I could only create the opportunity. I led David out of the room and into the parking lot.

"Hey! Hey! That's my boy. Where you going?" a wiry Hispanic man called out to me from the open doorway of Room 2. He was wearing a brown leather bomber jacket with a fur collar and dove-gray shoes. A tall slick-looking Black man was standing in the shadows just behind him. I didn't have to ask what their interest in David was. They were obviously drug dealers—the Black man was the cut-and-bag man; his pal was the lookout. I was willing to bet anything that David and Lori were their best customers.

"What're you doing with my boy?" the Hispanic man repeated. He probably thought I was a rival dealer trying to steal business from him.

I opened my jacket and showed him the .45 in my belt.

"No problem," the man said, throwing up his hands. He ducked back into his room and slammed the door behind him. There isn't a whole lot of love, compassion, or loyalty out on the street. It's all about turf and survival, and predators are everywhere.

I took David to the Middlesex County Adult Correctional Facility and let them hold onto him. Given his chronic oozing problem, they weren't very happy to have him. They ended up throwing a plastic poncho over him before they put him in a cell, where he immediately nodded off. He wasn't going to give them any trouble until he needed another fix.

I called the bondsman the next day and told him to call off the dogs on David's grandma. She got to keep her house, and David ended up in prison, where he's supposedly trying to kick. But prison is one of the worst places for that, because drugs are readily available inside and the drug fiends have nothing else to do with their time. Boredom and availability are a lethal combination.

As for Lori, I don't know what became of her. I do know that she never called her sister, so she's probably still out there, still shooting dope, continuing her slow downward spiral of de-evolution. It's a shame what she's doing to herself, but I've come to learn that a person can be helped only so much. Evolution cannot be imposed upon someone. The will to evolve must come from within. The truth must be faced.

2 It's Not What It Seems

Whenever I go to a new area to pick up a fugitive, I check in with the local police first, just to let them know what I'm doing. The reactions I get vary depending on how much experience these police have had with bounty hunters in the past. Some police departments couldn't care less about us because they don't take us seriously. Some go crazy, assuming right away that we're a menace and a threat to the community. Some can get pretty hostile, threatening us with arrest and prosecution. But occasionally we'll run across cops who welcome our presence because there are some things we can do that they can't. As long as we have the proper credentials and proper documentation for a fugitive's arrest, we don't need probable cause to enter a house. All we need is a reasonable suspicion that the person we want is inside. Also, since our targets are often repeat offenders, some police departments are quite happy to see us removing trouble from their jurisdictions.

I've been hassled by the police on a few occasions, but one time in particular stands out in my mind. One night in the spring of 1996, I was on my way home when I was stopped by the police for a burned-out taillight. It happened in a town in Union County, New Jersey, just a few miles from where I live. The patrolman who pulled me over insisted on seeing what was inside my vehicle. I was driving a Jeep Grand Cherokee at the time, so he could see through the windows that I had an assortment of metal boxes and gear bags in the back. His mustache started to get twitchy as he peered in with his flashlight. I obliged his curiosity, telling him who I was and what I was doing there, but when I let him take a look at my equipment, he immediately pulled his gun and called for backup.

What the cop found was the basic equipment that all the Seekers carry when they go out to make an arrest:

- A shotgun.
- A semi-automatic handgun (a 9mm, a .45 ACP, or a .357 magnum) with extra clips, a "red-dot" laser scope, and an Archangel holster, which is specially designed for drawing the weapon quickly.
- A laptop computer with a modem and a portable printer.
- A headset communications system with a twenty-one-mile range.
- Monocular night-vision headgear for hands-free operation.
- An air taser, which can send an electrical current through the air and knock a man down at ten feet.
- A Dazer, a small electronic device that emits a high-pitched frequency capable of incapacitating a dog without permanently hurting it.
- Hydrant, a military-grade mace that is mounted in the crook of the elbow and triggered by folding the arm. One cartridge can clear a crowded room.
- A small canister of mace for one-on-one confrontations.
- A telescoping ASP baton, an effective tool for subduing a difficult subject without inflicting serious injury.
- A digital camera with a long-range zoom lens.
- A Game Finder scope, which can detect body heat behind walls. We use it for searching vacant buildings, warehouses, and the like.

I don't know what freaked him out more—the contents of the gun box bolted to the floor or the array of high-tech surveillance equipment, particularly the infrared night scope. Even though I showed him the warrant I had for the arrest of a fugitive who was living in a nearby community, he refused to believe that I was a legitimate bail enforcement agent. He was convinced I was some kind of terrorist.

Two more patrol cars arrived, and I was arrested, read my rights, handcuffed, and put in the back of one of their cars. I didn't curse them out or resist in any way. Since I had permits for all my weapons, I just wanted to know what they were charging me with. But none of them gave me a real answer.

My vehicle was impounded and towed to the police station, where I was also taken and put in a holding cell. Without getting angry, I asked them the same question over and over again: What am I being charged with? I knew that if they didn't charge me with something, they'd have to let me go.

The sergeant in charge of the night watch came down to talk to me, but he wouldn't give me a straight answer either. All he would say was that it was pretty late, and that would delay things. But in fact, as I later found out, they were stalling while crime-scene technicians went through my Jeep, cataloging everything they could find. They also got into my laptop and perused my files. Since they were convinced I was a terrorist, I guess they were looking for letters to well-known international terrorist groups and formulas for explosives that I'd picked up on the Internet. They must have been disappointed with what they found.

It was getting near morning, and they still had nothing they could charge me with. My guns were legal, and it wasn't a crime to have any of the other equipment. But that's when someone on the force had a brainstorm: get a vacuum cleaner.

They vacuumed my Jeep cleaner than it had ever been and analyzed every last speck they found. By now it was getting on toward lunch the next day. They brought me a Big Mac, but I refused it. (I don't eat red meat.) I'd been asking for a phone to call my lawyer since I got there, but they'd stalled me on that, too, until the new sergeant on duty finally relented. I called my lawyer and asked him to come down to the station as soon as he could.

It was after one o'clock in the afternoon when my lawyer finally arrived, and after I told him what had happened, he told the police the same thing I'd been saying all night long: Charge the man with something or let him go. We were all in an interrogation room upstairs from the lockup—my lawyer and I, the day-shift sergeant, the patrolman who had originally stopped me (he'd gone home to get some sleep and then come back), and the captain of the precinct. The cops stared at us blank-faced when my lawyer made the demand, then went into a huddle, whispering among themselves. As they conferred, I noticed the sergeant pulling something out of his pocket.

The huddle broke up, and the captain cleared his throat. "We are charging Mr. Armstrong with possession of an illegal substance." The sergeant held up a plastic Ziploc bag. From where I was sitting, it appeared to be empty.

"May I see that, please?" my lawyer said, reaching out for it.

The sergeant didn't hand it over until he got the OK from his captain. My lawyer and I examined the bag, but we didn't see anything inside. I picked up the legal pad that my lawyer had been taking notes on, turned to a fresh page, and asked him to lay the bag down flat on the page. Against the clean yellow background, I finally saw it. A single brown-green seed as tiny as a sesame seed.

"It's a marijuana seed," the captain said gravely. He looked grim.

I almost laughed in the man's face. "Captain," I said, "I pick up fugitives from justice every day of the week, and seventy percent of the people I arrest are drug dealers or drug users. When I capture these people, I put them in my vehicle, and a lot of them are carrying drugs. Frankly I'm surprised that you found only *one* seed."

The captain frowned at me. "Is this your excuse for having marijuana in your vehicle?" he asked. "Other people brought drugs into your vehicle, and you knew nothing about it?"

My lawyer touched my forearm to remind me to stay calm. But I was calm. And rational, too, but that was the problem. I seemed to be the only one in the room who dared to make sense.

"Look," I said to the captain, "why don't you vacuum out the backseat of one of your patrol cars and see what you come up with? I'm willing to bet you'll find some illegal substances there, too."

"The point is," my lawyer said, picking up the ball, "my client's occupation puts him in close proximity to people who use and sell narcotics, people who can inadvertently leave their debris in his vehicle.

Furthermore, being in possession of one marijuana seed is not a felony, nor does it warrant overnight detention." He tossed the bag across the table, but it was so light it just fluttered like a falling leaf. "If this is what you're charging him with, then let's stop wasting everybody's time. I think Mr. Armstrong has spent more than enough time enjoying your hospitality, considering the degree of the alleged offense."

"Well," the captain started, but he didn't know what to say next. He looked to the sergeant and the arresting officer, but they had nothing to say either. "Well," he started again, "under the circumstances I think it would be best if we didn't pursue this matter any further." He picked up the bag and stuffed it in his pocket. "Mr. Armstrong, I'm sorry if we inconvenienced you. You're free to go."

I wasn't in the mood for being magnanimous, and I'm not the type to sugarcoat bullshit. I let my eyes convey my feelings for him, his officers, and the whole situation.

My lawyer whispered in my ear, "You can sue them for false arrest if you want. You have an excellent case."

I thought about it for a moment, then shook my head no, my eyes still on the cops. I worked in this area all the time. The case would get into the papers, and publicity is one thing a bounty hunter doesn't need. Besides, going to court would just eat up more of my time, time better spent tracking down fugitives.

"Will I be getting all my gear back?" I asked the captain. "And in the condition that I left it?"

"Everything will be returned to your vehicle," the captain assured me. "Check it before you leave. If anything is missing or damaged, please inform me immediately." He looked to the arresting officer. "Make sure that everything on the inventory list is back in Mr. Armstrong's vehicle."

The arresting officer's mustache drooped. "Yes, sir," he said and left the room with his tail between his legs.

Between the paperwork and the confusion locating all my gear, I wasn't out of there until late afternoon. When I finally drove out of the police station parking lot, I could only shake my head. I was clean, yet the cops were ready to throw the book at me simply because of what I do and what they didn't understand about it. I wondered what they'd have to say for themselves if the fugitive I was after had committed a violent crime while I was being held. I could have prevented that crime. Thankfully it didn't play out that way, and I was able to pick up the fugitive two days later.

Unfortunately, the police mentality in this country has not evolved much since I started working as a professional bounty hunter in 1984. In my opinion it has deteriorated. The quality of cops today is very poor because police forces don't hire the best people available. In the last ten years there has been a sharp increase in the number of incidents in which cops accidentally shoot other cops. More policemen commit suicide than any other single profession. The amount of domestic violence committed by cops is atrocious, and these are the people whose job it is to stop crime.

The us-versus-them mentality persists in urban precincts principally because the young men hired to patrol the inner city have had little or no previous contact with Blacks or Hispanics. Their first and only experience with minority groups is often with the small criminal element that's off track, and these officers start believing that the criminals they arrest are typical of their kind.

I believe that if we want to have better-quality police officers, then we as a society have to start producing better-quality men and women. *Everyone* must be encouraged to evolve to a higher level, progressing from what the ancient Egyptian philosophers referred to as mere "sapiens" (base creatures) to stellar men. But this process can begin only with personal accountability. A police force—like society in general—cannot be any better than the least evolved officer within its ranks.

3 Being a Seeker

Paul Robeson, the great African-American actor and social activist, once said that an artist must use his art to convey a higher message. I feel the same way. Bounty hunting is not my message; it's a means by which I can convey a higher message, the message of learning and evolution.

In the southern section of Newark, across the highway from Newark International Airport, is Weequahic Park, an island of greenery in the harsh urban landscape. The park surrounds a large, tranquil lake. In good weather the Seekers try to meet there at least once a month to kick back and talk about things. The only topic that is forbidden is work. We leave the bounty hunting and the fugitives behind so that we can concentrate on personal matters, world affairs, the future of the country, and the future of the planet. We set this time aside so that we can connect with one another as people.

These informal discussions are usually relaxed and far-ranging. Some of us have our favorite topics. The younger Seekers tend to want to talk about the "race problem." We don't discourage any topic, but those of us who are further along in our evolution don't consider racism a problem. It's only a problem in the sense that it's a smokescreen, a decoy, something designed to keep everybody down.

If people are preoccupied with hating one another, they can't evolve into better human beings or get a look at the bigger picture. By remaining in this primitive state, they are easier to manage and less of a threat to the powers that be. The absurdity of the situation should be obvious, but to most people it isn't. After all, what's the issue? Skin color. Would any reasonable person say that blue cars are more reliable than red ones? That gray coats keep you warmer than green ones? That yellow thread is stronger than pink thread? So how can anyone with an ounce of intelligence believe that a man with black skin is inferior to a man with white skin? To me, racism is almost a nonissue.

Many of my friends asked me why I didn't participate in the Million Man March, the day of atonement that took place in Washington, D.C., in 1997. I definitely would have attended if it had been the Million *Family* March. Why exclude women and children? Why exclude anyone? Anything that excludes a particular group is discriminatory, and what purpose does that serve? Also, based on the facts of my history, I have nothing to atone for. If a person can be truly and honestly accountable to himself, then he need not face any other judge.

In my life I have met an awful lot of people who sing variations on the same song:

> "I wouldn't have robbed that liquor store if my wife hadn't bugged me so much about not having money."
>
> "I *had* to steal that car. I needed to take my mother to the doctor."
>
> "If I'd had a good job, I would never have started dealing. But white people have kept me down my whole life."

Whenever I ask a fugitive why he committed whatever crime he's wanted for, I get the same old story. It's never his fault. Someone or something else forced him to do it. *The Book of 1,000 Excuses* is a well-worn volume. It's an exceptional person who will own up to his actions without a long song and dance.

My advice is this:

> If something is leaning so heavily on you that you can't think for yourself, get past it.
>
> If you're obsessed with thoughts of a new Lexus, either put it out of your mind or buy one and work harder to make the payments.
>
> If your wife is on your back twenty-four hours a day, perhaps you should get past her. Or better yet, help her to get past her petty fixations so that she can evolve along with you.
>
> If you believe that racism is keeping you down, get past it. Too many people use racism as a crutch, and a crutch keeps you a cripple.

Many so-called Black leaders cry racism at every turn, but they don't offer any concrete solutions. Perhaps it's because racism hasn't kept them down. But what have all their devoted followers gotten out of carrying their spiritual/political baggage? Not much, I'd say. The next time you hear their rally call, ask for the short-term *and* the long-term plans. In most cases there is no long-term plan.

If something is bothering you to the extent that it preoccupies your mind, you are giving that obsession life. You're creating your own monster and keeping it alive. But if you can get past it, the monster will die. Put it out of your mind. By doing this, you will have taken the first step in your own evolution.

As you might guess, I usually take the role of the teacher in our discussions, doing as much as 70 percent of the talking. This is because some of the Seekers are naturally quiet and prefer to listen. A few of our members have not yet fully recognized the importance of ideas and information and simply let it all wash over them. I'm always hopeful that being exposed to these discussions will open their minds and at the very least teach them how to think for themselves. The specifics of what we talk about are secondary to the process of exchanging ideas. If I can teach the younger Seekers how to learn for themselves, then I have conveyed my higher message, because I truly believe that it's the learners who will inherit the earth.

I tend to like to discuss politics and history, and since I do most of the talking, our talks often go in that direction. I like to point out inconsistencies in the behavior of our elected officials and will quote liberally from the Constitution and the Bill of Rights. The blatant illegality of the Internal Revenue Service is one of my favorite topics, as well as the myth that the Democrats and the Republicans represent opposing points of view. In fact, the two parties are far more similar than they want the public to believe. Genuinely unique political viewpoints have been bulldozed by the major parties in this country for most of this century, and I strongly believe that we must watch our politicians closely and scrutinize everything they do so that they don't overstep their bounds.

I'm capable of getting up on my soapbox from time to time. Luckily there's always someone in the group who will knock it out from under me if I start preaching. I remember one time a few years ago when the Seekers threw me a curve ball that almost rendered me speechless—which, if you know me, isn't easy.

It was a beautiful day in October. Summer had finally left the city, and the air was cool and crisp. The afternoon sun was glinting off the water, warming the green picnic tables where we had gathered. We had brought some food, and I was prepared to settle in for a good long discussion because we hadn't had one of these get-togethers in a couple of months. The summer had been very busy. I had brought along a few books that I'd recently read, one in particular that I wanted to discuss. It concerned a movement by some elected officials to adopt a New States Constitution that would in effect do away with the system of checks and balances and put the government's real power in the hands of a privileged few.

I dropped my pile of books on the picnic table, ready to get started, but I guess the others saw the soapbox coming out, and they rallied to head me off at the pass.

"So, Joshua," Jeremiah said, "what do you think about those Knicks? Is this gonna be their year?"

Rock and Job snickered behind their hands. Jedidiah was laughing out loud. They knew how I felt about professional sports.

"What's wrong with you?" Jedidiah said to Jeremiah, still laughing as he said it. "You know Josh doesn't waste his time with sports. Do you, Josh?"

Zora and Solomon didn't quite know what was going on, but the sly grins on the others' faces told me what was up. The older members were not in the mood for one of my lectures.

"Tell them when you last saw a game on TV," Job said to me with a knowing look. "Go on, tell them."

I shook my head and had to laugh. "To tell the truth, the last time I paid attention to any team was when Jim Brown was still playing."

The old-timers howled. Jedidiah slapped the tabletop, and tears sprang from Jeremiah's eyes he was laughing so hard. Solomon joined in, but Zora just looked puzzled.

"Which Jim Brown?" she asked. "The actor?"

Jedidiah set her straight. "The man was a football player first."

She shrugged. It didn't mean anything to her. "So Joshua doesn't follow sports," she said. "So what?"

"It goes deeper than that," Job said. "Tell her what you think of professional athletes, Joshua."

"They're court jesters," I said. "Modern-day court jesters."

Zora's eyes bugged out of her head. "Even Michael Jordan! You think he's a court jester?"

"He may be an outstanding human being, I don't know," I said. "But what do his fans get out of his playing ball? Not as much as he gets."

"But he's a positive role model," she persisted. I could see that she did not want to accept my point of view on this.

"Michael Jordan is an *unattainable* role model," I explained. "How many people do you see wearing his shoes, wearing his shirts, buying products he endorses? We see it all the time when we go out on pickups. There are people just scraping by, but they *have* to have a pair of Air Jordans. But how many of these people are *living* like Michael Jordan? How many of them are driving Lexuses? How many of them are living in mansions? How many of them take the day off to play golf? Any of them?"

Zora shrugged. "None of them, probably."

"But everybody wants to be like Mike. Isn't that what they say? 'I wanna be like Mike.'"

"But it's something to aspire to," Zora said.

"Yes, but is it a *good* thing to aspire to? Think about it. How many of us thought at one time in our lives that we could make it big playing ball? In reality, you stand a better chance of hitting the lottery than making it in professional sports. But some people carry that dream beyond reality. And what happens when they fail? Major dissatisfaction. They think they have nothing to live for. They stop evolving. Maybe they never even began evolving."

Zora nodded slightly. She was beginning to see my point.

"Individually, professional athletes may be fine human beings, but what they represent is not fine. They create mindless diversions that keep people from thinking. It's just something else to fill up TV time. The way I see it, it's just a waste of time that could be better spent reading or communicating with someone else or playing a sport to develop your own body."

Jeremiah dug into the small cooler he'd brought and pulled out a plastic tub filled with macaroni salad. "There he goes again," he mumbled to Jedidiah, who was rustling around in his own lunch bag.

"Yeah, we thought we could keep the preacher out of the pulpit for once," Jedidiah muttered, "but that was just a prayer. Joshua, do you ever stop preaching?" he asked with a grin.

"*Teaching,* not preaching. That's what I do."

"Yeah, whatever." Jedidiah pulled out a container of apple juice from his bag. "But you sure do talk a lot. You always have."

I knew he was just pulling my leg. Jedidiah doesn't talk as much as I do, but our basic beliefs are pretty similar. He didn't find my "preaching" that onerous.

"You really think I talk too much, Jed?" I asked, flashing a sly grin of my own. "Why don't you take over today? Tell us what's on your mind."

"Only one thing on my mind," he said, unwrapping a sandwich. "Eating lunch."

"Come on," I urged. "Share your wisdom with us."

He gave me a funny look. "You serious?"

"Absolutely."

"All right," he said, putting down his sandwich. "I'll give you some wisdom."

Jeremiah snickered as he chewed, and Job crossed his arms and lowered his chin, waiting for some verbal gems. The others turned in their seats to face Jedidiah.

"We're waiting," I said to him.

Jedidiah scratched his head and looked up at the trees. He narrowed his eyes, apparently thinking hard. He took a few moments to collect his thoughts. Finally he spoke. "Nah, that's OK," he said.

"What?" I said. "You don't have anything to say? Come on. Get the ball rolling. Pick a topic."

Instead he picked up his sandwich and took a bite.

"Jed, we're waiting," I said. "Enlighten us."

"No, no, no. I changed my mind," Jedidiah said, wiping his mouth with a paper napkin. "We all know you have this need to talk, Josh, so I don't want to deny you. If you stay quiet for too long, you may get sick or something."

Job and Jeremiah burst out laughing, and the other Seekers joined right in. They were so loud, their howls carried across the lake. I just shook my head and smiled. That's one of the great things about the Seekers: we manage to keep one another real.

Over the years, many people—both men and women—have asked me if they could join the Seekers. Bodybuilders, black belts, sharpshooters, con artists, ex-cons, tough guys of all sorts, reformed drug dealers, former prostitutes, even fugitives I had tracked down and brought to justice in the past come to me and ask if they can join. Each one makes a pitch, boasting of special skills or aptitudes that he or she alone possesses. But what most people fail to realize is that the externals don't count. I can teach a person how to fight barehanded. I can teach a person how to shoot a gun. I can teach a person how to coax information out of a reluctant subject. I can teach a person how to track down a fugitive, staying on the trail for days, weeks, and months on end. I can teach a person how to become a Seeker. But what I can't instill in a person is potential. Either you have it or you don't, and that's the main quality I look for in a candidate.

I also look for a flexible attitude. If you tell me that you want to be a Seeker because all you want to do is catch "dirty low-down bad guys," then I will definitely pass on you. If you've already got your mind made up about who the bad guys are, then don't bother coming to me. Put in your application with the police department.

If we know that we'll be losing a member, the Seekers often take on a trainee in the hope that this person will eventually fill the open slot. I remember one trainee in particular who didn't make the grade, a young man named James who had graduated from the police academy and was waiting to be called up. When the police department informed him that they wouldn't be hiring for a while, James came to me for a job. He did the required reading, passed the written test, and appeared to be an ideal candidate. Whenever we explained things to him in our training sessions, he was always respectful and attentive, and he was in superb physical shape, having black belts in two martial arts and a brown belt in a third. We all had high hopes for James.

To be accepted as a Seeker trainee, a candidate must come along with me on a pickup—nothing terribly difficult or overtly dangerous, just something to get his feet wet. When we felt that James was ready to progress, I took him with me to the Duncan Avenue projects in Jersey City. I had a lead on a man who had skipped out on a $25,000 bond. This fugitive was small potatoes compared with most of the ones we bring in, but he was charged with attempted rape, and I always go out of my way to take in rapists and child molesters, no matter what the bond is. In my mind, profit is secondary to getting these people off the street.

It was around 4 A.M. when James and I arrived at the projects. Piles of encrusted snow lined the streets, and a bitterly cold wind was buffeting my car as I turned off the engine. I could see that James was a little nervous, and I noticed that he was holding his gun in his lap. It was a .45 Smith & Wesson, same as the one I had under my jacket.

"Why do you have that out?" I asked him.

He seemed startled by the question. "I'm gonna need it, right?"

I just looked at him. "We're still in the car, James. Most likely you won't need it at all. Why don't you put it away before something happens?"

"Like what?" All of a sudden he was as jumpy as a cat. I wondered what had happened to all that martial arts cool he'd shown before.

"Come on, let's go," I said, flipping up my collar and getting out of the car.

I started across the street, but James hadn't gotten out yet. I looked back at him and waited for him to catch up. When he finally did, I asked him if he was all right.

"I'm fine, I'm fine," he said. "No problem."

I hoped it was just first-time jitters. I crossed the street, hunched over against the cold, then turned around to make sure he was still with me. I saw that James had his gun out again, carrying it carelessly at his side.

"I told you to put that away, didn't I?"

"Yeah, but—"

"Just put it away. You'll know when you need it."

He put it back in his belt clip holster and followed me into the courtyard of the projects, staying three steps behind me. The wind was howling between the high-rise brick buildings, and the floodlights on the corners cast an eerie glare over the blacktop. It was light, but it didn't exactly illuminate everything, and there were long patches of shadow where the light didn't reach. I noticed that there were frozen puddles all over the place, a lot of them hidden in the dark.

I was about to tell James to watch his step, but I stopped myself. James was a grown man. He didn't have to be told everything. If he did, he didn't belong in the Seekers. Besides, he was a black belt times two. I'd seen him working out in the gym. He had some truly beautiful moves, which he executed with grace, power, and assurance. If anything, the man was sure on his feet. My telling him to be careful of the ice would be an insult, so I held my tongue.

I kept my head down against the wind and forged on toward the entrance of the building where the rapist was supposedly living with his father.

"James," I said, "I think we'd better—"

"Whoa!" James suddenly blurted out.

Pow! The unmistakable sound of a gunshot. It struck a wall close by, and chips of broken brick tinkled down onto the dark ice. Instinctively I dropped into a crouch and pulled my weapon, scanning the courtyard for an attacker.

"Help me," James croaked. He was flat on his back on the ground.

My first thought was that he'd been shot by a sniper from up above. But I couldn't imagine how a single shot would have gone clear through him, then hit the wall eight feet off the ground. Then I saw that James had his gun in his hand again, and I could smell that it had just been fired.

"What happened?" I asked him. "You all right?"

"I slipped," he said sheepishly. He frowned at his gun as if it were a naughty puppy. "It just went off."

"Get up," I said, annoyed with him for not listening. "The whole project knows we're here now. Our man has got to be gone by now—unless he's deaf. No sense even going in there."

"I can't," he said in a quiet voice.

"You can't what?"

"Get up. I did something to my back."

I had to help him to his feet, which wasn't easy, because he was a big man and in a lot of pain. He couldn't stand up straight, and I had to help him walk back to the car. When I finally got him inside, I asked him why he had his gun out again when I had told him specifically to put it away.

He didn't answer me because he didn't have an answer. I'd asked him to do something, and he hadn't done it. It was that simple.

I drove him home, and we were silent most of the way. I pulled up to the curb in front of his house, took the car out of gear, and just stared at him.

"Should we try it again in a couple of days," he asked, "when my back straightens out?" But I could tell from the tentative way he asked the question that he already knew his fate.

He started to say something, but then changed his mind. He was probably about to make up some kind of excuse, then realized that in this situation no excuse was going to hold water with me.

"Sorry," he said quietly. He got out of the car and struggled up the walk to his house.

I see James in the neighborhood every now and then, and he seems to be doing fine. We say hello, and he asks how the other Seekers are, but he never asks if he can have another shot at becoming a member. Which is all for the best, I think. He wasn't cut out for it. Despite all his martial arts training, he lacked one crucial quality—self-control. Without a doubt he was disciplined, but there's a difference between discipline and self-control. Self-control comes from within. A boy becomes a man when he can tell himself what to do; therefore to become a Seeker, you must first become a man. My life—like all of our lives—is the tale of a journey to manhood. My journey is still unfolding.

4 Mentors and Guides

I was born in 1957 in Elizabeth, New Jersey, which is where I was raised. Though Elizabeth borders on Newark, in the sixties it wasn't plagued by the same urban woes. When the Newark race riots erupted in 1967, I watched them on TV. My only recollection of that event is that we canceled our regular Sunday visit to my cousins who lived in Newark. In Elizabeth crime was something that happened behind closed doors and under the cover of night. Drugs were not sold or consumed out in the open. Bad behavior was dealt with swiftly and strongly, and parents weren't afraid to be tough. If you got caught doing something wrong, you would without a doubt get your ass whipped.

My father was an arc welder for a grocery-store chain. My mother was a part-time teacher's aide and a part-time factory worker. My father loved music, and I can remember it filling the house, from either the radio or the record player. The only time there wasn't music in the house was when my father wasn't home or when he was listening to a baseball game instead.

My mother was a religious woman, but my father had no use for religion. Every Sunday she'd take me across town to the Baptist Church, and every Sunday my father would gripe from his armchair as we were getting ready to leave. "You're just giving the preacher your money for nothing," he'd say.

Most of the time my mother would ignore his comments, unless he decided he really wanted to get her goat. Sometimes my mother would be adjusting her hat in the hallway mirror or fussing with the collar of my jacket, just about to go out the door, and Dad would call to her from the living room, shouting over the bebop coming out of the radio. "That church service you go to ain't nothing but a show. You want to see a good show, I'll take you down to see James Brown sometime."

My mother's face would freeze and slowly harden. Her eyes would narrow down to slits, and I swear you could see the steam coming out of her ears. Comparing our minister to the Godfather of Soul was a heinous offense in her book, and it was guaranteed to start a fight. She'd storm into the living room, and they'd get into it big time, shouting and hollering for all the world to hear. Mom and I were always late for church on those mornings.

I was an only child and pretty much of a loner when I was growing up. I can't say that I had any really close friends back then. I did play a lot of baseball with the other kids in the neighborhood, but by the time I turned twelve, that had lost its appeal for me. Kids can be cruel to one another, and I had no patience for those kinds of needless mind games—who got picked to play on what team, who was the best batter, the best pitcher, the best fielder, the most popular. I preferred to stay home by myself rather than deal with that crap. But as I spent more and more time by myself, my mother started to worry about me.

"Are you OK?" she'd ask, standing in the doorway to my room.

"I'm OK," I'd say. I'd be lying facedown on the bed, my head hanging over the side, a book propped open on the floor as I scratched my dog's head.

"Why don't you go out and play? It's a nice day."

I'd shrug. "Don't feel like it."

"Should I be taking you to a doctor?"

"Nope."

"Look at me. Are you on drugs?"

I'd look her in the eye. "No. I'm not on drugs."

I was just profoundly bored. Everything bored me, school included.

I wasn't challenged by it, and my grades reflected my state of mind. I'd slide by with 70s until a teacher would crack down and start making some serious threats. Then I'd start getting 90s, which only proved that I could do it. I simply had no motivation.

One thing that did grab my interest was a birthday present I received from my father when I turned fourteen, a BB gun. It was a special model equipped with a gas canister that made the shots more powerful and accurate. I remember going out into my mother's garden and shooting at anything that looked like a good target. Since it was springtime, the flowers were my first victims. Once I had conquered stationary targets, I graduated to the bumblebees that buzzed around the flowers looking for pollen.

One afternoon after school when I was out stalking bees, I saw something I'd never seen before, a hummingbird. It was gray with a yellow belly and so small it seemed magical, like Tinkerbell. It flew like a bee but was much faster and more agile, beating its wings so quickly I couldn't even see them. It moved in perfect vertical and horizontal lines, up and down, right and left, going from blossom to blossom on the honeysuckle vines that covered our back fence. Without thinking, I raised the BB gun to my shoulder and squinted down the barrel, getting the bird in my sights and tracking it, studying its moves so that I could anticipate them. My finger rested lightly on the trigger. I followed the hummingbird up and down, right and left, keeping it in my sights as best I could, exhilarated whenever I could predict its moves, thrilled every time I had an opportunity to score a hit. It stopped at a blossom and hovered in place, dipping its needle beak in to sip the nectar. It was right in my sights, not moving, a clear shot. Without thinking, I pulled the trigger.

The crack of the gun hardly disturbed the warm moist spring quiet. The hummingbird tumbled down the honeysuckle vines. I looked at the ground, and my gut was suddenly in a knot. The little bird was in the dirt, not moving. I was scared and ashamed, afraid that someone would see what I'd done. I picked up a twig and prodded the bird, hoping it wasn't really dead, but it rolled over without resistance as if it were weightless. Its eyes were wide open and fixed.

I felt horrible. This wasn't what I had intended. I didn't mean to kill it. I never thought I *could* kill it. The bird was too elusive, too otherworldly. How could I possibly hit something like that? I wasn't that skilled. I should have missed.

But I didn't. I couldn't comprehend why or how it had happened, but it had, and the bird's tiny body shouted out my stupidity, my reckless disregard for its life. *What if it was my dog lying there?* I thought. I couldn't have felt worse if it were.

My first thought was that I had to immediately make it right. I ran into the house and found a box of Rice Krispies, the small individual-sized ones that came in a cellophane-wrapped pack of six assorted cereals. I tore open the box and the inner waxed paper bag and shook the Rice Krispies onto the grass. Food for the other birds, I thought, hoping an act of charity could contribute to my restitution for the killing. I crouched and pushed the hummingbird into the box. When I picked it up, the box hardly weighed any more than it did when it was empty, which only made me feel worse. The hummingbird was so small and delicate, so precious. How could I have killed it?

I found the trowel that my mother used for planting flowers and dug a hole in the soft soil at the back of one of the flower beds behind a stand of pink tulips. I wanted the bird to have a proper burial but not where anyone would see it. I was too ashamed. Tears rolled off my cheeks and into the hole as I dug, going deeper and deeper, subconsciously hoping that the better I concealed the evidence, the more likely the crime would be erased. I placed the box into the hole and quickly covered it up, my face completely wet with tears. I smoothed out the soil and crumbled it a bit with my fingers to make it blend with the rest of the bed.

But still I felt awful for what I had done. I ran into the house and went to my room. I had a bag full of Popsicle sticks under the bed, which I used to build things—little houses, airplanes, things like that. I picked out two sticks and fastened them together with a rubber band, making a cross. I ran back outside and stuck the little cross into the soil over the bird's grave. Then I carefully rearranged the bent leaves of the tulips. Only I would know that the bird was buried back there.

As I backstepped away from the flower bed, I happened to step on the barrel of the BB gun. I stared at it under my sneaker, not daring to pick it up. The gun was to blame for what had happened, not me. It had a hair trigger. It was too powerful for a kid. It was a bad gun.

I really wanted to believe all that, but I knew in my heart that these were just lame excuses. I stared down at the gun for a long time, trying to figure it all out, trying to put the pieces together so that I could absolve myself of the blame and get to keep the gun, too. But the truth was, I wasn't ready to handle a gun like that. I wasn't responsible enough. I'd let *it* rule *me*. I knew that wasn't the way it was supposed to be, so I promised myself that I would never let anything control me like that again. If I did something, it was going to be my own decision to do it. I did not want to be influenced this way ever again. When my father came home from work that night, I gave the gun back to him. He was puzzled because I had been so happy when I first got it. I just asked him to hold on to it for me until I was old enough to appreciate it.

Years later when I started carrying real guns for work, I would occasionally think about that hummingbird buried in my mother's flower bed. I carry weapons now, but only as a conscious act of survival. The guns don't make me a better or more powerful person. They're just tools. I'd prefer not to use them, but if I have to, I will.

A person does not evolve to a higher state by himself. We need mentors and guides to show us the way. I was fortunate enough to have several such people in my life, some more influential than others. I had some wonderful schoolteachers when I was growing up, people like Mr. Bernie Davis who taught African history, Miss Murphy who taught math, Ms. Wade and Mr. Caruso who both taught English, and Mr. Bergman who taught English in junior high. I was also lucky enough to study kung fu with two very dynamic instructors, Masters Alan Lee and Sid Austin. I studied martial arts for five years with them until I was out of high school.

Unfortunately, I didn't get sparked by school until I reached the eleventh grade at Thomas Jefferson High School in 1973. But even though my interest in school picked up in my last two years, I knew that it would be a waste of money for me to go to college. I was restless, and I wanted to be free and on my own. I didn't realize, of course, that I would have been freer in college. I was young, and I didn't see it that way. I had also been dating a girl who was getting pretty serious, and I was afraid that she'd tie me down if I stayed in Elizabeth.

I got it into my head that the place for me was Alaska. I'd heard that there was a lot of money to be made working on the Alaska pipeline, a direct hookup from the oil fields near the Arctic Circle to the lower forty-eight states. It also seemed like a romantic dream of the last frontier—rugged terrain, rugged men, and limitless opportunity. I had a friend from high school, Ellery Banks, who shared that dream, and six months after graduating, we boarded a bus in Newark and set out for the West. We believed that in Alaska a man would be valued for his drive and determination, and no one has more drive and determination than an eighteen-year-old male with big dreams but not nearly enough life experience.

We didn't have enough money to get us to Alaska, so we got off in Portland, Oregon, where we stayed for two months picking up odd jobs until we could save enough money to get us farther north. Our next stop was Seattle, Washington, but not long after our arrival we began to have second thoughts about our decision to go West. After paying for our bus tickets, we were nearly broke. Realizing our dream was harder than we'd ever imagined, and we feared we'd never make it to Alaska. Basic survival was our top priority now, and the first thing we needed to do was to find a *very* cheap place to stay. We found a room that fit the bill at the Blackstone Hotel, a hooker haven near the bus station.

The ladies who hung out in the lobby scrutinized us as we walked to the front desk to ask about a room. The old manager was confused when we told him we wanted to share a room and would he please tell us what the weekly rate was.

"You two looking to set up shop?" he asked angrily, glaring at us with eyes that were as yellow as his teeth.

"We're just looking for a place to stay for a while," I told him innocently.

I thought he was upset because he wanted us to pay for two rooms instead of sharing one. Neither Ellery nor I realized that he thought we were young hustlers looking to add a homosexual concession to the hetero delights the ladies offered. The manager clearly did not want that, but we were so obviously wet behind the ears, he eventually agreed to let us have a room.

"But don't you go squeezing the fruit unless you intend to buy some," he warned, nodding at a couch full of girls who were smoking and giggling at us. "Eddie don't like that kind of stuff unless you're a paying customer. You best stay away from him. Doc, too."

Ellery and I looked at each other. Who's Eddie, and who's Doc? we wanted to know, but the manager sounded so ominous, we didn't dare ask. We just took the key he gave us and went straight up to our room on the second floor.

The room was pretty spare—one double bed, a small table, two mismatched kitchen chairs, and a hot plate. The bathroom was out in the hallway, and there was a refrigerator downstairs on the first floor under the stairs that we could use if we wanted. When we checked it out, we were surprised to see so little food in it—a bottle of vodka, a lot of beer, the manager's lunch bag, and not much else. As soon as we got settled, we went right back out. The sooner we could find some work, the sooner we could move out of the Blackstone.

As we walked through the lobby on our way out, one of the ladies called to us, a shapely young woman with milk-chocolate skin and not much wrapping to cover it. Her breasts were as round as cantaloupes, and her plunging neckline went right down to the edge of the nipples. "Where you going, boys? You ain't gonna find nothing better out there. It's all right here." She jiggled her breasts, and I couldn't help but stare. I must have looked like a real hick because the other hookers slapped their hands and howled in delight. I didn't know how to respond to this, so I just looked down and walked outside.

Ellery and I pounded the pavement for the rest of that day, got up the next morning and did it again, then did it once more on the day after that. We tried to find work everywhere—restaurants, warehouses, construction sites, department stores, grocery stores, shoe stores, hardware stores, movie theaters, everywhere—but no one had any use for two eager boys on their first foray into the real world. By the end of the third day we were beyond discouraged. Privately I was seriously questioning our decision to come west. Maybe we should have stayed where we were in New Jersey. Maybe this whole trip was just asking for trouble. I considered the possibility of hitchhiking back home.

At the end of our third day in Seattle, we dragged ourselves back to the Blackstone, neither of us ready to admit defeat but both of us depressed by the trajectory our fortunes had taken. To get into the hotel, we had to squeeze past a gang of hookers sitting out on the stoop. Their pimp, the king of the Blackstone, was right in the middle of them holding court. His name was Eddie Benson, and he was as slick and badass as anyone I'd ever seen in Newark. He always wore black ankle boots with Cuban heels and a short black-leather jacket over a silk shirt open to the middle of his chest. He also wore lots of rings and bracelets on both wrists, and the fingernail on his right pinkie was long and pointed, a natural coke spoon. His car, a white Cadillac Eldorado with red leather upholstery, was parked at the curb.

Doc, Eddie's knock-down man, leaned on the fender, surveying the scene and looking out for trouble. Doc wasn't tall, but he was broad, and his biceps were bigger than my thighs. From the scowl on his face, I knew instinctively that he was someone who shouldn't be messed with. I felt that just making eye contact with either Eddie or Doc could be perilous.

As Ellery and I approached the stoop, the hookers quieted down. They were absolutely silent as we wove through them to get inside. I could feel Eddie looking at me, but I didn't look at him. I didn't want any trouble. I just wanted to get a job so I could get out of there.

The next morning Ellery and I got up early and started pounding the pavement again. But luck wasn't with us. We searched all that week, wandering aimlessly through the city looking for Help Wanted signs, but the few places that did have signs weren't interested in us, no matter how much we begged. By now we were desperate. After five days in Seattle we had come to the end of our money. That evening we went down to the corner grocery store and bought the last meal we could pay for, an ice cream sandwich, which we split in half. Ellery and I walked back to the Blackstone in silence, eating our dinner, both of us making believe that we weren't scared shitless. I didn't tell Ellery, but I was about ready to call my parents to ask them to wire me enough money for a bus ticket home.

I was chewing the last bite of the ice cream sandwich as we came up to the Blackstone. Doc was in his usual position, leaning on Eddie's Cadillac, arms crossed over his massive chest, but for some reason Eddie and his hookers weren't on the stoop that night. Doc was wearing a jade-green running suit, a pair of Adidas, and a heavy gold chain around his neck. As usual, I didn't look at him as I passed by.

For the first time since Ellery and I had been there, Doc spoke to us. His voice was like gravel in a coffee can. "Yo!" he said. "Eddie wants to talk to you. Both of you. Room one-oh-five."

"I have to go to the bathroom," Ellery whispered to me as we went into the lobby. "I'll meet you there."

"But—"

"I'll be right there," he said. "I promise." And he dashed up the staircase.

I looked back through the open front doors. Doc was staring at me.

Eddie's room was in a mysterious territory that neither Ellery nor I had ever explored, the first-floor hallway behind the staircase. I'd look down that hallway whenever I went to the refrigerator, but I had never set foot down there. That was where Eddie hung out and where his girls took their johns. What went on down there was none of my business, and I had hoped to keep it that way.

I glanced back at Doc one more time. He hadn't moved off that fender, and he was still watching me like a hawk. I had a feeling Ellery wasn't going to be coming down anytime soon.

I walked around to the back hallway and stopped to listen. One of the girls was laughing her head off in one of the rooms. In another room a radio was playing Wilson Pickett's "Land of a Thousand Dances." Harsh yellow light glared off the imitation wood paneling that lined the hallway. I glanced at the door numbers as I passed. Eddie's room was down at the end, next to an open back door.

A cool breeze came through that open doorway as I stood in front of Room 105 wondering what I should do. I heard voices through the door, but they were low and quiet, and I couldn't make out what they were saying. Maybe they were getting ready to kill me. But why? I hadn't done anything. I hardly ever looked at Eddie's girls.

My stomach was as tight as a fist, but I couldn't figure out why. I hadn't done anything wrong, so I had nothing to worry about, right?

But I wasn't convinced of that. It seemed that with people like Eddie, you could get on their bad side without even trying. I held my breath and knocked on the door.

"Come on in." I recognized Eddie's voice.

When I opened the door, I saw Eddie sitting on the bed, his back propped up against the wall. The girl with the chocolate-brown skin and the cantaloupe breasts was sitting on the edge of the bed, next to him.

"Go on now," he said to the girl. "Go make me some money." He was smiling devilishly at her. She stood up and gave him a defiant smirk, but I could tell this was just an act. It was clear that Eddie was in charge. I'd heard him chewing out one of his girls the night before, and the man had a vicious management style.

The milk-chocolate girl moved slowly toward the door. She had this sly grin on her face, and she was giving me the eye, which Eddie couldn't see. I pretended she wasn't even there. I didn't want Eddie to think I was trifling with his merchandise.

After she was gone, Eddie looked up at me. "You want your dick sucked?"

My eyebrows shot up into my forehead. I didn't know what to say.

"Not by me," Eddie clarified.

"No thanks," I said. "I'm fine."

Eddie chuckled to himself as he got up off the bed. He went over to a small kitchen table and dug into his pants pocket, coming up with a wad of dollar bills wrapped tightly with a rubber band. He took off the rubber band and peeled off a small pile of hundreds and laid them on the table. He went into his other pocket, pulled out a single car key, and laid it on top of the money.

I started filling in the blanks in my mind. Eddie wanted me to do something for him, something illegal.

"No drugs," I muttered, barely able to get the words out. "I don't mess with drugs."

Eddie tilted his head to the side and just looked at me for a moment. "Take it easy, blood," he said. "You're reading the wrong mind."

I was puzzled. So what did he want?

"This money is for you and your friend to get yourselves on your feet. A thousand bucks. Don't go wasting it on stupid shit. It's for food and rent. Now this here is the key to my Caddy. What I want you two to do is get yourselves a newspaper, check out the want ads, and find a job. Use the car. You just been looking around this neighborhood. Ain't no jobs around here. You got to expand your horizons. You understand what I'm saying?"

I was stunned, my eyes glued to the hundred-dollar bills on the table. "You mean you're *giving* us that money? For nothing?"

He shook his head. "Not for nothing. Definitely not for nothing."

Suddenly I was suspicious. "What's the catch?"

"The catch is, I don't want you and your friend to end up like me and Doc. You're both decent boys from good families. I can tell just by looking at you. But you won't stay that way hanging around here. Go find yourselves a better place to live. And get some honest jobs."

I got the impression that his advice was more a rebuke of himself. If he couldn't fix his own life, he'd at least fix someone else's. But I was still leery of such an outrageously generous gift coming from a pimp. I froze where I stood, afraid to get any closer to the money, afraid that it might commit me to something Eddie hadn't mentioned yet.

"Go on, blood, take it," Eddie said. "Just let me know before you take the car so I know it wasn't stolen." There was a melancholy warmth in his voice that I hadn't heard before. It was as if someone else were talking through him. He gathered the cash and the key and handed them to me.

I took them, still stunned. What if I got caught with a thousand dollars in cash in my pocket? How would I ever explain it? But I was no fool. A thousand bucks would give us a tremendous leg up. We wouldn't have to go back to New Jersey. We might make it to Alaska after all.

I looked Eddie in the eye for the first time since I'd arrived at the Blackstone. "Thank you," I said.

"Yeah, yeah, you're welcome," he said dismissively. I think he was uncomfortable with genuine emotions, particularly his. "Now go get that newspaper. Right now. Don't waste no time. You hear me?"

"I hear you. Thank you."

"Stop thanking me and just get the hell out. And close the door behind you."

I did as he said and rushed upstairs to find Ellery so that I could tell him about our sudden windfall. This was the kind of stuff that happened on TV shows like *The Millionaire,* not in real life. But it had just happened to us. Ellery's mouth hung open as I divvied up the hundreds on the bed. I think his mouth was still hanging open when we went out to get a newspaper and a hot meal.

By the next week we both had jobs. With the use of Eddie's car, we were able to widen our search to other neighborhoods, and it paid off. I found a shipping-and-receiving job at a factory. Ellery and I moved out of the Blackstone Hotel and into a small one-bedroom apartment in a better part of town. After I got my first paycheck, I was feeling good about myself, happy that I was making it on my own. But I also realized that it was all thanks to Eddie Benson, so I made it my business to take a bus back to the Blackstone to thank him properly. When I got to the hotel, I immediately sensed that something was different. Eddie's white Eldorado wasn't parked out front, and Doc was nowhere to be seen. There weren't as many pros hanging around the lobby either. The milk-chocolate girl was sitting on the sofa watching a movie on the old black-and-white television set that sat in the corner next to the unused fireplace. The reception was so poor you could barely see that there were people on the screen.

"What're you watching?" I asked her.

She looked up at me slowly, blinked once, and went back to the movie. "*The Invisible Man,*" she said absently. I wasn't sure if she recognized me or not.

"Where's Eddie?" I asked.

"Gone," she said.

"Gone where?"

She shrugged. "Eddie stabbed a guy out front a few weeks ago. He and Doc took off before the police came looking for them."

"You think he'll come back?"

She shrugged again. On TV the invisible man was unwinding the bandages from his head, showing one of the other characters that he couldn't be seen. I remembered that scene. I'd seen it on the *Million Dollar Movie* back home. But the image on this TV was too snowy to figure out what was really going on. She was just watching it to kill time. I wandered back to the bus stop and waited for a bus to take me to my new neighborhood, thinking about Eddie and all the money he'd given us, wondering why he'd done it. I suppose he might have been trying to make up for some of the damage he'd done in his life. Maybe he saw a little bit of himself in Ellery and me, Eddie before he started making the wrong choices. Maybe he wanted to keep us from making the same mistakes. Unfortunately, I never got a chance to ask him.

5 On the Bering Sea

I didn't stay with the shipping-and-receiving job for very long because something better came along, something that smelled of adventure. I was hired by the All-Alaska Sea Food Company to work on one of their floating processing plants, a mammoth ship with a crew of a hundred and twenty. Fish were caught, cleaned, frozen, and packaged all on that one vessel. Japanese fishing freighters unloaded their catches on these vessels for processing as well. The idea of working on a ship thrilled me. Not only would I be going out to sea, I'd be getting closer to my personal promised land, Alaska. My friend Ellery got himself a better job in Seattle, and he eventually came to like it, but I was the one who was going to be having the high-seas adventure.

The deck boss of the ship, a man named Lyle, recruited me for the deck crew, which caused quite a rift when the rest of the crew saw me coming aboard on my first day. There were only six Black men on the crew, and they all worked down in the hull on the production line. By hiring me and not promoting from within, Lyle had pissed off a lot of people. Even the eight women who worked belowdecks were miffed at him.

Part of the crew's resentment was racial, but mostly it had to do with status. The deck crew were the pirates of the ship, the tough guys, the elite. The deck crew got the best food and the best lodging. Members of the deck crew shared cabins with only one other person. The rest of the crew slept four to a cabin. I guess Lyle's thinking in hiring me was that I was young, strong, and willing, which was exactly what he needed.

The first real friend I made on the ship was a man named Leo Osten. Leo was a German immigrant, and despite the fact that he was sixty years old, he was one of the strongest men on board. He noticed that when I was off duty I preferred to read rather than play poker and get drunk. One day up on deck he struck up a conversation, and I was amazed at his breadth of knowledge. I knew I could learn a lot from this man, so I started to seek him out whenever I had some free time. Like me, Leo loved to read, and our discussions would go on for hours, usually concentrating on philosophy and religion. He told me all about the Baha'i faith, which he followed. Eventually we formed our own discussion group, which usually met in my cabin, where we'd listen to jazz, sip brandy, and talk. Even the captain joined us on occasion. Leo was like Socrates with a heavy German accent, always asking questions that would stir the pot and provoke further discussion.

One time we happened to be discussing racism, and someone pointed out that there were several members of the white supremacist group the Aryan Nation among the crew. I was anxious to hear Leo's thoughts on this, but he just listened to what the others had to say. Finally everyone quieted down, waiting for Leo to add something, but he didn't say a word. Instead, he pushed back his sleeve to show us his forearm. There was a small blue tattoo on his arm, so blurred with age I couldn't make out the writing. A small swastika, though, was still fairly clear.

"When I was a boy, they put me in the Hitler Youth," Leo explained. "I wore a uniform, went to the classes, and marched through the town with the other boys. I did all those things. But that was before I knew anything. I think back then I was like these Aryan Nation people we have now. They are ignorant, and ignorance will always find its own course. But once a person knows something, he takes a different course. Maybe someday these people will know something, and they will change." Leo rolled down his sleeve.

The discussion gradually picked up steam again, but I was still mulling over Leo's words. One thing he said struck me: Ignorance will always find its own course. I kept that in mind whenever I had to work with any of the Aryan Nation members.

Deck work is rigorous and sometimes dangerous. One job that no one ever wants is securing the decks when a storm suddenly blows in. Any loose pieces of equipment—barrels, booms, nets, cables, pallets, forklifts, anything—have to be lashed down to keep from losing them or having them become projectiles that can damage something else. The men who take on this duty run the risk of being hit by flying equipment or worse, swept overboard. A man overboard in the frigid waters off Alaska is an automatic casualty. It takes at least forty-five minutes to turn a ship that big around, and the man would die of shock long before anyone could get to him.

I remember one storm in particular, in 1978, because it had snowed heavily, and visibility was very poor. The deck was covered with snow up to our calves, so just walking was treacherous, not knowing exactly what was underneath it. By this time I had worked my way up to being in charge of the night crew. The head of the day crew was a surly individual named Jimbo, whose primary means of communication were grunts and scowls. In the off-season he lived with his wife and kids in Idaho, and he was one of the proud members of the ship's Aryan Nation club. My being on the deck crew could not have sat well with him, and everyone on board was just waiting for the day when Jimbo and I would lock horns. Fortunately, I didn't see much of him since he worked days and I worked nights.

The storm hit at midmorning, and it hit hard. The snow accumulated fast, and the winds picked up dramatically. As it was reported to me later, Lyle, the deck boss, asked for volunteers to go out and secure the deck. Jimbo volunteered immediately, but the few men who offered to go out with him weren't to his liking. It was a dangerous situation, and he wasn't about to go out with just anybody.

As usual, Jimbo didn't mince words. "I want someone who knows what he's doing. Someone who's not gonna get himself killed, and more important, who's not gonna get *me* killed."

Lyle got frustrated at this point. "So who the hell do you want?" he yelled.

"Go wake up Armstrong," Jimbo said. "He knows what he's doing."

There must have been some raised eyebrows when he said that, but Lyle was just grateful that Jimbo had finally made a selection. Immediately Lyle sent someone down to get me. I was a little surprised when I heard that Jimbo had picked me, but not that surprised. The situation transcended race or color; it was a matter of survival, pure and simple. Jimbo knew that he had to pick someone who was able enough to save his ass out there if it ever came to that.

Ten minutes later I was on the bridge ready for duty. The storm was raging outside the bridge window. The snow was coming down so thick we couldn't see the prow. Jimbo and I went down to the coatroom and suited up in silence—snorkel parka, wool mask and cap, double-layer gloves, insulated waterproof pants and boots. He didn't look at me or say a word, and since I had just been wakened from a sound sleep, I wasn't in much of a conversational mood myself. We went back up to the tower, where Lyle and the rest of the deck crew were gathered around the door that led out onto the deck. They were there to see us off.

Just as we were about to go outside, Jimbo finally spoke to me: "You take the starboard. I'll take port."

I nodded, and that was it. He opened the door, and we rushed out like paratroopers jumping out of a plane. The metal door slammed shut behind me, but I barely heard it over the howling of the wind. I could feel the biting cold on my face through my mask. I took a few steps and discovered that the deck was slippery under all that snow. I practically had to skate across it to maintain my footing. I was afraid that if my feet lost contact with the surface, I might trip over something hidden under the snow.

The ocean was a churning fury. Swirling walls of foam and water rose and fell like monsters out of the sea, blocking out the horizon and making my progress even more disorienting. Walking against the wind was like grappling with a sumo wrestler who was intent on throwing me overboard.

I headed for the starboard side; Jimbo went port. Besides looking out for loose equipment, we were supposed to keep an eye out for each other. If one of us was knocked down—or knocked unconscious—the heaving deck could pitch to one side and slide the man overboard.

Jimbo signaled to me that we should start with the stern, but as I moved toward the rear of the ship, watching him quickly became difficult. Snow was sticking to his parka, and he was blending in with the blizzard. I assumed he was having the same problem seeing me. Assuming, of course, that he *was* watching out for me.

We made it to the stern without finding any major problems, then turned around and headed toward the prow. At the bridge we had to split up to get around it. We wouldn't be able to see one another with the bridge in the way, but dozens of eyes were tracking us from the portholes. Crew members pressed their faces to the glass to watch our progress. The light inside seemed vibrantly colorful compared with the monochrome whiteness outside. But were these watchers worried about us or just curious to see if Jimbo and I would finally have it out? It seemed like the perfect situation for a showdown. No one would come out to stop us, and with the visibility so poor, he could come up behind me, shove me into the ocean, and later say it was an accident. I played out the scene in my mind like a movie, and before I realized it I had trudged beyond the bridge. The snow was coming down so heavily I couldn't even see the lighted portholes anymore, and undoubtedly the people inside couldn't see me. No witnesses, I thought.

I looked to my left, suddenly paranoid about Jimbo, but there he was, coming into view from behind the bridge on his side. He was moving a plastic barrel into a corner, using his knees to push it through the snow. As he secured it with a bungee cord, I could just make out his outline. It was like an abominable snowman sighting. I could see a figure, but I couldn't swear it was him.

Up ahead I could hear the squawk and bang of a loose boom, but I couldn't see it. I slowed down, afraid that if the wind shifted, the long metal arm would swing back at me and take my head off. I hunkered down and moved in a crouch. The sounds got louder, but I still couldn't see the source. It wasn't until I was just a few feet from the boom that I saw it. I stood up and reached out for the flapping ropes until I finally grabbed one, then quickly tied it off at the nearest cleat. When I looked up, I saw a snow-covered silhouette standing across the deck, like a ghost. I felt him staring at me. Was Jimbo watching out for me or looking for an opportunity?

I moved on, and Jimbo did, too. We stayed on our respective sides and made no attempt to communicate with each other. It would have been useless because the howling wind would drown out our shouts. Whenever I stopped to tie off a boom or secure a whipping net, Jimbo would stop and watch me, and I'd do the same for him. *But were we watching out or just watching?* I wondered. I was prepared to help him if he got into trouble, but would he help me?

It was slow going, incrementally slow. I felt as if I'd been out in the cold for a double shift, but in fact it couldn't have been more than forty-five minutes. The quarterdeck was just ahead. After that we'd be through. The quarterdeck is at the front of the ship. It's smaller than the main deck and up a flight of stairs, so it's pretty isolated. There were no portholes close enough to look out on the quarterdeck.

Jimbo and I climbed the port and starboard ladders simultaneously. The rungs and handrails were slick with ice. I kept thinking that every step I took could lead to a broken leg or worse. When I was halfway up, I glanced over the side at the ocean. Its roiling anger was hypnotic. It was anxious to take someone.

When I got to the top of the ladder, I saw that the quarterdeck was an unspoiled expanse of pure white. I stayed where I was on the ladder, the deck floor even with my waist. A loose boom on my side of the ship was pinned back by the wind, its ropes flying wild. It needed to be tied. I climbed the last rungs of the ladder and stepped out onto the deck. I felt like that other Armstrong, Neil, the first man who walked on the moon. The wind was brutal, buffeting my body, making me slide in place. I suddenly felt even more vulnerable to the force of the storm. As I approached the loose boom, it struck me how precarious the situation was. If the wind shifted abruptly before I tied off the boom, it could knock me out into the open sea like a bat hitting a baseball.

The ropes were blowing away from me, just out of reach. I had to hang onto the railing with one hand while I reached out for them. I caught one, but suddenly the deck fell out from under me as the boat dipped precipitously. A wall of water was poised to sweep over the deck. The boom swung forward. Instinctively I ducked to avoid the blow, hanging onto a rope and the handrail. Suddenly I saw him out of the corner of my eye. Jimbo was at the rail right next to me. I hugged the railing, bracing myself for the worst.

The water roared, pouncing like a tiger. My legs were swept out from under me, then an unexpected split second of silence came as the water embraced me completely, head to toe. I hung on, my focus totally on the rail. No one, nothing was going to pry me loose.

The water washed the deck clean of snow. The wind was roaring again. My whole face stung. My clothes were soaked, and the fur trim on my hood hung limply in front of my view. Jimbo was still right next to me, doing exactly what I was doing, holding on for dear life.

Somehow I had managed to keep my hold on the rope. The wind was too strong for me to move the boom back where it had been. I'd have to lash it to the handrail the way it was, pointing forward. I moved around Jimbo and started to tie off the rope, but ice was forming on it, and I had to work it a little before I could make a knot. After tying down the boom, I scanned the deck for other problems, but everything seemed secure. *We're through,* I thought with great relief. We weren't dead. We could go back inside.

But as I turned toward the ladder, I saw that Jimbo was just standing there, staring at me again. Ice had formed in his beard and on his eyebrows. I was close enough to see his eyes, but I couldn't read them. What was he thinking? What did he want?

He said something then, but I couldn't hear him over the howling wind. I signaled to him that I was going back. He didn't respond in any way, but he did follow me, taking the same ladder down to the main deck. From there we retraced our steps on our respective sides of the ship, double-checking for anything we might have missed. The walk out to the prow had felt like an eternity, but the walk back seemed to take no time at all. The faces in the portholes were waiting for us as we came up to the bridge. Seeing the bright light from inside gave me a rush. The heavy steel door swung open, waiting to receive us. Jimbo had gotten there ahead of me, but he waited for me to go in first. I didn't know if he meant anything by this gesture, but I really didn't care. I just wanted to get inside and warm up.

Leo Osten was there to greet me. "How did it go?" he asked me as I shrugged off my parka.

"OK," I said, but I was too tired to go into details.

On the other side of the room, Jimbo was peeling off his wet clothes, surrounded by the men from the day crew. Except for Leo, my crew was down below, resting up for their shift.

The captain came up to me and clapped me on the shoulder. "Good job," he said. "Go get some rest, and don't worry about your next shift."

I just nodded. I was so exhausted I could have fallen asleep right there.

"Go on," the captain said. "We'll call you if we need you."

I slung my parka over my shoulder and headed for my cabin. As I passed Jimbo and his entourage, I tried to make eye contact with him, but he was busy giving orders to his men.

My cabin mate worked on the day crew, so I had the cabin to myself for the rest of the day. Not that it would have mattered. I conked out immediately and fell into a deep sleep. Four hours later I woke up groggy and disoriented. I couldn't bring myself to get out of bed, so I just stared blankly at the ceiling for the longest time. After a while I sat up and reached over to the tape player. I put in a John Coltrane cassette, and the bittersweet tone poem "After the Rain" came on. The searching saxophone solo fit my mood. I lay back and listened, letting my thoughts drift like dust particles in a sunny room.

A sudden knock on the door stirred up those drifting thought particles. "Come in," I said.

The door opened, and Jimbo was standing there with his hand on the knob. "Can I talk to you?" he said.

"Sure," I said. "Come in." I swung my legs off the bunk and sat up.

He stepped inside and closed the door behind him, but he looked uncomfortable.

"Sit down," I said, pointing to the other bunk.

Reluctantly Jimbo took a seat on the edge of the bunk. I wondered if he was acting this way because he didn't like being in a Black man's cabin.

He cleared his throat and rubbed his nose before he spoke. "You did a good job out there today," he said. "I appreciate it."

"Thanks." I didn't know what else to say. I was stunned. Jimbo never complimented anyone, not even members of his own crew.

"Look, I'm not gonna get all sappy about this," he said, "but I think you're a good man, a good person. There aren't many people you can trust in the world, but I think you're one of them." He was looking me in the eye. "If you ever find your way out to Idaho in the off-season, you're welcome to stop by my place. There's good fishing on my land if you like to fish. And my wife is a mean cook. You'll leave fat, that's for sure."

I wondered if being out in that blizzard had made him color-blind. Did he really mean it? And if I did visit him in Idaho, how would he explain me to all his white supremacist buddies?

I managed not to say anything I might later regret. Instead I held my tongue and took the offer at face value. Perhaps being out in that storm with me had been a turning point for Jimbo. When it was just him and me out there, maybe he came to realize that skin color doesn't make one person better or worse than any other person. Whatever the color, it was just a color.

He stood up and pointed out my porthole. "Storm blew over," he said.

I looked outside for the first time since I'd woken up. The sun was setting over calmer waters. The clouds that lingered were benign pillows.

"See you around," he said, flashing a tight-lipped smile. He showed himself out, leaving me alone with the sound of John Coltrane's poignant lyricism.

I never took Jimbo up on his offer, and we never became bosom buddies, but we at least achieved a quiet respect for one another. And if he was preaching racist doctrine aboard the ship, I never heard anything about it. I'd like to believe that he left that nonsense behind. Ignorance follows its own course, but that's not the only course. People can evolve, and it could have happened to Jimbo. I certainly hope so.

After working for All-Alaska Seafood for almost two years, I went back to New Jersey to visit my family, and while I was there I happened to run into James Holloway, an old friend from high school. James had matured quite a bit since I'd last seen him, and I sensed from the way he talked that he had acquired a deeper understanding of the world. I asked him what he'd been doing lately, and he told me about an extraordinary man he'd met. The man's name was Kanya McGee, and he owned a bookstore in Harlem called the Tree of Life. James constantly referred to Kanya as his "teacher." When I asked what Kanya had taught him, James just smiled and said, "Everything that really matters."

I have to admit I felt a bit envious of James, but I didn't understand exactly why. James seemed to have learned a great deal in the few years since we'd graduated. Leo Osten had taught me a lot, and he had also planted a seed in me, a seed that now craved nourishing. I desperately wanted to learn more about everything that really mattered. I craved knowledge, real knowledge that I could use to improve myself. Kanya McGee seemed to be filling James's similar cravings, so I asked him to introduce me to his teacher.

Rather than take me to the man's bookstore, James took me right to Kanya's home in Harlem. He lived in a faceless twenty-two-story high-rise, but his apartment was something quite special. It took a while for Kanya to answer the door when we knocked, and when he opened it, he silently motioned for us to follow him into the living room. He sat down in a worn leather armchair by the window, snatched up a hardcover book that had been left open on the coffee table, and was immediately engrossed in it. Without looking up, he held up his hand, signaling for us to wait until he finished the passage he was reading.

James pointed to the sofa, indicating that I should take a seat. I felt I was entering the tent of a very wise old sultan. The walls were crammed with carved wooden masks from a variety of African tribes. A large wall hanging made from animal hide depicted an entire village—the people, their huts, and their daily activities. A stick of incense was burning in a ceramic holder on the mahogany coffee table, launching swirls of smoke that curved and bent through the room. The rug was a geometric Turkish pattern in red, yellow, orange, and brown. Kanya's slippered feet were propped on a wood and red-leather camel's saddle studded with hammered brass bosses the size of half-dollars.

I watched Kanya's face as he read. His skin was the color of burnished copper, and he wore heavy black-rimmed glasses. He reminded me of somebody famous, but it wasn't until later that I realized he could have been a double for Egyptian President Anwar Sadat, who years later would be gunned down at a political rally in Cairo.

When Kanya had finished reading, he closed the book and laid it on his lap. He greeted James, then looked directly at me. "Welcome to my home," he said. His warm voice permeated the room like the swirls of incense.

James introduced me and told Kanya that I was visiting from Alaska, that I was a voracious reader, and that I had a study group on board my ship. I asked him to suggest some books for further study.

He looked at me for a long moment. "Why do you read so much?" he asked.

I started to laugh. I thought the answer was obvious. "To improve my mind," I said.

"Your mind," he repeated, and nodded to himself, considering my answer. "But what about your *soul*?"

I got a sinking feeling that I was about to get a Sunday sermon about saving my soul from the hellfires of eternal damnation. But I was very wrong.

"It makes no sense to train your mind if you're going to ignore the soul. They're linked, you know. The mind can raise the soul to higher levels, higher than you realize. Individuals have to work to raise themselves. Once you start that process, you will be on your way to becoming a true man, a stellar man."

I nodded, not really getting everything he was saying, but the way he said it convinced me that there was something to his message.

"Do you watch much television?" he asked me.

I hadn't noticed a television set in the apartment, so I considered telling him what I assumed he would want to hear. But I sensed that lying to him would be the wrong move. "There's no TV on the ship," I said honestly. "But whenever I get back to the mainland, I do watch some."

"Whatever you watch, cut it in half," he stated flatly.

"I can do that," I said.

"The media," he continued. "Do you know where the word *media* comes from?"

I shrugged, but James was grinning. He'd apparently already heard this.

"Media was the name of an ancient witch in prehistoric England. She was a trickster, a befuddler of minds."

I thought I detected a hint of a grin on his face, but I wasn't sure. His face was as inscrutable as the Sphinx.

Our conversation continued late into the night. The more questions I asked, the more he would reveal. But if I sat back and tried to absorb his thoughts passively, he'd stop talking. Kanya was a coach of the mind. His goal was to make me use my intellectual muscle, to probe and stretch and reach for more.

"Can you show me how to evolve to a higher state?" I asked him.

He shook his head. "I can be a example for you, but you have to do it yourself. Every man is responsible for himself."

"But how can I start? What do I have to do?"

"Pay attention to the world around you, the people you see, how they interact. Pick out the stellar men and make them your guides."

I was fascinated by what he told me, and I wanted to spend more time with him, but unfortunately I was scheduled to leave for Alaska in two days. The next morning I went back to his apartment. Again I found him reading in his chair. I explained my situation and must have sounded pretty desperate. He smiled paternally and gave me his business card, which had his home phone number as well as his business number. "Whenever you want to talk, just call me," he said.

I knew he meant it, but I was impatient. I wanted to know more, and I didn't want to wait. I emptied my wallet and held out $150 in cash. "I want to buy some books," I said. "You pick them."

He laughed gently and leaned back in his chair. "I'll pick some books for you, books that I think you need right now. *The Kybalion,* of course. And two works by Professor Hilton Hotema, *Cosmic Creations* and *Awaken the World Within.* But I want you to keep one thing in mind. The wisdom that's right for you, Mr. Armstrong, doesn't come from a book. Your wisdom stems from your ancestors. Build an altar to them. Light white candles and offer libations. They are your past and your future. They are *you*. Think about that."

I did think about that, a lot. All the way back to Alaska on the plane

I stared out at the clouds, wondering exactly what Kanya meant by that. My ancestors are my past and my future. My ancestors are me. Did he mean my grandparents and great-grandparents? Or was he talking about family members who reached further back? Much further back. I started to read the books Kanya had sold me, hoping to find the answers.

Not long after I returned to work for All-Alaska, I was asked to join the crew of the *Elizabeth F,* a 125-foot crab boat. One of the *Elizabeth F*'s fishermen had fallen into the hull and broken his shoulder and pelvis, so they were in a pinch. King crab season was under way, and they needed a man desperately. The *Elizabeth F*'s captain asked my captain if he could spare a good man, and my captain asked me if I was interested.

At the time, Black fishermen were a rarity in Alaska, and the men who fished those waters were notoriously elitist. For instance, in all the ports in the northwest, there were bars that catered exclusively to fishermen, places like Sally's and the Bull Dog in Seattle and Alice's in Dutch Harbor, Alaska. Outsiders were not welcome in fishermen's bars, even if they worked in other areas of the fishing industry. When my captain told me about the job on the *Elizabeth F,* I wasn't sure I wanted to be the Rosa Parks of the Bering Sea. But the pay on the *Elizabeth F* would be better than what I was making with All-Alaska, plus I'd be working days, not nights. It didn't take me very long to make up my mind. I agreed to take the job.

The *Elizabeth F* specialized in catching king crab, the enormous spidery crustaceans that inhabit the Bering Sea near the Arctic Circle. We shared the waters with Russian and Japanese ships, all of us searching for those prized crabs whose legs tasted better than lobster tails and whose leg span was usually about three feet from the tip of one claw to the tip of its opposite. The decks of the *Elizabeth F* were lined with "cage bases," stations where six- by three-foot steel cages were winched in and out of the water. A fisherman was posted at each base to open the cages, lean in, pull out the trapped crabs, and, when necessary, refill the bait jars with cut herring. My job was to tend to a base, which is harder than it sounds. Cages were constantly going in and out of the water, and a fisherman had to work fast to keep up. Deckhands worked the winches from the deck above the main deck, and it was their job to secure the cages and lock them in before the fishermen started working on them.

Locking the cages in place was crucial, especially when the waters were rough. I was told plenty of warning stories about fishermen who'd lost their balance and fallen into their cages. To do the job right, you practically had to climb into the cage, and if you leaned in too far and it wasn't locked in place, not only would you plunge into the water, but the door could close on you and drag you down to the bottom. The chances of surviving an elevator ride like that were slim to none.

I'd been on the job for a few weeks and had pretty much gotten the hang of it. Or so I thought. One afternoon the sea started getting rough. A storm was coming, but the captain wanted us to keep fishing for as long as we could. This wasn't an unusual practice, and the captain wasn't being reckless. It was just a matter of economics. The prime crabbing season only lasted so long. The more we brought in while we could, the more profit we'd make.

By late afternoon, the sky was overcast and the ship was rocking, the deck pitching steeply. The crabs were plentiful here, so we kept on working at a furious pace. Whenever my cages came up, I tried to time it so that I'd lean in when the ship was briefly on an even keel. But it didn't always work out that way. Some crabs clung to the bars and had to be pried loose, and refilling the bait jar took a little more time, so I'd find myself leaning in when the deck was pitched downward, and there I'd be, staring straight down at the icy waves. A few times the pitch was so steep that the edge of the cage would actually dip into the water and lift me off my feet. But I kept working, wanting to haul in as many crabs as I could before we had to quit.

The sky was getting darker as the storm closed in. The wind was picking up, and the waves were getting higher, rocking the boat harder than before. The fishermen were yelling to the deckhands to keep the cages coming because the crabs were biting like crazy, coming in twos and threes now.

One of my cages came up, water dripping from the bars, and I could see that I had three in this haul. As soon as it banged into the locks, I opened the door and reached in to get them. One of them was stubbornly clinging to the bars in a far corner, so I had to climb halfway in to pry it loose. At that moment the deck took a sudden dip and sloped down dramatically. Instantly I lost my balance and was off my feet. What was worse, the cage was slipping. In his haste to pull up the other cages, my deckhand had neglected to lock mine in. I was staring at the water through the bars, and it was just a few feet from my face. The cage was going to take me down. I was literally in a dead man's locker, and the dead man was going to be me.

The pitch was too steep for me to back out. Even if I let go of the cage, I'd still tumble in. I yelled up to the deckhand, but there was so much commotion I don't think he heard me, and even if he had, he could never have reacted fast enough. I braced myself for the fall, hoping I could keep the door open with my leg and escape before it dragged me down too far.

But the deck suddenly tilted the other way, and the cage started to slide back toward the locks. My toes touched the deck, and I was able to pull the heavy cage back into place. The deckhand saw my predicament and quickly locked it in.

"Sorry about that," he called down to me, but I was too angry to respond.

I stopped to catch my breath, staring blankly at the stubborn crab gripping the bars of the cage. I realized that as I was about to go overboard, I had visualized a long descent to the bottom of the sea, my path lined with the spirits of deceased humans. I'm not a superstitious person, and I'm generally pretty skeptical about things that have no apparent explanation, but by all rights I should have been dead, and I wasn't. I wanted to know why.

Then I remembered Kanya McGee's thoughts about the development of the mind and the soul and how our ancestors can be our guides through life. *Could those spirits have been my ancestors?* I wondered. Maybe I was just lucky this time, or maybe it was something else that had saved me, something greater than luck. I decided that as soon as I got to shore, I was going to call Kanya and see what he thought about all this.

Days later I got to a phone and put in a call to him. He told me that it was quite obvious. My ancestors were protecting me. I believe Kanya was right. They were with me spiritually. Whether they literally saved me, I don't know, but I'm still here, and as Kanya has taught me, everything happens for a reason.

To this day I still call Kanya when I feel the need for guidance. For as many people as I have mentored in the Seekers, I still need my own mentors. We all do.

6 How Not to Do It, Part 1

In the off-season most of the fishermen I knew took other jobs, some of them as bounty hunters, and as the fish started heading for their spawning grounds, these part-time bounty hunters would start lining up assignments to keep themselves busy until the fish started running again. I found myself in Juneau late one Sunday afternoon in 1980, having a beer at one of the fishermen's bars while I read the newspaper. I was twenty-three years old at the time. The *Elizabeth F* had docked the previous day to unload our catch, the last of the season. While a group of my fellow laid-off crewmates hovered at the bar watching a football game on TV, I perused the want ads. I was trying to figure out what I could do for the next few months until we went back out to sea.

I was sitting by myself near the front window, and the view of the bay was distracting me. The sun was low in the sky, peeking through the clouds, turning the waters a dark blue-green. Blackhead gulls soared over the fishing boats, squawking and screeching, searching for scraps of chum on the decks. As soon as one of them spotted a morsel, they'd all dive-bomb it en masse. I put down the newspaper, crossed my legs, and gave in to the scenery. I'd come to learn that meditative moments like this should never be passed up.

I was gazing at the sunset, taking long breaths as I tried to empty my mind of all thoughts, when suddenly I became aware of someone walking toward my table. His heavy footsteps pulled me out of my state of tranquility.

"'Scuse me," the man said. "Your name Armstrong?"

I looked up and saw a cowboy. He was wearing a black cowboy hat, a suede vest with silver conchos sewn on the front, a wide belt with an oval brass buckle the size of a saucer, blue jeans that bunched at his ankles, and pointy cowboy boots with chunky riding heels. He had tiny eyes and a wide smile.

"Yes," I said. "My name's Armstrong."

"Jeffrey Ferguson," the cowboy said, putting out his hand. "I've heard a lot about you. They say you're some fisherman."

I shrugged modestly. "I do my job."

"Well, funny you should mention jobs." He pulled up a chair and sat down backward, leaning his forearms on the back. "I have one for you if you're interested. For the off-season."

I didn't know exactly what to make of this guy, so I cut right to the chase. "How's the pay?"

"Oh, don't worry about that. The pay'll be sweet, provided we get the job done lickety-split."

Jeffrey told me he worked on the deck crew of one of the other All-Alaska boats, and he'd heard about me from some of my old crewmates. I tried to imagine him working the decks in those fancy boots, but he knew what he was talking about, so I assumed he was for real. He was certainly brawny enough to work on a deck crew. It was just that he was so goofy—less like a cowboy than a caricature of a cowboy. He had an irrepressible good humor and a smile that just wouldn't quit.

"So what's the job?" I asked.

"Well, see, there's this guy who's wanted on an outstanding warrant in New York State. The guy's uncle put up his house to make bail for the guy, but he took off anyway, and now the bondsman is starting proceedings to take the uncle's house. The uncle got my name from the bondsman—I've worked for him before—and hired me to bring in his nephew."

I pulled my chair up closer to the table. "What did this guy do?" I asked.

"He was supposed to go on trial in Rochester for armed robbery and aggravated assault—his second major offense. It's a one hundred thousand dollar bond, which means ten grand for whoever brings him in. If we get him, we'll split it even. You interested?"

"Tell me about this guy first."

Jeffrey took off his hat and scratched his scalp. "The guy's name is Patrick Raoul Smithson," he said. "He's half Brazilian, half American Indian, but he's got a thing for Black women."

"What tribe does he belong to?" I asked.

Jeffrey shrugged. "How should I know? Does it matter?"

"It might."

He shook his head. "I kinda doubt it. See, he wasn't really brought up Indian. It wasn't until he went to prison for the first time that he got into his heritage. Calls himself a brave now, but it's all stuff he's seen in the movies. I don't think he ever really lived it himself."

"Interesting," I said as I picked up my beer and took a sip. I had a feeling there was more to this story, and if I waited long enough, Jeffrey might spill it.

"Don't get me wrong," Jeffrey said. "This Smithson is supposed to be a tough bastard. But it's not like he takes scalps or anything."

"How do you know all this?" I asked. "From the uncle?"

"Partly." Jeffrey pulled out a rolled-up manila envelope from his back pocket. "I got a copy of Smithson's criminal file and a copy of the warrant for his arrest. It's all right here."

He offered it to me, but I didn't take it. I wasn't so sure I wanted to get into the bounty-hunting business. It sounded pretty crazy to me. Of course, $5,000 would cover my expenses for a couple of months until the fishing boats went out again, and that would give me some time to do whatever I wanted. Still, I was suspicious.

"Why do you want *me* to go with you?" I asked Jeffrey. "There are plenty of other guys around here who do bounty hunting. They know the ropes. I don't."

Jeffrey pressed his lips together and tapped the rolled-up envelope against his chin. "Well," he started, taking a deep breath and blowing it out his nose, "to be absolutely honest, Smithson is known to hang out in Black neighborhoods. His uncle thinks he's in Seattle now, and I don't exactly blend, if you know what I mean."

"I know what you mean," I said. I was happy to see that he wasn't tiptoeing around the issue of race. A lot of people have a hard time talking about race, and most of them feel more comfortable pretending it doesn't exist—at least in public. I've met more than a few white people who would rather choke on the word *Black* than say it to my face.

"A Black fella won't stick out as much as I will in some of those neighborhoods down there," Jeffrey said. "Besides, I hear you're a city kid from out East. You know this kind of territory better than I do. And you used to live in Seattle, didn't you?"

I nodded, thinking that it would be nice to go back for a visit. I really liked it there. A job that would take me back sounded pretty good to me. "So what's this guy Smithson doing in Seattle?" I asked. "You have any idea?"

"He's got a sister there," Jeffrey said. "According to his file, he crashed with her the last time he was on the run. She's supposedly into the Indian thing, too. That's why she moved out West from New York. Wanted to get closer to her roots or something. He feels the same way."

"Seattle's not exactly a reservation," I pointed out.

Jeffrey shrugged. "All I know is what's in this file and what the uncle told me." He waved the rolled-up envelope like a testament scroll. That file was going to be his Bible. "Now if you're interested, we're gonna have to leave ASAP. Smithson probably won't be staying in Seattle long."

"Why not?"

"The Indian thing," Jeffrey said as if it should be obvious. "He wants to get back to nature, live in the woods, do all that Indian stuff. He told a prison psychologist that he and his people have been picked on by the white man ever since Columbus showed up, and he's sick and tired of it. He actually said he wants to 'return to the sacred land and seek refuge from the white man's tyranny.' That's a direct quote."

"'White man's tyranny,'" I repeated, chewing that over.

"So are you coming to Seattle with me or not?"

I looked at him and considered the pros and cons. Then I glanced at the newspaper on the table. The jobs in the want ads weren't all that enticing, and none of them would take me to Seattle. *What the hell,* I thought.

"Sure. Why not?" I said. "Let's go."

But by the time we made it to the outskirts of Seattle, I wasn't so sure I'd made the right decision. We'd left right away, traveling all night and into the next morning in Jeffrey's heavy-duty pickup truck, first getting on a ferry from Juneau to the northern tip of Vancouver Island, then driving straight through to Seattle. Somewhere along the way, Jeffrey had made the transformation from friendly cowboy to BOUNTY HUNTER. Little by little he started making it clear to me that he was the leader and I was his sidekick—sort of like the Lone Ranger and Tonto, ironically. I sat back and let him talk, which is my way. Talkers don't listen, and I'd rather be informed than out of breath.

"Now when we get to Smithson's sister's place," Jeffrey told me, "you just stick close and do what I say. If we're lucky, we'll catch him coming out of her apartment."

We were on I–5, heading south, just coming into town. The sky was the color of iron. A city map was on the dashboard, folded to Smithson's sister's neighborhood. If Jeffrey had asked me, I would have told him exactly where it was, but he was set on using the map. My last apartment in Seattle was about ten minutes from the place we were looking for.

"Are we going over to her place right now?" I asked.

"Why not? Waiting's not gonna help us any." His cowboy twang had gotten twangier overnight.

"We've been traveling all night," I said.

He glanced at me. "What's the matter? You tired?"

"Yeah. I think we'd be sharper if we got a little rest."

Jeffrey just made a face. "If Smithson runs off to the woods, we can kiss that ten grand good-bye."

He had a point, but I wasn't so sure the situation was as urgent as he was making it out to be. I'd read Smithson's file on the way down, and he didn't exactly sound like a noble Indian brave. When Smithson was flush, he liked to live large—cars, bars, women, casinos, and tattoo parlors. He had a thing for tattoos; most of his body was covered with them. This taste for extravagance must've been his Brazilian side. But whenever he got into a jam with the law or his money ran out, he went back to his Native American persona—strong, silent, evasive, and brutal when necessary. At one of his court appearances a few years back, he'd tried to sneak a stone tomahawk into the courtroom strapped to his leg. The tomahawk made it through the metal detector, but he hadn't anticipated being patted down, which he should have just assumed since he was on record for being a violent offender. Smithson's plan had been to take out the judge and the prosecutor.

I checked my watch. "It's almost noon," I said to Jeffrey. "Don't you think Smithson will be gone for the day?"

"How do you know he doesn't sleep till noon? My guess is he's pretty nocturnal."

But there was nothing in Smithson's file to indicate that.

Jeffrey signaled to take the next exit, pulled into the right-hand lane, and steered the truck onto the ramp. The first traffic light we came to was green, so he sailed right through. The next one turned red just before we got there. As we waited at the light, Jeffrey reached over to the glove compartment and rummaged around in there until he found what he was looking for, a long-barrel .44 magnum Ruger Redhawk with a genuine wood-grain grip. It almost looked like a six-shooter. I didn't know whether to laugh or what.

Jeffrey checked the cylinder to make sure he had a full load, then stuck it into the waistband of his pants.

"You getting in touch with your Wild West roots?" I asked.

"What do you mean?"

"That looks like something Buffalo Bill would have used."

"It's a good weapon," Jeffrey said defensively. "Very accurate."

"What if Smithson's got an Uzi?"

"Doubtful."

"But what if he's got a weapon that's a little more . . . modern?" I was trying to be tactful.

Jeffrey just shrugged. "So what? Automatics aren't all that accurate. Can't aim for shit with those things. I can pick a man's nose at a hundred yards with my Ruger." He patted the genuine wood-grain grip with obvious satisfaction. At the time, I didn't know enough about weapons to contradict him, but I've since learned through experience that Jeffrey's reasoning was shaky. Yes, revolvers are more accurate than automatics, but when you're out on the street and some bad guy is getting off three shots a second with his weapon, you're not going to have much time to take careful aim with your revolver. In the real world, the name of the game is firepower—how much and how fast. That's why so many police departments across the country have switched from revolvers to semi-automatics for their patrolmen.

The traffic light changed, and Jeffrey drove through the intersection.

"So where's mine?" I asked.

He glanced at me. "Your what?"

"Gun."

"Do you have a license?"

"No."

"Then you can't carry a gun."

"You want me to help you capture a violent felon without a gun? Which one of us is crazy?"

"Sorry, but if something goes wrong, the police will screw you to the wall. That's for sure."

"I think I'm getting screwed right now. What about that shotgun you got behind the seat? Can't I use that?"

Jeffrey shook his head. "Same deal. You need a license."

"We have to rethink this, Jeffrey." I was getting ready to bail out.

"Listen, if things get hairy, you can use the shotgun. But I don't want you carrying it around."

"Well, of course," I said. "No one carries a shotgun around in the city."

Jeffrey gave me a sour look. Apparently that's exactly what he had planned to do. I didn't realize until that moment how little Jeffrey knew about city life. From all that he'd told me, I got the distinct impression that his beliefs about urban America came from TV shows. I was traveling with the hillbilly Kojak.

Ten minutes later we arrived at Smithson's sister's place, a three-story brick apartment building in a blue-collar neighborhood. The street was crammed with parked cars, so Jeffrey double-parked his pickup across the street. As we sat and watched the building, a light drizzle started to fall. After a while the windshield was dotted with moisture that eventually coalesced into droplets that dribbled down the glass and stopped at the idle windshield wipers.

"Maybe we should hang back up the block," I suggested.

"Why?" Jeffrey seemed puzzled.

"Don't you think we look a little obvious double-parked right in front of the place?"

"Smithson's a scumbag, not a brain surgeon. If he was that smart, he would never have gotten caught the first time."

"He made it cross-country without getting caught."

Jeffrey scowled at me. He didn't appreciate my logic. "Just keep your eyes open in case Smithson shows his face."

But keeping my eyes open wasn't so easy. I had been up for the better part of twenty-seven hours. All I wanted to do was close my eyes and drift off for a while. Jeffrey, on the other hand, was amazingly alert, his gaze riveted to the front door of Smithson's sister's apartment building. He'd been up just as long as I had, so I figured if he could do it, I could do it, too. I forced myself to stay awake.

An hour later I was still forcing myself, but now it was becoming a real struggle.

"Go 'head, take a nap," Jeffrey finally said. "I'll wake you up if anything happens." His head was tipped back against the headrest, but his eyes were vigilant. He kept his hand on the grip of his Ruger.

"Thanks," I said as I leaned back. I pulled my cap down over my eyes and quickly fell asleep.

I don't think I'd been asleep very long when suddenly I was awakened by the sound of Jeffrey shouting. "Hold it right there, Smithson. You are under arrest, pal."

I blinked to focus my eyes. Through the wet windshield I could see Jeffrey leaning over the hood of the truck, squinting down the barrel of his revolver. I followed his gaze to the front steps of the apartment building where a man was standing, arms down by his sides, palms facing out. He was about average height, but he looked lean and athletic. He was wearing a red plaid shirt and jeans, and his long black hair was tied back in a ponytail. I recognized the grimace from the photo in the file. It was Smithson.

"Give it up, Smithson," Jeffrey yelled. "I've got you covered."

Smithson didn't say a word or move a muscle, but his calm made me nervous. I wondered if he had a gun. If he and Jeffrey started shooting it out, I was the one who'd most likely get hit. All I had was the truck door between me and Smithson, while Jeffrey had the whole engine block protecting him.

I ducked down and scrambled out of the truck, taking a safer position right next to Jeffrey. "Are you crazy?" I said to him. "You can't pull a gun in broad daylight. What if a cop comes by? He'll start shooting at *us*."

"It's all under control," Jeffrey said evenly, keeping his eyes on Smithson, who was still standing on the top step, not moving. Jeffrey had that Clint Eastwood glint in his eye.

I peered over the hood at Smithson. It seemed as if he was daring Jeffrey to make the first move.

Jeffrey shouted to him. "Put your hands over your head."

Smithson shouted back. "No."

Jeffrey's upper lip curled back. Cowboys don't like being dissed.

Suddenly Smithson leaped over the side of the brick steps and into the bushes. I caught a flash of his red shirt as he emerged from the bushes and slipped down the alleyway between the apartment buildings.

"Go get him!" Jeffrey yelled.

I hesitated, still thinking that Smithson might have a gun.

"Go on!" Jeffrey urged. "I'm too slow. You go."

He was right about that. Jeffrey was big and he didn't move very fast. I wondered if he'd brought me along just to be his bird dog.

I didn't like this situation, but it was no time for an argument. Smithson was here, and I wanted the money, so I ran across the street and peered down the alley. It was empty, but it was also narrow. If I went down it, I'd be a sitting duck when I came out the other side.

"Go on!" I heard Jeffrey shouting behind me. "You're gonna lose him."

Reluctantly I stepped into the alley. It was cool and damp in the shadows. And it was quiet. I moved forward, imagining Smithson's silhouette suddenly appearing at the top of the alley, like a shooting gallery target but with a real gun in his hand. My only option would be to drop to the ground. But then what? The odds were definitely not in my favor. This was insane.

Jeffrey was still yelling at me, but I ignored him and started back toward the truck in a low crouch. Then I heard someone else shouting from the back of the building. "Hey! What do you think you're doing over there?" At first I thought the person was yelling at me, but then I heard the wobbly clang of a chain-link fence, the sound of someone climbing it. I ventured cautiously down the alley to the back of the building where the commotion was coming from and peered into the concrete backyard.

An old man in khaki pants and a gray sweatshirt was frowning at the fence and the empty lot beyond it. When he spotted me, he turned his frown on me. "You with that long-haired fella?" the old man snapped.

I shook my head no.

"I just fixed that fence two goddamn weeks ago," the old man said, "and here this guy goes climbing it. Shit! It's not meant to take that kind of weight."

"Was this long-haired guy wearing a red plaid shirt?" I asked.

"Yeah, that's him," the man said in disgust.

I looked through the fence at the empty lot. It was covered with weeds, but none were tall enough to hide behind. Smithson was gone.

And so was my five grand, I thought.

"Didn't get him, huh?" Jeffrey said when I came back out of the alley.

I shook my head.

"Well, let's go talk to the sister then," he said, walking like John Wayne as he headed up the brick steps with his Ruger sticking out of his pants. I wondered if his intention was to scare Smithson's sister into giving him up. I'd always heard you catch more flies with sugar than with vinegar, but I was new to this game, and Jeffrey had done it before, so I kept my mouth shut.

I followed Jeffrey into the vestibule, where he scanned the buzzers on the grid. There were only six apartments in the building, and "D. Smithson" was in 3B. Her name was Donna, she was thirty-six, and she was divorced. I'd read it in her brother's file.

Jeffrey pressed a few buzzers that weren't Donna Smithson's. A voice came over the intercom. It sounded like an elderly woman. "Who is it?" she asked. Jeffrey put his finger to his lips, indicating that I should keep quiet. He pressed a couple of more buzzers, and this time he got lucky. Someone buzzed him in without asking who it was.

We pushed through the front door, and a head popped out of the first apartment, a cranky-looking bald guy in his sixties. "What do you want?" he snarled.

"A–1 Exterminators," Jeffrey said without missing a beat.

"It's about time," the man said, and slammed his door shut.

Jeffrey flashed a sly grin at me, proud of the slick way he'd gotten us into the building.

"What would you have done if no one had buzzed us in?" I asked.

"Broken the lock," Jeffrey said.

So much for slick, I thought.

We climbed the worn marble steps to the top floor. Apartment 3B was at the rear of the building. Jeffrey hitched up his pants and adjusted the Ruger before he pounded on the door with his fist.

"Who is it?" a voice inside screeched. The lady inside didn't sound like she wanted to be bothered. I noticed that there was no peephole in the door.

"Donna Smithson?" Jeffrey asked.

"Who wants to know?" She was right on the other side of the door. I pictured a witch from the unpleasant sound of her voice.

"I'm a friend of Patrick's."

"So."

"Is he in there with you?"

"No."

"I just need to drop something off for him."

"What is it?"

Jeffrey lowered his voice to a stage whisper. "I'm not gonna shout it out loud, for chrissake."

She toned down her voice a notch. "You here to pay him back?"

"Yeah." Jeffrey looked at me and shrugged.

"You got all of it?" she asked.

"Yup."

The dead bolt clicked as she unlocked the door. It opened a few inches. "Come on in," she said.

Jeffrey pushed the door open a little farther and peeked in. I looked over his shoulder. The apartment smelled of burned toast.

"In the kitchen," the woman called to us.

Jeffrey stepped into a small hallway, motioning for me to stay close. The living room was off the hallway on the left. There was a tangle of sheets and a blanket on the couch and crushed Bud cans and an overflowing ashtray on the coffee table. The bathroom was straight ahead, so I figured the doorway to the right had to be the kitchen. I wondered why she hadn't stayed in the hallway to greet us. Maybe she was hanging back with a shotgun or something. I slowed down, ready to make a quick exit if anything went wrong.

I watched Jeffrey as he approached the kitchen. When he got to the threshold, his body stiffened, but no guns went off. My curiosity got the better of me, and I peered in over his shoulder.

Donna Smithson was sitting at a Formica table, rubbing her temples with one hand, a cigarette smoldering in the other. I was flabbergasted. The Wicked Witch of the West's voice didn't go with the rest of her. The woman was gorgeous. She had long curly raven-black hair that circled her head like a storm and the beguiling Latin face of a flamenco dancer. She was wearing an oversized white V-neck T-shirt that went over her hips but revealed an awful lot on top. Unlike her brother, there was clearly more Brazilian than Native American in her genetic mix.

She looked up at us and frowned. "So? What do you want?"

"I have to find your brother," Jeffrey said.

"What about the money?"

"I just said that to get you to open the door."

"Fucker." She looked down and rubbed her temples. Hangover, I guessed.

"So where can I find him?" Jeffrey asked.

"What are you? Bounty hunters?"

"Bail enforcement agents," Jeffrey corrected.

Her laugh was a sarcastic cackle. "I figured. You look it."

Jeffrey glowered at her, but she seemed to get a kick out of annoying him.

Then she looked at me. "So what's your story? You don't look like one of his kind."

I couldn't suppress my grin. "No," I said. "I'm not like anyone."

"Yeah, right," she grumbled. Suddenly she noticed the Ruger sticking out of Jeffrey's pants. "What're you gonna do with that? Shoot me?"

"I've got no gripe with you, ma'am," Jeffrey said. "I just need to find your brother."

"Well, too bad, you just missed him," she said.

"We know that," I said. "Where'd he go?"

"How in the hell am I supposed to know? He comes and goes as he pleases. Doesn't tell me nothing."

The polite smile faded from Jeffrey's lips. "Come on now. We all know he's been living here. Why don't you make life easy on all of us and just tell us where he went?"

"I told you. I don't know where he went. He don't tell me nothing about nothing."

Jeffrey furrowed his brow and lowered his voice. "Ma'am, we are representatives of the law. We are not here on a personal vendetta."

"Like I care."

"Well, you should care. Aiding and abetting is a punishable offense in case you didn't know that."

"Where are you from? The fuckin' moon?"

Jeffrey's face went slack. "I'd appreciate it if you'd take that tone down a notch, ma'am."

"It's my house. I'll take whatever goddamn tone I want."

Jeffrey and Donna Smithson continued to go at it like a couple of nasty old crows fighting over a chicken bone. I tuned them out because I knew this wasn't going to net us anything. They were both just venting.

While they yammered at each other, I looked around the kitchen. Dirty dishes were piled in the sink, and all kinds of coupons were stuck to the refrigerator with a collection of magnets that all advertised a particular beauty parlor called the Mane Event. The linoleum was worn but basically clean, and the table was littered with prescription bottles, sugar packets, pens, bills, catalogs, and all sorts of loose papers. One piece of paper in particular caught my eye. It was pastel green and looked like a check stub. I leaned forward trying to read it, but I was too far away. The only thing I could make out was the logo of the company that had issued the check, Benny's Beanery. I'd heard of the place. It was a restaurant somewhere downtown. I glanced at Donna's meticulously manicured fingernails splayed out on the table. Obviously she didn't work in a kitchen, and she didn't seem to have the personality for waitressing. Her brother, though, might have found work washing dishes or bussing tables.

"Jeffrey," I said softly, trying to get his attention. "I think we should go."

"One minute," he snapped. "I'm not finished here."

"But—"

"Just hang on." He went back to bickering with Donna, who was bound and determined not to give him the time of day.

I leaned back against the door jamb and crossed my arms. This was obviously going to take a while. They had a lot more venting to do.

7 How Not to Do It, Part 2

When we finally left Donna Smithson's apartment, Jeffrey was so mad he was barely coherent. It wasn't until we were back in the truck that I got him to understand that I'd picked up a lead on Smithson. As we drove out of the neighborhood, I told him to pull over at a convenience store. I found a pay phone with a phone book, looked up Benny's Beanery, and got the address. As I'd thought, it was downtown, right near the Pike's Place Market in the most touristy section of the city.

I convinced Jeffrey that we should check into a motel and get a couple of hours' sleep before we went looking for Smithson again. For all we knew, Smithson might have left town already, but I had a feeling he hadn't. He had been pretty cool when Jeffrey was holding a gun on him, and I assumed we weren't the first bounty hunters to go looking for him. He'd had a pretty good run dodging the law, so maybe he wasn't worried about us. And if he figured we didn't know where he worked, he might just go there and put in a full shift, then crash somewhere else. We could only hope.

After getting some rest, we set out for Benny's Beanery at 11 P.M. The place was easy enough to find, but finding Smithson and nabbing him would be another story. It was Friday night and the place was packed. If we went in, and he spotted us, we could lose him in the crowd, and as I would later find out, crowds are unpredictable—there's no telling what they'll do. Sometimes they help you, sometimes they don't.

"Let me go in and take a quick look around," I said to Jeffrey. He was parked in a loading zone. Our rest had made him grumpy, and he had the Ruger stuck in his pants again. I didn't think it was a good idea for him to go in.

"Go ahead," Jeffrey said with a moody sniff. "I'll wait here."

"OK," I said, relieved that he wasn't insisting on leading the charge.

I went into the restaurant and headed straight for the bar, working my way through the crush so I could order a beer. It was a young singles crowd, most of them only a couple of years out of college. Some of the guys were getting pretty rowdy, trying too hard to impress the women. I retreated to a stand-up counter that looked out on the dining room so I could survey the place, checking the faces of everyone who worked there—waiters, bartenders, busboys, even the maître d'. Unfortunately, Smithson wasn't among them.

According to the file, Smithson had no history of working in restaurants, so if he was employed here, it was a good guess that he was probably in the kitchen, washing dishes or cleaning up. I worked my way over to the other end of the bar where I could peer through the swinging doors that led into the kitchen. Waiters and waitresses kept going in and out, banging the doors open, which gave me brief glimpses of the interior. I got a quick look at a couple of guys preparing plates at a stainless-steel counter, but neither of them was Smithson.

I picked up my beer and headed for the hallway where the rest rooms were located, and as I'd hoped, there was a doorway at the end that led into the kitchen. Being careful not to be seen, I leaned into the doorway and peered in. It was steamy in that part of the kitchen, and at first all I could see was the backs of two guys in white T-shirts hosing down dirty dishes in a sink that looked like a trough. A third person joined them. He was carrying a dirty soup pot that was big enough for a dog bath. This guy had a dark ponytail like Smithson's.

I stood perfectly still and watched him from the shadows. He was less than twenty feet away. I waited until he turned his head enough for me to see his profile. I was pretty sure it was Smithson.

But I wasn't sure what I should do. He was right there. I could grab him from behind, but then what? I didn't have cuffs, rope, anything. We'd just end up wrestling on the floor until someone broke us up—or called the cops. And that wouldn't be good. Jeffrey had already warned me that cops generally don't like having bounty hunters on their beat. If they took Smithson in, they'd run a check on him and find out he was a fugitive, and if they were the ones to send him back to New York, that would mean no payday for us. I went back into the bar, left my beer on the counter, and walked out of the restaurant.

"He's in there," I said to Jeffrey as I came up to the truck.

Jeffrey opened his door. "Let's go get him—"

I held the door closed to stop him. "Too many people inside. Why don't we go through the back?"

"Sure. Fine." I could tell Jeffrey wasn't really listening. He was still grumpy.

We drove around to the back alley and parked the truck, then walked toward the kitchen door. The streetlights were set far apart, casting long shadows. Jeffrey walked with his hand on the butt of the Ruger as if heading for a showdown at the O.K. Corral.

"You got cuffs?" I asked him.

"Course I got cuffs," he growled.

"Just asking," I said. I didn't want Jeffrey shooting Smithson because he had no other way to restrain the man. Dead fugitives aren't worth squat, and more important, I didn't want to end up being charged as an accessory to murder.

A single floodlight hung over the back door to Benny's Beanery. It cast a dim washed-out light that only partially illuminated the huge navy-blue Dumpster nearby. Jeffrey was ready to barge right in, but I held onto his sleeve.

"Smithson's doing scut work," I said. "Why don't we just wait and see if he comes out to the Dumpster? It'll be easier to take him out here."

Jeffrey gave me a wary look, but he didn't object. We moved into the shadows, our backs against a brick wall about two car lengths from the Dumpster. It wasn't long before someone in a white T-shirt and apron came out and heaved a heavy plastic garbage bag into the Dumpster. Jeffrey immediately reached for his Ruger, ready to move in. But the man was short and obviously Asian, and Jeffrey relaxed as soon as he realized it wasn't Smithson.

We waited in silence. Minutes passed. Someone else in a white T-shirt came out with more garbage, but this was a beefy Black man. Fifteen minutes later the Asian guy came out again.

Jeffrey turned to me and hissed in my ear. "You sure you saw Smithson?"

"I'm sure."

"Well, doesn't he do any work? Lazy no-good son of a—"

Suddenly a new figure appeared in the doorway, and Jeffrey stopped talking. This person was carrying two garbage bags, one slung over each shoulder. He came down off the steps and walked over to the Dumpster. His face was in shadow until he got up to the mouth of the Dumpster where the floodlight revealed his profile. It was definitely Smithson.

Jeffrey jumped out of the shadows. "Freeze, Smithson," he yelled, simultaneously pulling the Ruger out of his pants.

Ka-BOOM!

A muzzle flash strobe-lit the alleyway a split-second before the deafening blast bounced off the brick walls and plugged my ears. Smithson was running back inside.

"Go get him!" Jeffrey shouted to me. "Go!"

Again he wanted me to be his bird dog. But that didn't piss me off as much as the fact that he'd fired his weapon prematurely and without cause. Thanks to Jeffrey, Smithson had a head start on me again.

I bounded up the back steps and into the bright lights of the kitchen. I could tell from the darting eyes on all the alarmed faces which way Smithson had gone. I hurried out into the restaurant. Smithson had made it through the bar and was in the dining room now, leaping over tables like a hurdler. Some customers screamed, but the drunken ones cheered. I pushed my way through the crush at the bar to catch up with him, but the rowdy singles were all excited now. They were on their feet, craning their necks to get a look at the running fugitive, and of course, they were in my way. I plowed through them and made a mad dash for the dining room. The horrified maître d' held out his palms to stop me, but I didn't slow down one bit. The man backed out of my way before I crashed into him full tilt.

I ran out the front door and into the street, where packs of people were strolling along in the cool night air. I looked all around for a sign of Smithson—someone with a shocked look on her face, someone pointing—but there was no one. The scene was calm and pleasant. Too calm and pleasant. Smithson had escaped again.

"Why don't you let me hold the gun?" I said to Jeffrey when we reunited at the truck.

Jeffrey just gave me a withering look. "Why would I do that?"

I frowned at him. "All right, so now what do we do?"

"Start looking."

"Yeah, but where?" Since he had done this before, I was looking to him for guidance, but frankly I didn't have a lot of confidence in his supposed expertise. Jeffrey didn't have much finesse, and he'd jumped the gun twice, costing us the capture. I wondered if I'd be better off cutting my losses and going back to Alaska where I could get a job in a cannery until the fishing season started again. Low pay was better than no pay.

"Look," Jeffrey said, "we've got plenty of leads." He could see that I wasn't pleased with the way this operation was going. "We'll talk to the people Smithson works with at the restaurant. We can lean on his sister some more."

I was very skeptical. It was possible that Smithson's coworkers would give us something we could use. But the sister? Forget it. She wasn't going to tell us anything.

"Come on. Don't give up yet," Jeffrey said. "We just started." Jeffrey's pep talk wasn't making me feel any better. In my mind I kept seeing Smithson running off into the woods. After all, why wouldn't he? He knew he was being chased. The only thing that could possibly keep him in Seattle was our proven incompetence. If we were lucky, he didn't see us as much of a threat, which so far we hadn't been.

We stuck around the restaurant until it closed and, one at a time, caught the two kitchen workers we'd seen earlier going to the Dumpster. The Black man wanted nothing to do with us. He wouldn't even look at me when I tried to talk to him. Of course, Jeffrey was right behind me, and he looked more like a cop than a real cop, so I couldn't blame the man for refusing to talk.

The Asian man came out next, and I cut in front of Jeffrey to get to him first. "Stay here," I said firmly, taking off my cap and stuffing it in my pocket. "Let me talk to him alone." I was thinking honey and vinegar, and I wanted to try the honey without the vinegar this time.

"Excuse me, excuse me," I said, trotting up to the man. I kept my hands where he could see them so he wouldn't think I was coming to mug him. It was almost three in the morning.

The man gave me a suspicious sidelong glance. He was small but well built and in his mid-twenties, I guessed. I stopped trotting before I got to him and just walked the rest of the way. He quickly faced me and turned his body sideways, making himself a small target. His hands were positioned in front of him. Obviously he knew some martial art.

I smiled. "Easy, man, easy. I just want to ask you about that guy you work with. The guy with the ponytail."

"What about him?" The young Asian sounded like a California beach bum.

"I'm looking for him," I said. "Can you tell me where I might find him?"

"I don't know anything about him." The young man was resentful. I had a feeling that if he knew anything, he wasn't going to tell me.

"His sister sent me to get him," I said. "There are some pretty rough characters out looking for him. She wanted me to warn him." I hoped that he hadn't recognized me as the "rough character" who had chased Smithson through the restaurant.

"You're too late," the young man said. "Some guys were already here. He ran off." I could see from his posture that he was beginning to relax.

"You know where he went?"

The man shrugged and shook his head.

"Shit!" I said. "I was gonna get him out of here. His sister's gonna be pissed now. You sure you don't know where he might be?"

The Asian man shook his head, but his expression was more sympathetic. He didn't seem to mistrust me as much as he originally had. "I don't talk to Smithson all that much," he admitted. "I do know he has a girlfriend, though. He might be with her."

"You know where she lives?"

He nodded toward the docks. "Somewhere out that way." He was indicating the poor Black section of town.

"You don't happen to know her address, do you?"

He shook his head.

"You know her name?"

He shook his head again. "Tall Black girl. Good-looking. Sort of a Tina Turner type, but not blond. Redhead. An obvious dye job. I saw her when she came by one night, but that's all I know about her." He turned and went on his way.

"Hey, thanks," I called after him.

I started walking back toward Jeffrey, who was walking toward me. "You find out anything?" he asked.

I sighed. "Start looking for redheaded Tina Turners."

For the rest of that week we hung out in the 'hood trawling the streets, looking for Smithson and following any tall Black woman with dyed red hair who crossed our path. We'd follow a woman home, then stake out the place hoping that Smithson would show his face. Amazingly, there were more women who fit the description than we ever expected, and Jeffrey wanted to grill every one of them, but I managed to keep him under control. Even if we did find Smithson's girlfriend, she'd probably clam up and then tip off Smithson that we were in the neighborhood. I figured we'd be better off just taking in the scene for the time being.

But one long day of searching for redheads and staking out their apartments led to another. As we cruised the same streets over and over, the shops, beauty salons, and grocery stores all started to look alike. Even the redheads started to look alike, and by the third day I was half-convinced that I was just seeing the same ten redheads over and over again.

"How tall was that Chinese guy?" Jeffrey asked me early in the morning of the fourth day while we sat in the truck. I was watching the steam rise from my cup of tea, soaking in the quiet as a golden sun peeked over the roofs of the apartment buildings directly in front of us. I ignored his question, hoping he'd respect the serenity just a little while longer.

But Jeffrey was oblivious. "'Cause I was thinking," he went on. "He was a little sucker, that Chinese guy. Just an average-sized redhead would look tall to him. Maybe we should start checking out shorter redheads."

I stared at the twisting swirls of steam, trying to lose myself in their snaky dance. I didn't mean to be rude, but Jeffrey was not teaching me anything about bounty hunting. His prior successes had to have been flukes. I suspected he'd just lucked out and gotten assignments to find fugitives who were a lot dumber than Smithson. If we were going to pull this one off, I knew I'd have to take some more initiative.

"Think we should go back and talk to the sister?" Jeffrey said. He'd been asking me this several times a day for the past three days. "What do you think? Should we try it?"

I just shook my head, which had become my standard response.

"Maybe there are some Indian clubs in town. You know, where they all get together and do Indian stuff. Maybe we should check them out."

I didn't even bother to answer that one.

"You know, you're not being very helpful today," he said. "I thought you'd have some ideas, you being from the inner city and all, but—"

"Ssshhhh." I raised my hand for him to be quiet. "Look." I pointed. "Over by the coffee shop."

Standing in front of the coffee shop across the street where we'd just bought our breakfast was a man with dark hair pulled back in a ponytail. He was wearing black jeans and a white T-shirt.

"Is that him?" Jeffrey whispered as if the man could hear us.

"I don't know," I said. The man was mostly turned away from us, but from this distance it certainly looked like Smithson.

"Let's go check him out," Jeffrey said in a low growl.

"Be still for a minute," I said. Jeffrey was ready to yank the line before he even knew if he had a genuine bite.

The man with the ponytail was just standing in front of the coffee shop as if he was waiting for someone. A few minutes later a woman came down the sidewalk. She was wearing lime-green pedal pushers and high-heel sandals. Her hair was the color of pomegranate seeds. As she approached the man, she spread her arms and gave him a big hug and a kiss.

"That's him!" Jeffrey had one hand on his gun, the other on the door handle.

I laid my hand on his shoulder. "Let's be cool this time," I said.

I pulled the bill of my cap down over my eyes. "Let me go see if it really is him. If it is, I'll signal to you."

"What's the signal?"

"I'll stretch my arms over my head, like I'm yawning, OK? When you see that, pull up with the truck *nice and slow,* and we'll take him together."

"OK, OK. As soon as I see you stretching, I make my move." Jeffrey was raring to go.

"But not until I give you the signal," I stressed as I got out of the truck and shut the door.

I started toward the coffee shop, keeping my head down as if I had a lot on my mind and someplace important to go. I crossed the street and approached the couple, who were still locked in an embrace. I could see the woman's face but only the back of the man's head. I walked closer, maintaining my determined pace. As I passed them, I finally caught a glimpse of the man's face. He had a parrot nose, thin lips, and long dark eyelashes. I was pretty certain this was Smithson, but I wasn't absolutely sure. I decided to go into the coffee shop and get a better look at him through the front window.

But just as I was about to enter the coffee shop, I heard an engine roaring and tires squealing. Out of the corner of my eye, I saw Jeffrey's faded red pickup barreling down the street.

Oh, no, I sighed to myself.

"Give it up, Smithson!" Jeffrey was yelling at the top of his lungs, waving his Ruger out the window. "You are under arrest, pal." He was charging hard, like a cowboy on a horse out to rope a calf.

The man with the redhead clearly was Smithson because as soon as he heard his name, he bolted like a jackrabbit, running right past me. I was furious at Jeffrey for screwing up again, but I wasn't about to let Smithson get away this time. I knew we weren't going to get another chance, so I took off after him.

Smithson dashed across the street, paying no attention to the traffic. I followed, putting my faith in the drivers' brakes. Horns honked, tires screeched, but I didn't look right or left. I just kept my eye on Smithson.

He headed the wrong way down a narrow one-way street. Jeffrey tried to follow him, but oncoming traffic blocked his path. Smithson then cut across a parking lot jammed with cars, weaving his way in and out. I suppose he thought he'd be able to lose me in there, but he hadn't counted on the tenacity of a man who needs money and who doesn't particularly want to work the night shift on the processing line in a cannery.

Smithson was physically fit, and he moved with the quickness of a tight end. I was pretty fit myself from working on a fishing boat, but I wasn't sure I was as fast as he was. I decided to conserve my wind and not yell to him the way Jeffrey had. He wasn't going to listen to anything I had to say anyway. Besides, I had no weapon to threaten him with. It was just me. My only choice was to stay on his tail and hope to wear him down, the way a jackal will trail an antelope for miles and miles waiting for the antelope to tire out.

But after four blocks of running, Smithson showed no signs of tiring. He stayed about twenty feet in front of me, and whenever I started to close that distance, he sprinted ahead to open it up again. After doing this a few times, he turned his head and looked back at me. "You're not gonna get me," he shouted.

I didn't respond. We were in this for the long haul. I couldn't afford to waste any energy.

Smithson kept running. He ducked into alleys, cut through empty lots, and zigzagged down busy streets, hoping that the traffic would interfere with my progress. But I stayed right with him. Cars and storefronts slipped by in a blur. I became less and less aware of where I was. My focus was exclusively on him.

It wasn't until he'd veered toward the water that I realized how far we'd gone. We were heading for Fishermen's Terminal. Huge factory trawlers loomed over the docks just ahead. Dozens of smaller vessels were in berth—trollers, crabbers, longliners, gillnetters, and seiners. We must've covered at least a dozen blocks to get there, but I tried not to think about that. It would just make me feel more tired if I knew how far we'd run.

The ground abruptly switched from blacktop to the weathered gray planks of a boardwalk. Smelling the crisp salt air, I suddenly realized what a beautiful clear day it had turned out to be. The sky was blue, and the sun was sparkling off the sound. My lungs ached, and my legs felt like rubber, but I didn't seem to mind it. I just kept going and going, keeping my pace, running like a machine, left, right, left, right, left, right . . .

Smithson glanced back at me. His face was flushed and looked haggard. Still he managed to scowl at me, telling me again that I wasn't going to get him. Our feet pounded the boards, his steps a counter-rhythm to mine. He was heading for one of the factory trawlers whose gangplank was down. Those ships are mazes inside. The processing floor is almost as big as a football field, crammed with a dizzying array of machines and conveyor lines. If Smithson ran aboard, he could easily lose me in there. I had to stop him now.

As tired as I was, I kicked it out and closed the gap between us. He didn't realize where I was until I was right behind him. He poured it on, trying to get away from me, but I reached out to grab whatever I could. His ponytail was flying behind him like a flag, there for the taking.

I snatched his hair and yanked back as if I were trying to control a runaway horse. I got a fistful of shirt with my other hand, and suddenly we weren't running anymore. He'd stopped and was now struggling to break free. I dug my heels in, set on taking him down.

But when Smithson saw that flight wasn't an option any longer, he took the other alternative—fight. He moved in on me with a hip check, knocked me down on my back, and pounced on top of me. I held on to his hair and tried to push him off at the same time. But Smithson was vicious. He went right for my eyes, clawing at my face. I turned my head and pushed off with my heel, flipping over on top of him, but he kept the roll going and flipped back on top of me. I'd had five years of martial arts training when I was a kid, but my time in the dojo hadn't prepared me for a desperate man fighting for his freedom. Smithson fought like a tiger, determined to gouge my eyes. I finally had to let go of his hair to protect my face, but his single-minded determination to blind me left him vulnerable to other attacks. I got my knee between his legs and slammed it into his groin—once, twice, three times, as many as it took to get him off me. Finally he groaned and rolled off, curling up into himself. He struggled to his feet, ready to run again, but I had had enough. I lunged at his legs and hugged his ankles. He hit the planks hard, face first. At this point I didn't hesitate. I straddled his back and pinned his arms to his sides with my knees, then grabbed his ponytail and pulled back as far as his head would go. As soon as he realized that I was going to snap his spine if he kept it up, he stopped struggling.

"All right . . . all right," he gasped. We were both breathing hard. I didn't even try to speak. I held him at bay like this for five, ten, twenty minutes—I wasn't sure how long because I was so exhausted.

"Well, all right!" Jeffrey lumbered up to the scene. I was amazed he'd found us, but somehow he had. His steps were heavy, and they jangled. For a second I thought he was wearing spurs until I saw that the jangling was coming from the leg irons and handcuffs he was carrying. He secured the leg irons on Smithson while I was still on top of him, then put on the handcuffs while I held the man's arms. Smithson didn't resist. He was too tired.

I climbed to my feet and looked down at the man. He just lay there on the dock like a big tuna.

Jeffrey clapped me on the shoulder. "Well, we did it," he said. He was smiling like the new mayor on election day.

"Yeah," I said, still trying to catch my breath. "We did it." I was too tired to correct his choice of pronouns.

Jeffrey escorted Smithson back to New York by himself and collected our fee. True to his word, he wired my half to me right away. The money sweetened my bitter feelings about Jeffrey's incompetence. He had a lot of nerve calling himself a professional bounty hunter. But over time I had to admit that he had taught me one valuable lesson: how *not* to catch a fugitive.

8 Evolution

I left Alaska and went back to New Jersey to live in 1984. I was twenty-seven, and it had been eight years since I left home. I felt it was time to do something different, something more permanent. I just didn't see myself being a fisherman for the rest of my life.

After that first job with Jeffrey in Seattle, other part-time bounty hunters had asked me to help them out. I'd gotten interested in the whole process of finding fugitives, and eventually bounty hunting became my regular off-season gig. Some of the bounty hunters I'd worked with were a little better at it than Jeffrey was, and I'd learned the basics of the trade from them. After a while I got pretty good at it, but along the way I came to the realization that fugitives from justice were simply people who had not had the right guides and mentors in their lives to help them evolve. Everyone needs positive examples, people like Kanya McGee and Leo Ostin. But at this point I didn't see how bounty hunting could fit in with my ancient Egyptian beliefs. In many ways they seemed to be at odds with one another. After all, how can you raise a person's self-esteem to help him evolve when you're hauling him away in handcuffs and leg irons?

When I got back to Elizabeth, I became something of a local curiosity, the brother who had gone to Alaska to work on the pipeline, become a fisherman, and ended up learning how to be a bounty hunter. The stories of my adventures in the Northwest started to spread from my friends and family to the community at large, and inevitably these tales grew taller. People gawked at me on the street. Some even seemed disappointed that I wasn't more "colorful," as if they expected me to be wearing a fur hat and carrying a hunting knife with an elk-horn handle on my belt.

One day I happened to run into John Brennan, an old friend from high school. John's father was the chief of police in Elizabeth. We went back to my parents' house and sat at the kitchen table, kicking back, drinking beer, and catching up on old times. After he filled me in on what had become of some of our old classmates, he mentioned that he'd heard the rumors about my exploits in Alaska.

"You must be looking for work now," he said. "I told my dad about you, and he said he'd love to have you join the force. He thinks you'd have a great future as a cop."

I just nodded and let the whole concept sink in for a moment. I had never in my wildest dreams imagined myself as a cop. John was right that I needed to find work, and jumping from bounty hunting to law enforcement did seem like a logical step, but somehow the idea of being a cop didn't sit well with me. For one thing, I didn't want to be restricted by a bureaucracy. Most of the people I knew in law enforcement were in it only for the pay and the benefits. I also didn't like the us-versus-them mentality that many—maybe even most—policemen eventually develop.

From what I've seen over the years, most cops sooner or later become intoxicated by the sense of power they get from wearing a gun and a badge. To them, everybody *out there* is a scumbag. But those scumbags are almost always poor and Black or poor and Hispanic. For these officers, police work is just a matter of hauling in scumbags, day after day. That's a mind-set I didn't share back then and I don't share now. Even as I considered John's suggestion, I knew in my heart that I would never be able to work with people who held such a narrow view of the world.

"I appreciate you and your father thinking of me," I told John, "but

I don't think the police force is right for me." I ran my thumbnail through the label of my beer bottle. At this point I wasn't sure any job was going to be right for me. In Alaska I had been respected as a top-notch fisherman. Any job I'd get in Elizabeth was going to be a come-down from that.

John took a sip of his beer. "I hear what you're saying," he said. "No problem. It was just an idea."

"Yeah," I said absently. I was staring at the light shining through the dark green bottle in my hand.

"So what *are* you planning to do now that you're back?"

I shrugged. "Don't know. I've got a few ideas but nothing definite."

"Oh," he said.

I was still thinking about bounty hunting, but not the way I'd seen it practiced in the Northwest. I didn't say anything to John, though, because I wasn't ready to talk about it yet. I had to get it down on paper first.

Not long after I had that talk with John, his father happened to introduce me to a man named William Davis. William was in his early sixties, stood six feet tall, and weighed 225. He had a lot of gray in his hair and a lot of wisdom to go with it. He was one of the first Black men to serve on a U.S. Navy vessel, and he'd been an Equal Employment Opportunity officer with the post office, which is the equivalent of a federal agent. As a young man he'd played sax in a jazz band, touring throughout the country. When I met him, he had just gotten his private detective's license. We got to talking about his new line of work one afternoon, and I told him about my bounty-hunting experiences in the Northwest. William's plan was to work solo, offering his services to attorneys and private individuals, but I saw an opportunity here. Bail enforcement agents in New Jersey must have a private detective's license. I thought that if we became partners, I could set myself up as the bounty-hunting division of our joint venture. But instead of proposing this outright, I held my tongue. I didn't want to go into this half-cocked. I wanted to do it right, and I wanted to do it differently.

Every bounty hunter I'd met so far was basically a misguided individual with a gun. I envisioned something better, a company of professional bail enforcement agents that would maintain high standards and observe a strict evolutionary code. When William and I parted after that first meeting, I promised I would stay in touch. In fact, I intended to get back in touch sooner than he thought.

That night I sat down and started writing out a proposal for William in which I outlined all my ideas for a different kind of bounty-hunting operation. Intelligence, advance preparation, and humanity were the cornerstones of my vision. I worked on the proposal for two weeks until it expanded to a fifteen-page document. I envisioned a bounty-hunting team that would combine compassion and street smarts. The members of this team would constantly seek to improve themselves physically, mentally, and spiritually, all in equal measure. They would be committed to self-mastery, and their knowledge, understanding, and wisdom would be evident in everything they did. In other words, they would be examples for both the community and the fugitives they sought. They would be a team of highly evolved individuals, or stellar men as they're called in ancient Egyptian philosophy.

I presented my proposal to William, who accepted it after just one reading. Soon after that we became partners. William eventually moved to North Carolina to pursue other interests, leaving me his share of the business. But that proposal was the blueprint for what would eventually become the Seekers.

As sole proprietor of the business, I continued to develop the ideas I had outlined in my original proposal. Initially I worked alone but later took on another partner, Calvin, a man who shared my vision for a new kind of bounty-hunting operation.

Calvin was an exceptionally creative individual who had a keen sense of what was going on out on the street. A trained graphic artist, he had a gift for creating convincing disguises, such as florist and deliveryman uniforms, which helped us get the drop on our targets. Calvin was also very clever with gadgets, and though our funds were limited, we didn't skimp on equipment. We tried to have as much state-of-the-art technology as we could afford, which at the time included long-range listening devices, various kinds of mace, camouflage suits, the latest semi-automatic handguns, nonlethal ammunition, and advanced restraining systems. What we didn't bother with were things like phony badges and revolving lights for our cars, which turned out to be a smart move on our part.

Our primary focus was on obtaining as much information as we could before attempting to make an arrest. We soon learned that the more we knew about a fugitive—his habits, his family, his friends, his women—the easier it was to take him by surprise and without incident. Waking a fugitive out of a sound sleep in the wee hours of the morning was our preferred approach. People are usually too scared or too sleepy to put up much of a fight in that kind of situation, and our capture rate improved significantly as a result.

By keeping a low profile—unlike every other bounty hunter working in the field at the time—we kept from getting on the bad side of the police. This is not to say that we were invisible to them. Just the opposite. We'd go in and out of the local police stations, delivering fugitive after fugitive, leaving the cops scratching their heads and asking, "Who the hell are those guys?" For a time we were known as the "Black Ninjas of Union County."

But our anonymity didn't last forever. Our capture rate became so impressive, the top brass began to take notice. Not only did we consistently bring in fugitives, we also did our paperwork and kept meticulous files on all our cases. We were so professional in the way we operated, the police just assumed that we had permits for the guns we carried, when in fact at the time we didn't have any permits at all. (The first bondsmen to hire us believed that having a warrant for someone's arrest gave a bounty hunter automatic permission to carry a gun. As soon as we found out he was wrong about that, we quickly applied for gun permits.)

Because of us, the police we dealt with started to change their attitude about bounty hunters. In fact, the Union County Sheriff's Department actually considered putting us on permanent retainer, but political opposition forced them to scrap the idea. The cops' main objection was that we weren't "academy trained."

Calvin and I worked together for only fourteen months. His attention was needed at home after the deaths of a few close family members. We were a good team, and I missed him when he left.

One of my hardest cases ever was the first case I took after William Davis left me in charge in 1986 and before Calvin joined me. It was a time of accelerated evolution for me—I was progressing professionally, and I felt good about the way I was doing it. Every day seemed to present me with a new challenge. But even though I now had a clear vision of what I wanted to do with my life, I was totally on my own as to how I was going to do it.

Up to this point I had been concentrating on local pickups, occasionally venturing across the river into New York City but mainly tracking down fugitives in Union, Essex, and Hudson Counties in New Jersey. These criminals weren't minor leaguers by any means. Drug dealers made up about 80 percent of my successful captures along with a few attempted murderers, some rapists, and a couple of other violent offenders. I'd thought I was doing pretty well, all things considered. Then came Donald Tate.

Even though I had been picking up some pretty mean characters, none of them had exactly been cash cows. Their bails had been relatively low, so my 10 percent fees hadn't really netted me all that much. I was making ends meet but just barely, and if I was ever going to expand the business, I would need some working capital. One of the bondsmen I was working for at the time understood my situation, and after I proved myself to him, he offered me a big catch, a violent criminal who had already served some time and had just skipped out on a court appearance on a new charge. Bail had been set at $125,000 because the man was a repeat offender. That meant $12,500 for me if I brought him back; $25,000 if I had to go out of state to do it. Immediately I thought of it as seed money for my burgeoning business. All I had to do was find this man named Donald Tate.

But Tate was unlike any of the other fugitives I'd ever picked up. He was a real hardcase, a street thug and a career stickup artist who had perfected his technique in prison. He was in his forties, but he was reputed to be in incredible physical shape. I was told that he usually managed to elude the police by just outrunning them, scrambling up chain-link fences and leaping rooftops like a special-forces commando. This time around he was wanted for armed robbery and drug dealing.

Tate may have been a physical marvel, but I figured he couldn't be that smart, because he'd made the one stupendous mistake that so many bail jumpers make: when he ran off he left a very unhappy woman behind. As a result, it didn't take much finessing for me to get Tate's current whereabouts from Patty, his former live-in lover. Patty was a petite woman with short straight hair. From what I'd heard, she was a real firecracker, but when I showed up at her apartment, she was sulky and depressed. When I asked her where she thought he could be, she told me without hesitation. She knew for an absolute fact that Tate had gone to another part of the state to hide out with one of his aunts.

By the end of that day I had found Tate's aunt's apartment, thanks to the tip from Patty, but I couldn't just go barging in. I had to make sure he was in there before I entered her property. Breaking down a door when the fugitive wasn't there could get me into a lot of trouble. If Tate's aunt called the police, they might very well encourage her to file charges against me. Not only would that tie me up with legal hassles, it would give the aunt an opportunity to warn Tate that a bounty hunter was on his tail. If the police held me up for a day, which would be about the minimum I could expect, Tate could flee to just about anywhere. I had decided not to waste time checking in with the police because I was afraid to let Tate's trail get any colder, and anyway I didn't expect him to be all that much trouble.

Instead of approaching the house—a three-story white wood-frame box on a street full of mismatched architectural styles—I staked out the place for a few days first. I sat in my car and just watched, hour after hour, periodically going away for a while, then coming back, parking in different places, but always watching. After a while it became pretty obvious from what the old woman was bringing home with her groceries and what was going out in the trash that she wasn't living alone. She didn't look like the type who could go through a case of Budweiser in less than a week. I figured Tate had to be in there. It was time to make my move.

The next morning I waited for Tate's aunt to leave, then quietly I went inside, intending to take Tate by surprise. The back door was locked, but it wasn't a dead bolt, so it took me about fifteen seconds to open it with a thin strip of plastic. Once I was inside, I pulled my gun out and climbed the stairs to the aunt's second-floor apartment, intent on doing a systematic search going from room to room. But the first room I entered was the kitchen, and there was Tate sitting at the table eating a bowl of cornflakes. He was wearing a ripped T-shirt, gray sweatpants, and untied work boots. He looked a little bleary, as if he'd just gotten up.

I leveled my gun on him. A television was on in the next room. If there was someone else in the house, I hoped that person wouldn't try to interfere with the arrest.

Tate was glaring at me, the dripping spoon poised in front of his mouth. He had a face like a pit bull, and I got the impression that he'd just as soon kill me as look at me.

"Stand up, Donald," I said. "You and I are going back to Newark."

Tate didn't say a word, and his face didn't betray his intentions. In the flash of an eye, he leaped out of his seat and crashed through a closed window with no hesitation whatsoever. Shattered glass and splintered wood rained down on the linoleum floor in his wake. I rushed to the window and saw Tate down on the grass two stories below. He'd landed on his feet and hit the ground running, charging into the open lot next door like a runaway horse. He jumped a fence at the far end and quickly disappeared. I didn't even try to go after him. I knew I'd never catch up.

Instead I went back to see Patty. It was after 11 A.M. when I rang her buzzer, but I had apparently woken her up. She came to the door in her bathrobe, but when she saw it was me, she didn't want to talk. I made it clear to her that I wasn't leaving until she told me something. Her eyelids were drooping, and she kept mumbling that she just wanted to go back to sleep. I followed her inside and took a seat on the couch. I wasn't going to browbeat her, but I wasn't going to leave either. As I made myself comfortable, I pointed out to her that Tate was on the run, and it was very likely he would show up here looking for a place to crash.

"Imagine what would happen if he found us together in your apartment," I said.

Patty suddenly looked sick. "No," she whispered, her eyes bugging out of her head. "Not here. I don't want no more trouble. If you promise to get out of here, I'll tell you where he might go."

Finally she gave me something I could use. Tate had a lot of family down in West Anniston, Alabama, she told me. He had one uncle he was particularly close to, and he'd hidden out with that uncle before, she said. Now that Tate knew someone was after him, I had a feeling he just might head south again. The next morning I packed up my car and headed for Alabama.

As soon as I arrived in West Anniston, I went straight to the police department to inform them of what I was doing there. I asked to talk to the chief, and predictably he wasn't very welcoming, especially when I showed him the permits I had for the guns I had taken with me. A Black bounty hunter from New Jersey with enough firepower to take on an entire platoon was one fish this good old boy didn't want in his little pond. But instead of making a fuss, I simply showed the chief Tate's file.

"I'll go back to my motel, pack my things, and head on home if that's what you want," I told him. "Of course, then Tate'll be *your* problem. That you can count on." I pointed out that nearly every crime Tate had ever committed—and the list was long—included either a gun charge or an aggravated assault.

The chief rubbed his chin as he thought about it for a while, then took off his gold-rimmed glasses and leveled his gaze on me. The rattle and drone of his rickety old air conditioner filled the space between us.

"Here's the deal, son," the chief finally said. "Y'all go do what you have to. *But* if you shoot anybody other than this fella Tate, I guarantee you won't be leaving Alabama for a long long time. Y'all hear what I'm saying?"

I understood perfectly.

Hoping to make my stay in Alabama as short as possible, I got right down to work and staked out the uncle's house, hoping to corner Tate again. The house was a ramshackle tar-shingled structure that seemed to have been added on to several times. It was on the outskirts of town where the houses were spaced far apart, so I couldn't watch from my car without looking suspicious. Instead I hid the car in the pines, then walked through the woods and watched the rear of the house from behind a tree.

I saw a lot of people going in and out, but I didn't think any of them were Tate. Undaunted, I came back the next day and the day after that, taking up different positions in the woods, patiently watching the comings and goings of the Tate clan. Using binoculars I studied their faces, and sure enough, by the end of the week I finally spotted Donald. But there was a problem. Tate had six grown cousins who lived in that house, and they all stuck close together. Whenever Tate went out, he brought a whole pack of these big-ass country boys along with him. Now it wasn't that I was afraid of them, but I was afraid that I might accidentally shoot one of them if things got out of hand. And I had no doubt that the police chief would make good on his threat. What I had to do was come up with a way to nab Tate when he and his cousins were off guard so I could take him with minimal interference.

Later that evening I happened to drive by a lumberyard on my way back to my motel, and suddenly I got an idea. The lumberyard was closed, but I pulled into the lot anyway. I found a pay phone just outside the front door and dialed Tate's uncle's number.

When the uncle answered, I told him I was the manager of the lumberyard. "Listen," I said, "I can sure use some men out here. I got a big load coming in tomorrow, and I need to unload it right away. Can you help me out? I'm paying ten bucks an hour."

The uncle seemed interested, but he sounded leery. "So who told you to call me?" he asked.

"Junebug," I said without missing a beat. In the deep South everybody knows somebody named Junebug.

"Well, how many men y'all need?" the uncle said.

"How many you got?"

"Well, I got six boys and me."

"That's good. I can use all of you."

"I got a nephew visiting me, too."

"Sure, bring him along. I got plenty of work. You know the Hardee's out on the highway?"

"Yeah."

"Y'all be there at five tomorrow morning. I'll buy breakfast, and from there we'll go straight to the yard."

"Sounds good to me, mister. Just gimme your number in case something comes up."

I gave him the pay phone number, and after we hung up, I waited.

A half-hour later he called back with some lame question, which I had totally expected. He was checking to see if I was for real.

The next morning at four-fifteen I arrived at Hardee's and parked at the edge of the lot in a space where I had a good view of the front door. Then I settled back and waited. Over the next half-hour a few cars and pickup trucks pulled in, mostly farmworkers stopping for something to eat before their day began. But by five minutes to five the place was still pretty empty, and I wondered if Tate and his clan were really coming. Tate knew there was an open warrant for his arrest, which made him fair game for any bounty hunter. Maybe he had gotten hinky and told all his relatives to stay away. It was also possible that Patty had called him and warned him that I was coming down to get him; strange love works in strange ways. But whatever the reason, if they didn't show up, I didn't have a Plan B to fall back on.

Then at five on the dot two cars pulled in, and one of them was Tate's uncle's rusted-out station wagon. Eight men piled out of the two cars, and each one looked like a mean variation on Donald Tate, pit-bull face and all. Even the uncle looked pretty nasty, despite his woolly gray hair. Standing in the middle of them was the man himself.

I got out of my car and walked briskly to the front of the restaurant, getting there just ahead of the crowd of cousins. When I got to the glass doors, I stopped and turned away as if I were lighting a cigarette, but I was actually reaching for the gun inside my jacket. As Tate's cousins filed in, I waited, pretending that I was having a hard time getting my lighter started. I was waiting for the right moment to make my move. Just as Tate was about to go in, I wheeled around, leading with my gun, and kicked the door closed in his face. Most of the cousins were already inside.

"On the ground!" I shouted. "Now!" I stuck the barrel of my 9mm in his face to make sure he saw it.

"Shit!" Tate grumbled, scowling at me as he slowly raised his hands to his shoulders and reluctantly got down on one knee.

I took out my handcuffs, but the cousins in the restaurant quickly came back outside as others started to gather around. Their initial confusion quickly turned into rage.

"What the hell you think you're doing?" one of them shouted. This cousin had a scar across the side of his shaved head that ran from the corner of his eye to the top of his ear. It looked as if someone had taken a whack at him with an ax.

The others chimed in, grumbling and closing in on me.

"Go inside," I said to them. "This doesn't concern you."

"Don'ch'all leave me here," Tate called out to his kin.

"We ain't goin' nowhere," the man with the scar shouted. He was trying to stare me down, nostrils flaring.

Tate was standing back up now, a smug look on his face. I was carrying a mace canister, and I considered using it to gain control of the situation. But there was always the possibility that one or more of them was carrying a gun. Using mace could set off a firefight, and I could just see the headlines: SHOOTOUT AT HARDEE'S. NEW JERSEY BOUNTY HUNTER ARRESTED.

OR NEW JERSEY BOUNTY HUNTER DEAD.

I pulled out the mace canister anyway and held my ground. "Go back inside," I repeated firmly. "I told you, this doesn't concern—"

Suddenly, out of the blue, seven police cars roared out of the woods that bordered the parking lot and screeched up onto the sidewalk. Bubble lights were flashing, and the sirens were so loud they scared the birds out of the trees. All of a sudden I felt as if I were in a *Dukes of Hazard* episode. Those good old boys from the police department had been tracking me all along. A dozen cops scrambled out of their vehicles with weapons drawn and quickly surrounded us. Without being told, the cousins linked their fingers on top of their heads and backed up against the front windows as twelve officers in identical uniforms with identical revolvers stood in the same three-point stance, barrels leveled at the bunch of us, me included.

The chief ambled up to the scene and stood between two of his men. He crossed his arms and nodded at Tate, who was standing closest to me. "This here the fella you looking for?" he asked me.

"That's him," I said.

"You sure?"

"Positive."

"Well, then, handcuff him."

The cousin with the ugly scar spoke up. "Listen to me, Chief. That's my cousin Donald and—"

The chief cut him off. "You boys go on inside and get yourselves some biscuits and gravy. This here's official business. It don't have nothing to do with y'all."

With twelve revolvers trained on them, the cousins weren't about to argue. They shuffled inside, muttering the whole way.

"You need leg irons?" the chief asked me testily. "I'll lend you some if you need 'em." From his tone of voice, I could tell that he didn't exactly approve of the way I was handling this arrest.

"Thanks, Chief, but I've got everything I need in the car."

I cuffed Tate to a belly chain and led him over to my vehicle. He came along without any trouble. I put him in the front seat, strapping him in with the seat belt. Then I handed him a book. "Here," I said. "It's gonna be a long ride."

He just sneered at me and let it drop to the floor.

The chief watched as I secured the prisoner. After I slammed the door shut, he took me aside. "You sure you gonna be all right alone with him?" He seemed skeptical of my abilities.

"I'll be fine," I assured him. "I've done this before."

"All right then," he said, and headed back to his car.

All seven police cars escorted me to the city limits. People stopped and gawked, wondering what the occasion was. I don't think West Anniston had ever seen a parade that big. The police cars stayed with me until I got on the interstate.

A few weeks later the chief called me to find out what had become of Tate, and we had a nice talk. We've stayed in touch over the years, and as hard as it may be to believe, we've become pretty good friends. We've visited each other several times, and whenever I get down to Alabama, we like to kick back and go fishing together.

Donald Tate was tried and convicted on all charges, which earned him another stint in prison. He served his time and was eventually released. I don't know where he is now, but I have a feeling he hasn't changed his ways any. The whole way back from Alabama he didn't once look at the book I'd given him. He just bitched and slept. Donald Tate was one person who simply refused to evolve.

9 The Criminal Element

My personal evolution kept pace with my professional development as I tried to reconcile my ideals and beliefs with day-to-day living in the real world. I sought to merge the street person in me with a person who could live above the streets. To this end, I started meditating more, reading more, and discussing what I read with my peers and associates. I questioned everything. I studied what I saw around me—the poverty and the crime, the good and the bad—and I looked for the causes, not just the effects. My goal was to become a stellar man in a world that desperately needed stellar men.

In the spring of 1987, I received a call from the police in a nearby community asking if I would help them with an unusual situation. It had started with a routine arrest. A young man named Peter Hawkins had been arrested and charged with assault against his aunt's boyfriend. It had started as a domestic situation—a family dinner, too much to drink, people getting testy and telling each other off, and one person, Hawkins, taking it all a little too seriously. The aunt's boyfriend had berated him for not being able to hold down a job and had questioned Hawkins's intelligence. Hawkins, who was self-taught and actually very well read, became highly offended. He considered himself an inventor who just couldn't catch a break in life, and in fact he had applied for patents on several ideas that he'd come up with. Some of the other people in the house considered Hawkins a nerd and a dreamer, so they egged the aunt's boyfriend on until Hawkins couldn't take it anymore. Hawkins found a tack hammer in the kitchen and banged his tormenter over the head a few times. His aunt got hysterical and called the cops. She and her boyfriend, who wasn't hurt seriously, pressed charges, and Hawkins was taken away in cuffs. It was his first offense, but since it was a felony, the police held him for three and a half days until his older sister could arrange for bail.

In jail he was treated like any other thug, and he resented that. His pleas to speak to the police chief were ignored, of course. To the police, he was just another member of the "criminal element" and was processed just like the rest. Hawkins had been thoroughly humiliated by the whole experience, and naturally he wanted revenge. A long letter addressed to the chief arrived two days after his release. "When you least expect it," the letter said, "I will set off a bomb so powerful and devilish, you will either die or wish you had."

The next morning at police headquarters, an opinionated sergeant at the front desk waved a photocopy of the letter at me. "You see this?" he shouted. "This guy Hawkins is sick, deranged. These people are fucking dangerous. Guys like this shouldn't be put away. They should be *exterminated*."

I wanted to get away from him, but I had just come from the chief's office and was waiting for a copy of Hawkins's file and his mug shots. A secretary had gone off to make copies for me.

"When you find this cocksucker, you put him in a cage," the sergeant said, jabbing a finger in the air. "Tie him up tight and bring him to me. I'll take care of him." The sergeant was an Italian-American who certainly knew how to spit venom. He was compact and muscular, but he also had a growing belly and a horrendous wig, the kind that looks so bad you have to wonder why the person can't see it for himself.

The sergeant continued his tirade despite the fact that I wasn't responding. "Did you read this letter? Did you? Where does someone get off saying stuff like this to the chief? Not just to the chief, to *anybody*. This Hawkins guy ain't human. Human beings don't go around making bombs and threatening decent people. This guy's a mad dog. No, he's *worse* than a dog."

The secretary came back with my photocopies, and I thanked her. I could tell from the tight set of her mouth and the fact that she kept her eyes down that she didn't approve of the sergeant's attitude either. I suppose she felt that if she looked me in the eye, she'd be showing her true feelings, and that wouldn't be good for her job security. The police mentality divides the world into two camps: pro-cop and anti-cop. There's nothing in between, and the poor woman didn't dare reveal anything that could be interpreted as a sign of dissent.

"Hey, you get him, baby," the sergeant called after me as I started for the exit. "But leave some for me. You hear?"

I just nodded and went on my way. Though he didn't know it, the sergeant had just confirmed an ancient Egyptian belief for me: some people start off so low in life that evolution is virtually impossible for them.

When I got back to my car, I took some time to study Peter Hawkins's file. The police had made an effort to find him, but he wasn't at his mother's apartment or with any relatives they knew about. He had no previous criminal record, and the way he'd reacted to being arrested indicated that he considered himself a decent individual who at least on some level knew right from wrong. I wondered if the police might be overreacting. Perhaps the fact that Hawkins was an amateur inventor spooked them. They clearly believed he was capable of making a bomb, but was he capable of using one to commit murder? That was the question. In any case their fear was obvious, and the chief figured it wouldn't hurt to have the Seekers out there looking for Hawkins, too.

Human nature is fairly predictable, particularly when a person is under stress. Guilty or innocent, a person who feels squeezed will react in certain ways. Nine hundred and ninety-nine times out of a thousand, a person on the run will go where he feels safe, a place that he has connections to, and *that* is usually his undoing. Once I uncover a fugitive's personal connections, then I know where to start looking for him.

In this case Hawkins had caused a great deal of turmoil within his family by beating up his aunt's boyfriend, then threatening to blow up the police chief. It was possible that Hawkins might have gone to stay with a relative, but I had a feeling he might not risk that. He would probably be wondering how his family felt about him in the wake of his violent outburst, and he would fear that they might turn him in. From experience I knew that he would trust only someone he felt very close to, a sibling or a cousin who was around his age. Or a very close friend.

I called Mr. Baines, my information analyst, and ran down the situation. He suggested a few possibilities for tracking down Hawkins, including contacting places where he might have bought the supplies for making a bomb. But I was a little dubious about that approach. If Hawkins was as smart as they said he was, he'd be careful to cover his tracks. And anyway, how much could a store clerk tell me about a customer's current whereabouts? My aim wasn't to assemble a detailed FBI-type file on him. I just wanted to find him before he did anything violent. On a hunch I asked Mr. Baines to check into Hawkins's patent applications. The police hadn't taken that route, and there might be something useful there.

In the meantime I paid a visit to Hawkins's mother, who lived by herself on the first floor of a four-family house near the Newark-Elizabeth border, a block away from Weequahic Park. I mounted the front steps to the porch and rang the doorbell. No one answered.

I rang it again. Still no answer.

I knocked. Nothing.

I cupped my hands around my eyes to block out the glare and tried to look through the lace curtains in the front window. Suddenly I heard the door opening.

An elderly woman in a pink terry-cloth bathrobe stood at the door. She had steel-gray hair, and she was leaning on a walker. She wore thick glasses and squinted out at the daylight like a mole. She was trying to figure out who I was.

"Mrs. Hawkins?" I said, moving in closer so she could see me.

"Talk louder," she said. "Don't have my hearing aids in."

"Mrs. Hawkins," I said, raising my voice, "my name is Joshua Armstrong. I'm looking for your son Peter. Is he here?"

The woman looked totally confused. I figured she still couldn't hear me, so I said it again louder, but it didn't help.

"My Peter's a good boy," she said. Her expression had suddenly turned sad.

"Is he home now?" I asked.

"He's a good boy," she said.

"I know he's a good boy. Do you know where I can find him?"

"He comes to see me all the time. He brings me the coffee that I like."

Mrs. Hawkins was either a little senile or it was a good act and she was covering for her son. I considered the possibility that he was hiding inside, but I had a feeling he wasn't. If he'd had an extensive criminal record, I could see his mother lying for him, but Peter Hawkins didn't fit the profile. Also, the aunt who had filed charges against him was the baby sister of this woman, and his mother might not automatically side with her son against her sister. Maybe Mrs. Hawkins was still trying to sort it all out for herself, and that's why she was telling me her son was a good boy.

I tried one more time. "Mrs. Hawkins?" I said loudly.

"Yes?"

"Do you know where I can find Peter?"

"What?"

I raised my voice even more. "*Where's Peter?*"

"Peter's working. Where else would he be?"

I already knew from the police report that Hawkins worked nights as a custodian at an elementary school, but he hadn't been back to work since his arrest.

"Thank you for your time, Mrs. Hawkins," I said. "Sorry to bother you."

"Peter's at work," she called after me. "You go find him there."

"I will," I said, and headed back to my car.

I checked my watch, wishing that Mr. Baines would call me back, but it was much too soon. What he did usually took some time. Fortunately, there was another person I wanted to talk to, Hawkins's sister Clarice. She was the one who put up the title to her car so that her brother could make bail. But that was when he had been charged only with assault, and bail had been set at $10,000. The bomb threat was going to up the ante considerably.

Clarice, who was married and had three teenage children, was at least ten years older than her little brother. I caught up with her at the bakery in South Orange where she worked. She was a big woman whose high-headed posture let everyone around her know she was the boss. Two college kids worked there with her—a gangly young man who did the heavy work out back and an attractive young woman who worked behind the counter. I came in the back way and found Clarice standing over a row of layer cakes set out on a long worktable. A stainless-steel bowl of vanilla frosting was wedged in the crook of her elbow. She iced those cakes with the ease of a master, using a broad knife with a ridged edge that scored tight parallel lines around the sides.

When I told her why I needed to find her brother, she tossed her head and sniffed, refusing to accept my version of reality. She preferred her own. "It'll all be cleared up before the court date," she said with absolute confidence. "My aunt and her boyfriend will drop the charges. They just need a little time to cool down."

Apparently she hadn't heard about the bomb threat. "The assault charge is beside the point now," I explained to her. "Your brother threatened to kill the chief of police. They could charge him with attempted murder of a law enforcement officer. That's a heavy charge. He could end up spending the rest of his life behind bars."

"I think you're exaggerating," she said. "My brother's not like that." She kept her eyes on her work, but I noticed that her previously perfect lines were getting a little wavy.

"I'm not exaggerating," I persisted. "If the cops catch him, they'll haul him in like a mad dog. And they'll *prosecute* him like a mad dog. Now I don't think your brother is that hard-core. If I find him, and he lets me bring him in without a big scene, a good lawyer might be able to work something out."

Her lines had gotten so messy, she put down the knife. Her voice softened. "Would they really put him in prison? Do you really think that could happen?"

"Without a doubt. Unless you help me."

She pressed her lips together and thought about it. The distant sound of a radio filled the silence. Way in the back the college kid was sifting a fifty-pound bag of flour into a big mixing machine.

She heaved a sigh, her eyes watery. "I don't know what to tell you, Mr. Armstrong. Peter is . . . weird."

“How is he weird?” I asked.

“He’s a loner. He doesn’t have any friends. Except for that old man he hangs out with.”

“What old man?”

Clarice knit her brows and shrugged. “His name is Mr. Young. That’s what Peter calls him. I don’t know what his first name is.”

“Where does he live?”

She shook her head and shrugged again. “Somewhere in Newark. They work on inventions together. That’s all I know.”

She started to sob. I touched her shoulder. “This is helpful,” I said. “Thank you.”

A deep, shuddering sigh rattled her chest. She held on to my sleeve. “But what’s going to happen to my brother?”

“I don’t know. Most of it is up to him.”

“You find him,” she said. “Please?”

“I’ll do my best. I promise.”

I left the bakery and went back to my car. Just as I turned the key in the ignition, my cell phone started to vibrate in my pocket.

I pulled it out and pressed the answer button. “Hello?”

“Joshua, I have some information for you.” It was Mr. Baines. “I don’t have any new addresses for Peter Hawkins, but I did check with the Patent Office in Washington. Turns out Hawkins has two patents on file—one for a toilet seat for the handicapped, the other for a device that will automatically turn off the burners on a gas stove if they’re left on too long. The patents are both held jointly with a man named Earl Young.”

“Excellent,” I said. “Do you have an address for this Mr. Young?”

“One-oh-three Prince Street, apartment seven D as in David.” He gave me the phone number as well.

“Fantastic,” I said. “But keep checking around in case this doesn’t lead anywhere.”

“Will do. I’ll call you if I get anything.”

I hung up and put the cell phone back in my pocket.

I knew the address he’d given me very well—103 Prince Street was the second tower of the Prince Street projects. I’d been to that building many times chasing down leads and had even made a few arrests there.

I pulled my Land Cruiser out onto South Orange Avenue and headed for Newark to pay a visit to Mr. Earl Young.

When I got to Prince Street, it was late afternoon. I parked across from Earl Young's building, turned off the engine, and took in the scene. It was a warm spring day, so a lot of people were hanging out—girls playing jump rope, teenage boys horsing around with a basketball, women sitting on benches and gossiping while they kept an eye on their toddlers. Having no idea what Earl Young looked like limited my options. I would have to go inside and knock on his door, but I wasn't sure yet how to handle this. If Hawkins was in there with him, and he was as desperate as he seemed to be, I would have to be very careful. I didn't want him setting off any suicide bombs with me on the premises.

But that got me to thinking. What if Hawkins had seriously flipped out and he really did have a bomb? And if he'd made it in Mr. Young's apartment, what else could he have up there? He could have enough explosives to level the building. I tried to rid my mind of Hollywood portrayals of mad bombers, wild-eyed fanatics who can't be reasoned with, but people like that do exist, so I wasn't going to take any chances.

With so many people hanging out by the entrance, I didn't want to approach the building. The less I was seen, the better it would be. People watch their own turf, and they pay attention to faces they don't know. I didn't want to be singled out as a suspicious character because it could get back to Mr. Young and possibly Peter Hawkins.

I took out my cell phone and dialed Earl Young's number. It rang eight times before anyone picked up. "Hello?" The voice was croaky, as if the man had just woken up.

"Earl Young, please?"

"He's not here."

"My name is James Albright," I said. "I'm with the Social Security Administration. It's important that I talk to Mr. Young."

"He's not here right now. You'll have to call back." The man's voice had cleared. He sounded younger than someone who'd be collecting Social Security.

"Is there a better time for me to call?" I asked.

"Hmmm . . . not really. You said this is important?"

"Yes. It concerns something that could affect his benefits."

"I can take a message."

"By law, I'm obligated to tell him directly."

"Can he call you back then?"

"By all means." I gave him my cell number.

"OK," the man said. "Mr. Young probably won't be back until after five, so he'll have to call you tomorrow."

"That'll be fine. Thank you."

I hung up and tapped the cell against my chin as I stared out the window at the building. I was willing to bet that the man I had just talked to was Peter Hawkins. He didn't sound as if he was foaming at the mouth, but voices can be deceiving.

I weighed my alternatives. If Hawkins was in there and Earl Young wasn't, it would be a good time to take Hawkins. No chance of hurting the old man in a scuffle. But when I thought about bombs and explosives, the idea of confronting Hawkins directly seemed like a disaster waiting to happen. Finally I decided to wait and do my usual thing—a predawn wake-up call from the Seekers. I only hoped Hawkins wasn't sleeping in a vest made out of dynamite sticks, cradling a plunger in his arms.

As I watched the building from my car, I put in a call to Rock. He wasn't a formal member of the Seekers at the time, but he was the perfect man for this job. He was big and tough, and he was an electronics specialist. There was no telling what the two inventors had rigged up in that apartment, and I certainly didn't know how to defuse a bomb. I asked Rock to meet me there at 3 A.M.

I watched the building for a few more hours, but no one who looked like Hawkins came out. I left to get myself some dinner at around nine and came back about two hours later. Using my cell phone, I dialed Mr. Young's number again.

"Hello?" It was the man I'd talked to earlier.

I changed my voice and made it more gravelly. "Rufus? That you?"

"You have the wrong number."

"I'm looking for Rufus Young. He there?"

"You've got the wrong Young. No one named Rufus here."

"Is this nine-three-nine . . . ?" I made up a phone number.

"Not even close." The man hung up on me.

It was definitely the person I had talked to earlier, but was it Peter Hawkins? I was just going to have to take an educated guess and hope I wasn't wrong.

I sat and watched the building for the next four hours. As mellow jazz from the tape player filled the space inside my vehicle, I witnessed the street changes as they unfolded. Just before midnight, a group of young men congregated and hung out on the benches. They alternately harassed the young women who passed by and made threatening moves at one another, always pulling back just before it got real. They seemed menacing, but it was basically just ritualistic behavior, a misdirected show of manhood and power.

By one o'clock the crowd had thinned out considerably, and by one-thirty the young men were all gone. People still came and went, but they walked with brisk determination, eager to get wherever they were going. None of them wanted to linger outside the projects at this hour.

By two-thirty it was peaceful, not a soul in sight. The scene outside finally matched the mellow sound track playing inside the Land Cruiser—piano, bass, and brushes on snare and hi-hat. A thermos cup of hot tea on the dashboard steamed a section of the windshield. I sipped from it idly, my eyes ever vigilant.

In my side mirror I saw a green Ford Explorer moving slowly up the street. I checked my watch—it was five minutes to three. The Explorer pulled up right next to me and stopped. Rock was sitting behind the wheel. I smiled and nodded at him.

He found a parking space farther up the block and walked back to the Land Cruiser, getting in on the passenger side. We shook hands, and I offered him some tea as I filled him in on the details. He listened intently as I explained that Hawkins was an amateur inventor who might or might not have a bomb factory up on the seventh floor.

He nodded thoughtfully. "Guess we won't know till we get up there," he said evenly.

I was happy to hear this. Like all the other Seekers, Rock had adopted the fundamental Samurai ethic: if a man is ready for death at all times, the fear of it will never control him. We went over the details of how we would get into the apartment and discussed contingencies in case Hawkins did have a bomb. When I checked my watch again, it was three-thirty, time to get started.

We got out of the Land Cruiser, crossed the street, and went toward the building. Getting in was no problem because the front door lock was broken. Things rarely get repaired in a timely fashion in the projects. Rock and I took the stairs. We didn't want a noisy elevator announcing our arrival.

It was cold in the stairwell, and light bulbs were out on several of the landings. The stairs were littered with soda cans and cigarette butts; broken glass crunched under the soles of our boots. On the seventh floor landing, we pushed through a battered metal door and slipped into the hallway. It was thirty degrees warmer on the other side of that door, and the warm smells of fried food hung in the air.

We got our bearings and located apartment 7D. There were two dead bolt locks on the door. Getting in was going to take a little doing. Rock and I had both brought along a set of lock picks, so we split the duties: he took the top one and I took the bottom. We worked quietly, and within five minutes we had them both open. Putting away the picks, we pulled up our masks and took out our guns. I put my hand on the knob and looked Rock in the eye. He nodded. I turned the knob slowly and pushed the door with my forearm, but it didn't budge. I tried the door again, leaning my shoulder into it this time, but it wouldn't open. There were other locks on the other side of the door, barrel locks on the jamb or a police lock, which is a heavy iron bar propped up against the back of the door and held in place by a bracket in the floor.

I crouched and felt under the door. There was an inch-high gap between the bottom of the door and the floor. I reached into the pocket of my jacket and pulled out a directional smoke canister. Striking a match, I lit the wick on the canister. It sparked and sputtered for a moment, then I pointed the lit end under the door, and the canister started to hiss. Smoke was pouring into the apartment, but only a few negligible wisps leaked back into the hallway.

Within minutes I heard someone stumbling around inside. A loud clang sounded—the metal bar of the police lock hitting the floor, I assumed. The person fumbled with the dead bolts and rattled the door-knob, confused and disoriented because the locks were already open.

Rock and I braced ourselves. When the door finally flew open, a cloud of smoke escaped, but the man trying to run out didn't. Rock pushed him back inside and got him in a bear hug. I snatched up the smoking canister and ran to the bathroom where I dropped it in the toilet to extinguish it.

With my gun in my hand, I followed the sound of the man's coughing. Rock had hauled him into the living room and set him down on the couch. I turned on a lamp to get a good look at his face. Through the drifting smoke, I could see that it was definitely Hawkins.

"That's him," I said to Rock, and he immediately turned Hawkins over on his belly.

I pulled out a pair of handcuffs and cuffed his wrists behind his back.

Hawkins was a big man, but he was overweight and out of shape. A white T-shirt and briefs were stretched tight over a soft belly. He was lying on a tangle of sheets and a blanket. Apparently he'd been sleeping there. Behind his round metal-frame glasses, his eyes were wild with panic. He was struggling to get his breath, but the more he hyperventilated, the more smoke he took into his lungs. He was trying desperately to yell, but he couldn't get enough air. Rock and I didn't have any problem with the smoke because of our masks.

As Rock sat him back up, I noticed a Formica kitchen table pushed up against the wall. It was piled with all kinds of tools and hardware—bolts, nuts, nails, pieces of wood, strands of wire, cans, bottles, screwdrivers, pliers, a glue gun, a small acetylene torch. Cardboard boxes full of more junk crammed the floor around the table. This was obviously the inventors' workshop. I caught Rock's eye and nodded toward the table. I wanted him to check it out while I searched the rest of the apartment for Mr. Young. If there actually was a bomb in all that clutter, I certainly wouldn't be able to find it.

Rock called to me as I headed down the hallway. "I don't see anything that looks like a bomb," he said.

"What in the hell's going on in here?"

Instinctively I trained my gun at the figure coming out of the bedroom. A very old man in a plaid flannel bathrobe was coughing and squinting at me like Mr. Magoo. I assumed that this was Mr. Young.

“Peter,” he said in a grouchy voice. “What the hell’s going on in here? What’s burning?” He didn’t seem to notice my gun or my mask as he brushed past me and went toward the living room. “Peter,” he said. “Answer me.”

Hawkins started to stammer, “I . . . I . . . .” But he couldn’t put a coherent sentence together.

“You have to get dressed,” I said to Hawkins firmly as I followed Mr. Young into the living room. “You’re coming with us.”

Hawkins suddenly became frantic, sucking air like a sump pump. “No,” he said between breaths. “Wasn’t me . . . I didn’t mean it . . . No!”

“Peter,” the old man demanded. “Are these boys friends of yours?” He apparently didn’t realize that his friend was handcuffed.

Everybody ignored him. Rock took Hawkins by the arm and tried to get him to stand up, but Hawkins squirmed and flailed his head. Rock insisted, however. He wrapped his big hand around Hawkins’s upper arm and pulled him halfway off the couch.

“No!” Hawkins screamed. Now he was blubbering like a child, tears springing from his eyes. I could understand being scared, but this kind of behavior was demeaning.

“Do you boys know what time it is?” the old man demanded. Again we ignored him. Rock and I knew better than to take our focus off a fugitive before he was completely under control, even if he was a big baby. But I kept glancing back at the old man just in case he had a notion to rescue his young protégé.

By now Hawkins had slithered down onto the floor and was having a fit. “Listen to me,” I said to him as Rock and I fought to get him on his feet. “Relax. You hear me, Hawkins? Be a man.”

We finally stood him up, but he immediately let his legs go limp and dropped to the floor again. Rock was getting fed up with this nonsense. He hauled Hawkins up roughly and pushed him down onto the couch. I grabbed Hawkins’s face by the jowls and made him look me in the eye. “Calm down and listen to me,” I said, raising my voice. “You threatened a police chief. You’re already in big trouble. It’s gonna be a lot worse if the police have to come in here and help us haul your ass away.”

He was inhaling through his mouth but not exhaling.

“Now stand up,” I said.

Rock didn't wait to see if Hawkins would obey. He immediately yanked Hawkins up by the arm. I unrolled a restraining belt from my pocket and put it on him, buckling it in back. Then I replaced his handcuffs with the ones on the belt so that his hands were attached to his hips on short chains.

"OK, sit down," I said.

Rock sat him down.

I found a pair of sweatpants and sneakers on the floor next to the couch. Lifting his legs up one at a time, I got him partially dressed. A shirt and a jean jacket were hanging on the back of a chair. I balled them up and stuck them under my arm. If Hawkins calmed down, he could finish getting dressed later.

"What the hell're you boys doing? And why're you wearing those masks?" Mr. Young still didn't quite get it.

"Peter's coming with us," I said to him. No sense confusing the man with more details than he could handle.

We led our wobbly-kneed fugitive to the door, trying our best not to disturb the junkyard clutter.

"Can I ask you a question?" I said to the old man as we were about to leave. "You don't have any explosives in here, do you?"

"Any what?" He seemed insulted by the question.

"Explosives," I said. "Dynamite, fertilizer, anything like that."

"You must be some kind of fool," he said to me. "Why would I keep explosives in a building full of people?"

"How about him?" I said, nodding toward Hawkins. "Would he?"

"Not in my house he wouldn't. You wouldn't do something that foolish, would you, Peter?" There was a hint of doubt in Mr. Young's voice, but Hawkins was too hysterical to respond. He was panting like a dog, emitting high wheezing sounds from his chest. His eyes kept going in and out of focus. He could have been doing drugs, but I doubted it. He was just an emotional mess.

I quickly told Mr. Young where we were taking Hawkins and why, but we didn't stick around to discuss it. The way Hawkins was carrying on, I was afraid he'd have a heart attack. It was amazing to me that I had ever imagined Hawkins as some kind of diabolical genius. He didn't look as if he had the nerve to set off a pack of firecrackers.

We whisked Hawkins out of the apartment and into an elevator. I wanted to get him outside as fast as possible, and the stairwell presented too many problems. He could trip on the steps or create a commotion that would echo through the whole building.

Hawkins wasn't light by any means, and once we got him out the door we practically had to lift him off his feet to get him moving, Rock on one arm, me on the other. He blubbered and wailed the whole way. "Don't kill me! Please! Please!"

"We're not going to kill you," I kept telling him, but it did no good. He just kept it up.

We got him into the passenger seat of the Land Cruiser and fastened his seat belt. I wanted him up front so I could see what he was doing.

"You're gonna kill me. I know it. *I know it!*"

I slammed the door on his hysterics. Rock just shook his head. Neither of us had ever seen a fugitive carry on like this. It was unsettling having to listen to him, and I didn't look forward to the drive to the police station. It almost made me wish for a nice violent tough guy. At least I knew how to handle those.

"Why don't you follow me in your car?" I said to Rock. "We may have to switch along the way. I don't know if I'll be able to take this for the whole ride."

"I hear what you're saying," Rock said. He headed back to his car.

I went around to the driver's side and got in. But before I started the engine, I turned toward Hawkins and looked him in the eye. "Listen up," I shouted over his howls. "What kind of man are you, screaming like that?"

That stopped his howling for a second. He stared at me and sniffed. "You're gonna kill me," he whimpered. His face crumpled, and he started blubbering again.

"Stop crying," I said. "You're a disgrace to yourself and your whole family. You did something wrong, now face up to it."

He kept blubbering. His face was completely wet with tears.

I started the engine and pulled out into the street. "Is this how you want to be seen?" I asked. "How would you feel if you saw your father acting this way? Or your grandfather?"

He got quiet.

"It wouldn't make you feel proud, would it?"

"No," he said in a small voice.

He seemed to be coming to his senses. I drove down the street and didn't say any more. I figured he should be alone with his thoughts for a while. At the end of the street, I stopped at a red light.

Suddenly Hawkins exploded. "Please don't kill me. Please! I know my aunt's boyfriend hired you to kill me. He's evil. Please don't do it!" He was worse than ever.

The light soon turned green, and as I turned onto Springfield Avenue, I calmly tried to explain to him that I was not a hit man hired by his aunt's boyfriend, that I was a bail enforcement agent bringing him to the police. I didn't dare use the term *bounty hunter*—no telling what that would do to him.

Rock was right behind me, but it would've been stupid to change cars now since we'd just started out. I wished I could figure out some way to calm Hawkins down because I really didn't want to hand him over to the police in this state. They already thought he was some kind of freak. If he came in like a raving lunatic, they'd treat him like a rabid dog. Especially that sergeant at the front desk.

As we drove down Springfield Avenue, I put a mellow tape into the tape deck, hoping that music would soothe his nerves, but it didn't. It only made more noise.

Then all of a sudden he really started kicking up a fuss. "Police!" he shouted. "Help me! Help! They're gonna kill me! They're stone-cold killers!"

He'd spotted a police car coming toward us from the opposite direction, and now he was bouncing up and down, trying to throw himself against the door to get the policeman's attention.

I was fed up with him now, so I decided to give him what he wanted. I stopped the car and rolled down my window, waving for the cop to stop. The police car passed by, made a U-turn, and pulled up behind me. The cop inched forward cautiously in the right lane until the vehicles were side-by-side. I rolled down the passenger-side window to let the cop see what I was dealing with.

The cop was a Black man in his mid-thirties. He rolled down his window and stared at Hawkins, who was having a hard time explaining his situation because he was hyperventilating again. The cop stayed in his car. "What's the problem?" he shouted to me.

I leaned forward so I could see his face. "*He's* the problem," I said, indicating Hawkins.

"I know you, don't I?" the cop said, pointing at me. "You're the bounty hunter. About a year ago you picked up a guy who slammed into my buddy's unit on purpose. Sent him to the hospital with a spinal fracture. We were real glad you got that son of a bitch."

I nodded, relieved that for once I wouldn't have to explain myself. I told him about Hawkins and the bomb threat and how he'd been carrying on since I'd apprehended him. Naturally, being a cop, the man bristled at the thought of a violent threat against another officer.

"Would you do me a favor?" I asked the cop.

"If I can."

"Would you please tell this guy that I am not going to kill him?"

The cop nodded. "No problem."

"Officer, stop him!" Hawkins yelled, suddenly getting his wind back. "He wants to *kill* me."

The cop gave Hawkins a hard look. "Excuse me, sir," the cop said. "*Excuse me!*" he shouted over Hawkins's blithering. "*This man is not going to kill you. You will be perfectly safe in his custody.*"

Hawkins quieted down, but more out of confusion than understanding.

The cop lowered his voice, but he spoke to Hawkins in a firm, no-nonsense manner. "I advise you, sir, to stop yelling and resisting arrest. If you do not cooperate, Mr. Armstrong is authorized to use more severe restraining methods to keep you under control. If you force the issue, I guarantee you will not like the consequences. Do you understand what I'm telling you?"

Hawkins nodded. His eyes were wide, and his mouth was shut—just the way I wanted him.

The cop held a stern look on Hawkins. "Do you need an escort?" he asked me.

"Not necessary," I said. "I think he'll be OK now. Thank you."

The cop nodded and made a U-turn around me, driving away. I put the Land Cruiser in gear and stepped on the accelerator. Rock, who'd stayed in his car farther down the block, followed behind.

After I'd driven a mile or so, I glanced over at Hawkins. He was being *too* quiet. "You OK?" I asked.

"Yeah. I'm OK," he said sullenly.

"Why're you so quiet all of a sudden?"

He was gazing out the window. "I'm trying to act like my father. And my grandfather."

"I see." I turned my attention back to the road. I was happy to hear that something had penetrated. Perhaps the seeds of evolution were germinating.

"What's going to happen to me?" he asked in a sad but calm voice.

"I don't know. It all depends on you."

"Me? What do you mean?"

"Did you actually have a bomb?"

"No, of course not."

"Tell me the truth," I said.

"I swear. I was just angry. They humiliated me. All of them. My aunt and her boyfriend. And the cops who put me in jail."

"And you wanted to take it out on someone."

He exhaled slowly. "Yeah . . . I guess . . . ."

"So you went right to the top and threatened the police chief. That was pretty stupid."

"Yeah, I know . . . ." He looked pretty glum. I'd say he was showing signs of remorse.

"Now I want you to tell me the truth, Peter. And don't lie, because this is important. If the police search Mr. Young's apartment or your mother's house or the school where you work or anyplace else where you go, will they find the ingredients for a bomb?"

He made a sour face. "No."

"Think hard. All that stuff you use to make your inventions—could someone use any of it to rig a bomb?"

"Well, yeah, I suppose, but . . . "

"But what?"

"If you know how to do it, you can go into anyone's house and rig up some kind of explosive. Ammonia, paint thinner, mothballs, baking soda, batteries, wire, stuff that everyone's got at home—that's all you need."

“Make sure you tell that to your lawyer when you get one.”

“You think I’m gonna need a lawyer?”

“Definitely.”

He released a long sigh of hopelessness. Peter Hawkins was no tough guy. He was just someone who let his anger get the better of him.

“Listen,” I said to him. “You made a mistake, but I don’t think you really intended to do any harm.”

“I didn’t.”

“I’ll talk to the chief for you. You’re gonna be charged with something for sure, but maybe they can reduce the charges. I’m not making any promises, but I’ll see what I can do.”

“Thank you,” he said softly. “I appreciate it.”

We didn’t say another word for the rest of the way back. I drove into the parking lot of the municipal building and found a space near the entrance to the police station. Hawkins was cooperative when I opened the door and undid his seat belt, but he was shocked when I freed his hands from the restraining belt. “Take off the belt,” I told him. “Throw it in the back.”

He seemed reluctant to touch the belt, as if I really didn’t mean it.

“Go on, take it off,” I said.

He reached behind his back and unbuckled it, then tossed it in the back with the rest of my equipment.

“Come on,” I said, stepping away from the door to let him out. “I want you to walk in there like a man.”

He didn’t say anything as we walked in together. It was a little after five in the morning, and the station was quiet. The desk sergeant on duty was the same sergeant who had advised me to bring Hawkins back in a cage. A paper cup of coffee was positioned in front of him, steam swirling up. As we walked in, he peered at us over his half-glasses.

“Mr. Armstrong,” he said, taking off his glasses, “what brings you in at this hour of the morning? And more important, did you bring any doughnuts?”

“This is Mr. Hawkins,” I said. “We have some business here.”

“Business?” The sergeant apparently didn’t recognize the “mad bomber’s” name.

“Yes, business,” I said. “Would you call the lieutenant on duty for me?”

"Sure." The sergeant picked up his phone and was about to press the lieutenant's extension when he stopped and gave us a leery squint. We said nothing. After a long moment he finally made the call.

The lieutenant—a middle-aged Hispanic man with thick salt-and-pepper hair—came out right away. He knew me from previous arrests that I'd made in town.

"This is Peter Hawkins," I said to him. "He wants to turn himself in."

The lieutenant's eyes widened. Obviously he recognized the name right away, but he didn't believe it. *This is the mad bomber?* he must've been thinking. "Come with me, Mr. Hawkins," he said, reaching out to take Hawkins's arm.

"One minute," Hawkins said. He turned around and threw his arms around me, hugging me tight. "Thanks, man. I don't know what else to say to you. Just thank you. Thank you."

I was as shocked as anybody, but I returned the hug and told him not to worry about it. "Just be a man and it'll be all right," I whispered in his ear.

The lieutenant took him downstairs for processing. When they were gone, I turned to the sergeant, who was staring at me as if he'd just seen a pig fly. "Something wrong?" I asked him.

"That was him? The bomb-threat guy?"

I nodded.

"Why didn't you tell me?"

"I did. I told you his name."

"You know what I mean. I would have liked to—" He stopped himself before he said something he'd regret later.

"What time does the chief get in?" I asked.

"Eight."

I took out one of my business cards and gave it to him. I'd just had new ones made up on gold-colored metal with black lettering. The sergeant scrutinized it with one raised eyebrow.

"Ask the chief to call me as soon as he can," I said. "I have to talk to him."

"About what?"

"The criminal element," I said as I headed toward the door. "You have a nice day."

Rock was standing in the parking lot waiting for me. "How did it go?" he asked.

"It'll be all right, I think. Let's go get some breakfast."

We went to our individual cars and headed for a good diner I know in the area. At eight o'clock I called the chief myself and explained Hawkins's situation. The chief wasn't exactly in a forgiving mood, but the subsequent police investigation failed to uncover any explosives, so the charges against Hawkins were confined to making terroristic threats against a police officer. Hawkins was tried and convicted, but because it was his first offense he received a one-year suspended sentence. And from what I was told, he didn't cry or carry on once at his trial. Evolution, I had more reason to believe, *is* possible.

10 The Capture That Changed My Life

By 1989 the Seekers as a group was beginning to take shape. The roster at the time included Jedidiah and Rock and two individuals who took the Seeker names Max and Colt. The additional manpower naturally allowed us to take on more cases and cover more areas, but the greatest benefit was the increased amount of information the five of us could gather and share. Each man also had his own set of street contacts, which made us that much more effective. In this phase of our development, each member basically worked solo or occasionally with a partner if the situation called for a backup. I was working alone the night I brought in the capture that changed my life.

His name was Lorenzo Franks. He was twenty-two years old, and he'd been charged with grand theft auto, possession of a weapon, and resisting arrest. According to the file I got from his bondsman, Lorenzo had gotten high, stolen an Oldsmobile Cutlass, gone for a joyride, tried to outrun a police car, and when he was finally caught—forty minutes and thirty-eight miles later—the cops found a box cutter in his pocket. He was arraigned and released on a $50,000 bond. This case was about as routine as they come, so there was no need for a backup. Lorenzo did not have an extensive record; his only other run-in with the law was a minor possession charge—he'd gotten caught smoking pot in front of City Hall in Manhattan. Lorenzo was no rocket scientist. For me he was a ground ball. Find him, grab him, deliver him, earn five thousand bucks. Simple.

Well, yes and no. Finding him wasn't all that hard, but the journey I had to take to get there provided me with a startling and valuable lesson that altered my thinking about the world and what I was doing in it.

By all conventional indications, Lorenzo was the product of a lack of understanding, a misguided person who bounced from one situation to another, letting fate and chaos steer his course. I checked out his last known address, which was his mother's apartment in the projects on Staten Island. His mother was away visiting relatives in Virginia when I dropped by late one afternoon, but his nineteen-year-old sister, Joyce, was home. Joyce immediately made it clear to me that she did not look up to her big brother.

"Lorenzo's in the Bronx," she told me when I asked where he was living. "With his cow."

"Excuse me," I said.

"His cow," she repeated vehemently. "Her name is Vera Wilson, and she's big as a cow. Has kids like a cow, too. One right after the other. Four of them. None of them are Lorenzo's . . . I don't think."

Joyce was sitting at the kitchen table, and she wasn't exactly small herself. Her schoolbooks were spread out around her. She was going to college. I asked her if she knew the address where Lorenzo and Vera lived.

"A place called the Washington Motel," she said. "I've never been there, but my mother went once. She says it's a dump. Everybody who lives there is on welfare. She said she won't ever go back, and I told her not to. Lorenzo's just a bum and that's all he'll ever be."

I nodded as if I sympathized with her. I could see that she wanted a supporter, but really all I wanted was information. Though I didn't realize it at the time, I hadn't gotten as far as I thought I had on my evolutionary journey.

"Do you know Lorenzo's apartment number?" I asked.

"I'll get it for you." Joyce went into another room and came back with a black address book. "Three K," she said. "And when you find him, tell him to get his shit together this time. Maybe they'll send him to a prison where he'll learn a trade."

"Maybe," I said.

I thanked Joyce for her help and moved on to the next step, surveillance. That night I drove to the Washington Motel, parked in the lot, and just watched. As Joyce had said, it was a welfare motel and a very busy place because of that. When a family was in dire need and the city had no place else to put them, they'd end up here in a rented room until a more appropriate living space could be found. The trouble was, appropriate living spaces were hard to come by, and a lot of these families had been living here for months with four, five, even six people occupying one room.

It was early November, and the weather had suddenly turned wintry. No snow, but a bone-chilling cold gripped the East Coast. I sat in my car and watched people going in and out of the motel. Most of them were Black, a few Hispanic. The men looked either cocky or resentful. The women seemed to be either beaten down and docile or angry and aggressive. Of course, these were the night owls. I refused to believe that all the residents were this extreme.

The Washington Motel was a three-story U-shaped building. I estimated that there were at least a hundred rooms, and all of them were off long interior corridors with no easy access from the outside. I would have to get inside to find apartment 3K, which might pose a problem. A police substation now occupied what had been the front office of the motel.

I waited until after 2 A.M. when the cold had driven nearly all the residents inside before I made my approach. I pushed through the front doors and was immediately confronted with a uniformed officer sitting behind the front desk. He was a Black man with a suspicious gaze, who stared at me poker-faced, waiting for me to state my business.

The red carpeting in the lobby was stained and threadbare in places. There was no furniture except a single folding chair, which was occupied by a sleeping man in a parka so big and puffy it seemed to be propping him up. A scratched brown-painted metal door was to the right of the front desk. A woman came in after me and showed an ID card to the guard. He pressed a button under the counter, and the door buzzed. She whipped it open and slipped inside before it stopped buzzing.

"Something you want?" the cop asked me after the woman was gone.

"I'm looking for somebody who lives here," I said.

"Who's that?"

I took out my bail enforcement agent ID, a photo of Lorenzo, and the warrant for his arrest and laid them on the counter. The cop studied them for a few moments, then looked up at me from under his brows. "Bounty hunter?"

I nodded.

Unlike a lot of other cops I'd dealt with, he seemed unfazed. He'd probably dealt with bounty hunters before.

"I don't know this guy," he said, tapping his finger on Lorenzo's photo.

"You saying he doesn't live here?"

"I didn't say that. There are plenty of faces I don't know in this place. You know what room he lives in?"

"Three K," I said.

He checked a printout attached to a clipboard. "I've got a Vera Wilson in 3K."

"That's his girlfriend."

"Mmmm." The cop nodded, but I couldn't tell what his attitude was. I expected him to tell me to get the hell out.

He got off his stool, took a few steps back, and leaned into a side room. I could hear him conferring with someone else, asking about Vera Wilson's boyfriend in 3K. I couldn't hear what the person inside the room was saying. The cop came back to the counter with my warrant and the photo.

"She ain't supposed to have anyone boarding with her. It goes against the welfare rules."

I nodded, waiting for him to disappoint me.

"You can go in and look for him, but you gotta leave your guns here. You can have 'em back when you leave."

I laughed. "You must be joking."

He shrugged. "Those are the rules."

"I can't do my job without—"

He cut me off. "You can take cuffs, leg irons, and mace. That's it."

I could see there was no room for negotiation. The precedent had apparently been set a long time ago.

"You need to see my registration for the gun?" I asked.

He shrugged. "That's up to you. If the gun's here, you're not gonna be using it, so the registration doesn't make any difference to me."

I didn't like the idea of going after a fugitive unarmed, but considering Lorenzo's record, I doubted I'd be needing it. I unclipped my holster from my belt and laid it on the counter.

"I need to pat you down," he said.

I shrugged, resigned to the rules, but first I pulled out my taser and showed it to him. "Can I bring this?"

"Nope." He took it from me and stashed it under the counter with my gun. Then he came out from behind the counter and frisked me—body, arms, and legs. When he was through, he went back to his post.

"Any dogs in there?" I said, nodding toward the metal door.

"A few."

I wondered how effective mace would be against a pit bull. Dog dazers hadn't come on the market yet. I had a feeling mace would just make a mean dog meaner.

"Go ahead," the cop said. "I'll buzz you in."

I hesitated, still unsure whether this was a good idea. I considered going home, then coming back in the morning to wait for Lorenzo to come out, but I never liked to work that way. Trying to take a fugitive when there are other people around is always risky—friends will try to run to the man's rescue, sometimes onlookers will get involved, the wrong people end up getting hurt. But going into a building like the Washington Motel underequipped could be disastrous, too. Still, I kept telling myself that Lorenzo wasn't hard-core. He might try to run, but he wasn't the type to put up a fight. If I took him by surprise, kept it quiet, and he didn't have any buddies around, it would be all right. Three ifs weren't too many, I thought.

"You going in or not?" the cop asked.

"I'm going," I said.

He hit the buzzer, and I pushed through the door. A long corridor with a scuffed vinyl floor stretched into the distance. It seemed to be at least half a city block long. Fluorescent lights on the ceiling gave everything a silvery gray tint. The door slammed shut behind me. I felt as if I were being locked in.

I took a closer look at the back of the door and saw a bunch of perfectly round dents in the metal, at least twenty of them. I stuck my finger in one. They were bullet holes.

"Crazy people." The woman who had just been buzzed into the building was coming out of a nearby room. She walked toward me, buttoning up her coat. "Crazy people did that," she said.

"What do you mean, crazy people?"

"These boys in here, they get new guns and they have to try them out. They poke their heads out their door and just shoot down the hall. And in the middle of the night when people are trying to sleep. Scares me half to death."

"The cops let them bring guns in?" I asked.

The woman shrugged. "They try to stop it, but those boys, they always find a way." She flipped a scarf around her neck and pulled the door open for herself. It slammed shut behind her, echoing down the hall.

Crazy, I thought. I also thought about my gun back at the front desk. I didn't know which was crazier—people taking practice shots down a hallway or me being in here without my weapon.

I walked toward a lighted red exit sign in the middle of the hallway and took the stairs. The stairwell was littered with junk food wrappers and crushed soda cans. Underneath the Twinkie wrappers, Big Mac boxes, and Popeye's Fried Chicken bags, there were dozens of empty crack vials. They shattered under my feet as I climbed the steps. I knew that people put all kinds of crap into their bodies, but the accumulated debris of not just bad habits, *dangerous* habits created a frightening abstract picture. The body is supposed to be a temple, but that message obviously went unheeded here.

As I rounded the landing onto the second floor, I found more junk food wrappers and containers—Ring Dings, Snowballs, Whoppers, Milky Way bars, Butterfingers, Skittles, Coke, Orange Crush, Yoo-Hoo—not to mention hundreds of stomped-out cigarette butts. A purple and green plastic tricycle had been left in a corner of the landing. Kids consumed a lot of this junk food. I was willing to bet that some of these kids hadn't ever eaten a decent meal.

I made my way up to the third floor and opened a metal door. The third floor hallway was identical to the one on the first floor, uniformly depressing. The quiet was eerie; I could hear the fluorescent bulbs on the ceiling buzzing like flies. I glanced at the numbers on the doors to get my bearings. Room 3K was farther down the hallway, past where it made a ninety-degree turn to the left.

Walking down that lifeless hallway was like walking underwater, but when I turned the corner I suddenly stopped, startled by an unexpected figure. A little boy, maybe five years old, was lying on the floor. My heart started to pound. I thought he was dead. But then I saw that he was clutching a pillow, and his chest was rising and falling with his breathing. The boy was asleep. But why was he sleeping out here?

I hunkered down next to him. He was wearing green corduroy pants, white socks, and a gray Mets sweatshirt. He had a blanket, but he was sleeping on top of it, and I could see from the way he was hunching his shoulders that he was cold. I stroked his hand with the back of my finger until his eyes fluttered open.

"Hey," I said softly. "What are you doing out here?"

He closed his eyes and frowned, angry that I had woken him.

"Don't you have a bed?" I asked.

"Sleepy," he said grumpily. He opened his eyes and tried to glare at me, but he couldn't keep them open.

"Where are your parents?" I asked.

He just looked at me, his head falling off the pillow.

"Come on now. Where are your parents? I'll take you home."

Without lifting his head, he pointed to the nearest door.

"Why aren't you in there with them?"

"Too much talking."

"You can't sleep when people are talking?"

He shook his head. "Too loud."

I couldn't just leave him out there. I had to do something. I was about to knock on the door when I noticed that it wasn't closed. I pushed it open a few inches. "Hello," I said.

No answer.

I peeked in. The TV was on, tuned to an interview show where some guy in a suit was joking with a glamorous blonde in a little black dress. The sofa bed was open, and a man was sprawled out diagonally on top of it. He was wearing a green flannel shirt and gray sweatpants, nothing on his feet. A tiny kitchenette was on the right side of the room. Seated at a small Formica table, a woman was sleeping on her arms.

"Hello," I repeated, and stepped into the room.

Neither of them stirred. I moved closer to the man. His breathing was shallow. A needle was lying on the bed covers next to his hand.

I went over to the table where the woman was sitting. A tablespoon, a cigarette lighter, a pack of Kools, and a tiny empty plastic bag were spread out around her. The bottom of the spoon was charred black. The woman was wearing a black turtleneck, one sleeve pushed up, one all the way down.

A wave of sadness washed over me. I just stood there, frozen, as if I were soaking wet in the middle of a blizzard.

These two were blissed out on heroin. The woman, who was small and mousy, had cooked it up, and they had shared a needle. The little boy's father—if this was his father—had hogged the bed. He was a big man, well over six feet tall.

I stood there, confused and helpless. I didn't know whether to hate these people or pity them. Were they responsible for their own miserable lives because they refused to evolve? Or were they the victims of circumstance, born into poverty and unable to escape it?

I'd come to believe that the first thing to destroy a society is unawareness. Everything else that's bad falls into place behind it—drug addiction, theft, prostitution, violence, murder. These two people didn't realize how far they'd sunk. They were on welfare, yet they had to support two heroin habits. Maybe they were working under the table somewhere—unless they were so far gone they couldn't handle regular jobs anymore—but if they weren't working, then he was probably stealing whatever he could to scrape up enough cash for their next fix. Breaking into houses, stealing radios out of cars, stealing whole cars, shoplifting, taking money from church boxes, snatching purses from women on the street—nothing was too low for a drug fiend. I'd seen it firsthand. When drugs become a person's god, that deity is demanding. Tribute must be paid constantly.

If the man couldn't steal enough for the two of them, the woman undoubtedly sold her body to feed the demon. Watching her blank, deluded face made me want to cry. I couldn't help but think he had dragged her down into his own self-destructive spiral. That's the way the story usually went.

Later, when I'd had a chance to think about it and do some reading on the subject of relationships, I learned that at one time this woman held the power to raise her man from his animal existence simply by withholding sex from him. I know that seems like an old-fashioned, even backward notion, but for people in these kinds of dire circumstances it's a viable solution.

Romantic love is a high that lasts about as long as any other narcotic, and like a drug, the craving for it can take over a person's entire life. I learned from my readings in ancient Eygptian philosophy that the relentless pursuit of romance can make people obsessive, single-minded, and blind to the true fullness of their lives.

But that desire for romance can also be used to good effect. By denying sex when necessary, a woman can capture her man's focus and with some effort begin to reform his behavior. At one time these two people might have been entwined in the sweet vines of romance, but as I stood in their apartment surveying their sorry state, I could see that their relationship was now a tangle of weeds, plants that bear no fruit and exist simply to exist.

The little boy, of course, was a fruit of his mother's love. He was a gift that these people could not begin to appreciate. Tragically, he was entangled in their messed-up lives, and it would be a miracle if he ever escaped from this impoverished upbringing. I feared for this boy's future. He had probably never had a decent meal. His parents had never cared enough to give him a safe place to sleep. He'd seen the adults he depended upon for his own survival shooting poison into their veins. He'd probably never had a book read to him and as a result would probably never read a book himself. How could a person brought up this way *not* go wrong? It occurred to me that someday this innocent little boy could be a felon. In ten years he could be sleeping on a ward in a juvenile detention center. In twelve or fifteen, a bounty hunter might be holding a warrant for his arrest.

But why? Because he consciously decided to become a criminal? Or because he never had a choice? An individual must choose to evolve, but he has to become informed that there are options and possibilities. If a child's existence is so debased and animalistic that mere survival is his sole concern, how can he ever evolve? If a person is constantly looking down for scraps of pleasure and opportunities to copulate, when will he ever look up and see what else there is in life?

I was sickened by the whole situation. I didn't know what to do. My impulse was to take the boy away and save him, but that would be kidnapping. I thought about taking him downstairs to the cop behind the desk, but what could he do? This boy undoubtedly wasn't the only child living at risk in this building. The police would have to take all these children. And then what? They'd be transferred to social services and placed in foster homes where they'd live with the stigma of being one of life's rejects, where care would be provided but would never be a substitute for a parent's love.

I stood there and pondered the dilemma for a long time, and finally I came to the conclusion that I shouldn't mess with the nest. I went over to the bed, grabbed the man by the wrist and ankle, and eased him onto the floor, then I went out into the hallway and picked up the boy, setting him down on the bed and tucking him in. I threw a blanket over the man, hoping that he wouldn't wake up angry and cold and take it out on the boy. My prayer was that someday this boy would meet someone who cared enough to guide him. If I had been sufficiently evolved at the time myself, I might have undertaken that responsibility. To this day I think back on that child with some regret.

From the doorway I took one last look at this family before I shut the door behind me. As I walked down the hallway heading for Room 3K, I wondered what kind of upbringing Lorenzo Franks had had. He was from the projects, but his sister was, too, and she was going to college. She was trying to better herself. What had happened to him?

I tried to imagine all the possible reasons for Lorenzo being in his current state. He was older than his sister. Maybe there had been a drug problem in the home when he was young that didn't exist by the time she was born. Maybe he and his sister hadn't been brought up in the same household. Maybe she had been sent to live with relatives who were better role models. Maybe he had been abused or even molested as a child. There were lots of possible reasons, but the point was, I was here to apprehend him, and in my heart I wanted to feel sorry for him. I was relating him to that little boy I'd just tucked into bed. Lorenzo was a fugitive from justice; I was supposed to view him as a criminal. But after seeing what I'd just seen, how could I? Like so many others, Lorenzo was probably as much a victim as he was a felon.

When I got to Room 3K, I stood there and stared at the door for a moment. In the distance I could hear the faint thumping bass line of a rap song booming from a passing car out on the street. I thought about giving Lorenzo a pass, but I knew that would be an empty and misdirected act of kindness. If I didn't pick him up, someone else certainly would.

I quietly tried the doorknob, and as expected, it was locked. Picking the lock didn't seem like a smart idea. It was just a single room. Whoever was in there would no doubt hear me and most likely react as if I were a burglar. Lorenzo might even have a gun, and I didn't. But considering his nonviolent record, I decided to take the direct approach and knocked on the door.

No one answered, but I could hear voices inside. Someone was shushing someone else. I knocked again.

"Who is it?" A man's voice came through the door. He was whispering.

I hunched my shoulders and bent my head, so that whoever was on the other side of the peephole wouldn't get a good look at my face. "I'm looking for Lorenzo," I said.

"What for?"

"His mama sent me. It's important."

"What do you want?"

"I came all the way from Staten Island. I gotta talk to him."

I heard the dead bolt unlocking. I quickly pulled up my mask. The canister of mace was in my hand in my pocket. The door opened halfway, and Lorenzo Franks himself was staring back at me. As soon as he saw the mask, he went to slam the door, but I already had my foot inside. I rammed my shoulder into the door and forced my way in.

"Don't move," I said, holding the mace can extended.

Lorenzo put his hands up to protect his face and backed into the kitchenette. The pole light next to the bed was the only one on in the room. Lorenzo was wearing boxer shorts and a V-neck T-shirt.

I quickly scanned the room, which was identical in layout to the little boy's room down the hall but more crowded. A woman was sitting up in bed, clutching her chest. Three small children were curled up on an air mattress on the floor. A crib was jammed into a tight space at the far end of the room between the bed and the window.

Lorenzo must have been asleep. He was squinting and shielding his eyes from the light. "I ain't got no money, man. I swear."

"I'm not here to rob you," I said.

"Don't hurt them," he pleaded. "Don't hurt the kids. Please."

I was impressed that his first concern was for the children.

"You skipped out on your bail, Lorenzo. You know you can't do that. You have to come with me now."

"What about my mama? You said my mama sent you."

I shook my head. "I just said that to get you to open the door. I don't know your mama." No sense adding that burden to his troubles. No man wants to believe that a family member would ever give him up.

The woman was sobbing, making panicky little squeaking sounds. One of the kids was half-crying, half-moaning. The other two were awake but quiet. The baby was sound asleep.

"Get dressed," I said to Lorenzo.

"But—"

"I said get dressed. These children need their sleep."

He sighed and reached for a pair of pants hanging over the back of a kitchen chair. He looked defeated and resigned to his fate, but he was cooperating.

"Are you a user?" I asked him. "Tell me the truth."

"Hell, no." He seemed offended by the question.

"Is she?" I nodded at Vera.

"No."

"Good." I dug into my pocket and came up with a fistful of bills. It was at least a hundred dollars. I laid it on the table. "This is for the children," I said to Vera. "For food. Nothing else."

She was still too panicked to respond.

Lorenzo was putting his shoes on. I tried to keep my eyes on him, but I couldn't help glancing at the kids. I was thinking about that other little boy. I was worried about all of them, having to live here and absorb all the negative influences that infected this place.

"Get your coat," I said to Lorenzo when he finished tying his shoes.

"Aw, man! This ain't right," he complained, but he stood up and got his coat anyway.

"If you have anything you want to say to your woman, go ahead and say it now."

He made a face at me as he went over to the bed and sat down next to Vera. "I'm sorry about this, baby," he said. "I love you." He kissed her and hugged her. He stood up and looked at the baby for a moment, then stooped and touched the little ones on the head one by one.

"Anything else you need to do?"

"Yeah, get a new life," he grumbled.

Or improve the one you've got, I thought to myself.

"OK, let's go," I said. I took him by the arm and led him to the door, the mace ready in my other hand.

When we got out into the hallway and closed the door, I put him up against the wall. "Hands up," I said. He leaned against the wall with his hands above his head. He knew the drill. I pulled down one wrist and cuffed it, then the other. He'd been cooperative, so I hadn't cuffed him in front of Vera and the kids. That would only embarrass him and leave the kids with a terrible lasting impression.

I turned him around and led him down the hallway toward the stairwell. "Now what?" he asked.

I explained the procedure. He'd be held at the Essex County jail until his court date came up, which could end up being several weeks. Since he'd skipped out on his bail once, it wouldn't be granted again on the same charges. If he was eventually convicted, he'd go straight from jail to prison. I didn't tell him that in all likelihood this walk we were taking right now would probably be the last one he'd be taking on the outside for at least a year.

As we walked down the hallway, he kept looking back. He seemed anxious. "If I go to prison, those kids ain't gonna remember me by the time I get out."

"But they're not yours, are they?" I asked.

"Don't matter," he said. "I'm the one they call Daddy. I'm the one who takes care of them. Besides Vera, I'm the only one who cares about those kids." His eyes were wet.

"They'll remember you," I said as we pushed through the door to the stairwell. "That'll be your incentive to keep your nose clean in prison so you can get out sooner."

"Yeah, right . . . "

Lorenzo was confused and upset, but I hoped that his feelings for those kids would stay with him. He seemed to genuinely love them.

I brought him in without incident, and his fate unfolded pretty much as I had predicted. He was convicted and sentenced to a year in prison. I don't know if he ever went back to Vera and the children after he got out, but I hope he learned a lesson as profound as the one I learned the night I went to pick him up. The Washington Motel was my trip to hell and back. It didn't show me anything I hadn't seen before, but it did show me how the failure to evolve happens. Before I went into the Washington Motel, I thought crazy people shooting firearms down hallways was scary. But that kind of behavior is only a symptom, not the disease itself. A child brought up wrong is far scarier. A child brought up wrong can be fatal.

11 Self-Control

Temptations abound in this world like old-fashioned mousetraps, each one set with an enticing piece of cheese. Without self-control, a person can easily be lured into one of these traps. The Seekers' reputation was expanding, and we were being hired to do more out-of-state pickups. In 1991 Jedidiah, Zora, and I traveled to southern Florida to pick up a big-time Colombian drug dealer named Carlos Herrera who had blown off a court date in New Jersey. Herrera was a genuine drug lord, and our biggest fish yet.

Like most of the Latin kingpins, Herrera considered an indictment nothing more than a minor bureaucratic nuisance, something for his lawyers to deal with. His energies were concentrated on moving weight from his homeland to ours, so I guess that made him a citizen of the world—at least in his mind—and a citizen of the world doesn't have to abide by the laws of any one country. I have no idea where people like Herrera get this attitude, but maybe they don't have bounty hunters in Colombia. "Facing the music" must mean something different down there.

The outstanding bond on Herrera was $250,000. The judge in New Jersey had known that the risk of flight was great in this case and that

Herrera's primary residence in this country was in Florida. The judge probably would have set the bail even higher if he'd thought he could get away with it, because granting bail almost guaranteed that Herrera would leave the state and not come back. To make bail, Herrera had given his bondsman $25,000 (10 percent of the total) and the deed to a mansion he owned on the Jersey shore. The bondsman later found out that the deed was almost worthless since Herrera had already defaulted on two home-equity loans that were secured by the house. To get his money back, the bondsman would have to get in line behind the two banks, and the house wasn't worth enough to satisfy everyone. A loss like this was too big for the bondsman to absorb, so his only alternative was to find Herrera and haul him back to court. He knew it wouldn't be easy, and he doubted that just any bounty hunter could even get close to a major leaguer like Herrera. The bondsman had heard about the Seekers and our unorthodox methods, so he decided to give us a try.

The first thing I did was to find out where Herrera was currently living. I was pretty sure he wouldn't be at the Miami address that was in his file. Herrera was no kid; he'd been around for a while. People don't survive that long in the drug business unless they're smart and cautious. The house in Miami was probably occupied by someone, but I knew it wasn't going to be Herrera. Fortunately, we had some contacts down there who were able to help us out. The word on the street was that Herrera had moved his family up to a place in Pompano Beach. My contact got me an address, and Jedidiah, Zora, and I started packing.

We flew down to Florida, then rented a Ford van and headed for Pompano Beach. As a precaution we took the license plates off and replaced them with a set of Florida plates we got from a junkyard so that we couldn't be traced back to the rental agency. We informed the Pompano Beach police that we had done this when we checked in with them and showed them the warrant for Herrera's arrest.

We spent the next few days checking out the address I'd gotten from my contact, as well as the town in general. Herrera had a spectacular, ultramodern house with cathedral ceilings, lots of skylights, and huge asymmetrical windows. It was surprising that a criminal would have so many windows in his house. Surveillance techniques are very sophisticated, and windows like these would just make the job that much easier. Of course, if Herrera didn't think anyone knew about this place, why wouldn't he have nice big windows? Besides, it was unlikely that he'd ever be seen handling dope in his own house. He was too smart to allow it to enter his door. Only a mad dog makes a mess where he sleeps.

The neighborhood was a few blocks away from the ocean. It wasn't as posh as Palm Beach, but it wasn't too far behind. Every house on Herrera's street was spectacular, and that presented us with a problem. Whenever we go out on a pickup, we try to draw as little attention to ourselves as possible, and in an exclusive neighborhood like that, we had to be extra careful. Just driving around might be seen as unusual behavior, and the wealthy don't hesitate to call the police or their private security guards if they feel threatened. Obviously we didn't want Herrera to see us being pulled over by a cop in front of his house. He'd flee in a minute if he thought something was up.

Before we could proceed, we needed a good cover. I went to a local sign maker and had two plastic signs made that we could stick onto the doors of the van: "J & J Roofing." I put a toll-free 888 number on the signs, which was connected to an answering machine back home in New Jersey. I was able to change the outgoing message by phone: "You have reached J & J Roofing. Your call is important to us. Please leave your name and number, and we'll get back to you promptly." While the signs were being made, Jedidiah and I went to a local rental company where we obtained a set of roof racks and a twenty-foot aluminum ladder. We changed into jeans, work shirts, and work boots, and by the end of the day we had our cover.

In the meantime, Zora put on a skirt and heels and checked out the local bars, hoping to pick up some morsels of information about Herrera and his family. Over the next few days she went back to the same establishments at the same time every day in order to infiltrate the scene. At one place she noticed a Hispanic gentleman in his sixties who was always sitting at the bar late in the afternoon sipping a dark rum straight up while he read a Spanish-language newspaper. Invariably his crumpled hat was on the bar by his elbow. He had the soulful face of a poet, she said, but his hands were rough and callused. He always wore a light-colored short-sleeved shirt, khaki pants, and black lace-up work boots that were as lined as his face. Zora had a feeling he was the type who knew everybody's business.

The next time she went to the bar she nodded and smiled at him but otherwise left him alone, chatting with the bartender instead. On her next visit, she overheard the man telling the bartender in Spanish about his life as a young man in Havana before Castro took over. He said he had worked at one of the grand gambling casinos before the Communists closed them all down. Zora joined their conversation, saying in Spanish that she used to deal blackjack at Bally's in Atlantic City. The three of them spoke for a while about casinos in general, comparing the old Havana establishments with Las Vegas and Atlantic City. They didn't talk long, but it was enough to put Zora on speaking terms with the old gentleman.

The next day I went in by myself so that I could see the man for myself. I ordered a beer and took it to a table across from the bar. When Zora walked in ten minutes later, the old gentleman seemed glad to see her. She took a seat next to him at the bar and greeted him warmly. The bartender asked if she wanted the "regular." She nodded and he brought her a glass of red wine. "So," the old gentleman said in his heavily accented English, "may I ask what you are doing here in Pompano? You seem to be new in this area."

She frowned and exhaled a long sigh. "I'm looking for someone. Someone who owes my father money."

"Really?" He knit his brows and suddenly seemed very concerned with her situation.

She reached into her bag and pulled out a photo of Herrera. It was a snapshot that had been confiscated from Herrera's Jersey shore house. He was shirtless, sitting in a lounge chair, his skin deeply tanned and shiny with suntan lotion. He was smirking playfully at the camera. She showed the photo to the old gentleman. "By any chance do you know this man?" she asked. "His name is Herrera."

The old gentleman studied it for a moment, then laughed scornfully. His cordial attitude suddenly made a U-turn. "I cannot help you," he said abruptly. "I do not sell drugs."

"I'm not looking to buy drugs," Zora protested. "I'm looking for this man Herrera. He hired my father to put a new roof on his house, but the place is empty. My father paid for the materials out of his own pocket. He had to custom-order these special shingles that Mr. Herrera wanted. Very expensive. So expensive, my father will never be able to sell them to another customer. If Mr. Herrera doesn't want my father to do the job, fine, but he should at least pay for the damn shingles."

The Cuban gentleman scrutinized her face. "Are you the police?" he asked frankly.

"No, I'm not the police," she said indignantly.

The man pointed at the photo in her hand. "This man is very dangerous. Don't make trouble with him."

"I don't want trouble. I just don't want my father to get screwed. People take advantage of my father because he's too nice."

The old gentleman sighed. "Don't make trouble. Listen to me."

"I *don't* want trouble," she insisted. "All I want is an answer. Does he want my father to do the job or not? I just want to talk to somebody, but it doesn't look like anyone even lives there anymore."

"Yes, yes, Señor Herrera does live there. I know because I know his house." The old gentleman was trying to placate her.

"But nobody's ever home whenever I go there," she said.

"I know the gardener who works for this man. My friend—the gardener—he told me he has to do much extra work whenever this man is away. My friend is very busy now."

"What does your friend have to do?"

"Turn on lights, turn off lights, move the cars. You know, make it look like someone is home. For almost one week he has been doing this."

Zora nodded as if she was beginning to understand. "So does your friend have to spend the night there, too?" she asked.

A devilish grin spread across the old gentleman's face. "I don't think so. My friend has a jealous wife."

She grinned. "Are you sure about all this? Not just about your friend's wife, I mean."

"Yes, I am very sure."

"Well, that's good to know . . . I guess." She finished her wine and ordered another. "Can I buy you a drink?" she asked the man. "For your kind help."

He shrugged humbly. "If you like."

She ordered him another rum, and they drank together for a while longer. I finished my beer and headed for the door, catching Zora's eye as I passed the bar. We made eye contact but didn't say anything. Outside in the parking lot I called Jedidiah on my cell phone. I told him to meet me at our motel. Zora would join us as soon as she could.

It was after three o'clock in the morning when Zora drove the van past Herrera's house. She'd cut the headlights two blocks back to avoid being seen. I was in the passenger seat next to her; Jedidiah was in the backseat.

"Right here," I said, pointing through the windshield.

She pulled the van over to the curb and parked in the shadow of some overhanging pine boughs.

"I'll be in touch," I said as I opened the door. We were all wearing wireless headsets with earplug receivers and microtransmitters so that we could communicate in whispers. Jedidiah and I were also wearing night-vision monocles, so that we could see in the dark. Unlike the standard binocular models that cover both eyes, these state-of-the-art devices leave one eye unencumbered to prevent the wearer from becoming disoriented. With our increasing success, the Seekers had started investing in better, more technologically sophisticated equipment. I got out of the van and crossed Herrera's front lawn to get to the back of the house.

A black Mercedes was parked in the driveway and a maroon Cadillac was in the open garage. The Mercedes was the one the gardener moved twice a day, parking it a little differently each time. There were no lights on in the house, which was normal for this time of night, and no other vehicles were on the property, which was good. I didn't want to walk in on the gardener stretched out in one of Herrera's guest rooms.

I walked across the inlaid stone patio, past a set of sliding glass doors that led into a sunken living room, and went directly to a corner of the house where the roof sloped down low. I pulled up a patio chair, hitched my backpack over both shoulders, and hauled myself up onto the roof. I crouched on the edge of the roof and paused to hear if I'd wakened anyone. When I was satisfied that it was safe, I walked up the steep incline heading for the nearest skylight. The doors and windows were undoubtedly wired with alarms, but skylights are rarely wired. Using a prybar from my pack, I forced the skylight open and climbed through. I dropped down onto thick carpeting in the upstairs hallway.

I drew my weapon—a .45 semi-automatic—and started searching the house, top to bottom, to make sure no one was there. I was still worried about that gardener. If he or anyone else was there, I'd probably have to abandon the plan and leave right away because I couldn't in good conscience hold the person captive until Herrera showed up. On the other hand, if I let the person go, he or she would probably alert Herrera and then he'd never come back.

Quickly but carefully I went from room to room, gun pointed up and at the ready. After checking the bedrooms, I decided to go down to the basement and work my way up to the ground floor. In the basement I found Herrera's enormous game room, which was equipped with a twenty-foot mahogany bar, two pool tables, a foosball table, a pinball machine, a poker table, and a Ping-Pong table. Plush brown leather sofas and lounge chairs were arranged in conversation groups all around. I went over to one of the pool tables and ran my hand along the felt.

Behind a closed door next to the bar, I found the more utilitarian part of the basement. The washer and dryer were on one side of the room; a workbench was on the other. A humming freezer locker as big as two stacked coffins was against the wall in the middle of the room. I opened it and looked inside. There was a petting zoo's worth of red meat and poultry in there as well as several half-gallons of gourmet ice cream and sherbet.

I checked out the workbench. A vise was bolted to one end of it. Various tools were scattered on top—pliers, a tiny screwdriver set, small-gauge box wrenches, nylon-tipped drift punches, split-end screwdrivers, plastic-face hammers. Curiously, there were no woodworking tools of any kind, not even a saw, and the space was amazingly clean for a workbench. The can of gun oil confirmed my suspicions. This space was dedicated to cleaning, repairing, and modifying guns.

I climbed the stairs to the first floor of the house, which was magnificent and surprisingly tasteful. Criminals who get rich quick typically buy things that are gaudy and showy, and their homes tend to look like Las Vegas casinos. But not this place. Whoever had done the decorating liked the incongruous, pairing spare lines and open space with religious folk art. The chairs and sofas were all right angles in a plain dove-gray fabric. The walls were white, the floors a light-colored natural wood. But the paintings were incredible explosions of color. Dying saints, Madonnas, a manger scene, Christ on the cross. It wouldn't surprise me one bit if Herrera were a devout Catholic. Belonging to an organized religion seems to give some people the psychological freedom to participate in heavy-duty criminal activities. I understand that confession is a sacrament, but when people don't learn from their mistakes, the whole concept ought to be rethought. If you keep on committing the same sins and you just keep going back to your priest for absolution, what's the point? What about responsibility and accountability? The legal system has provisions for repeat offenders; religions should, too. If you coddle a man in his bad habits, he'll never learn how to change.

I was staring up at a larger-than-life-size painting of the Virgin Mary done in bright shades of red, yellow, and orange, the frame studded with small pieces of mirror, as I spoke into my headset microphone. "All clear," I said softly. "Come on in, Jed."

Two minutes later I heard Jedidiah drop through the skylight with a soft thud on the thick carpet. He came down the stairway and joined me in front of the painting.

"Looks like we have to wait for Mr. Herrera to come home," I said.

Jedidiah nodded, but the question was, how long were we going to have to wait? We sat in the den for a while, leafing through fashion and home-decorating magazines for lack of anything better to do. After an hour or so, we started wandering through the house to combat the boredom. Because it was very late at night and we were completely on our own, there was an undeniable voyeuristic titillation associated with our snooping. We had no intention of stealing or destroying anything—that goes against the Seeker principles—but we were curious. And the more we found, the more we wanted to look, because Herrera had the best of everything.

In the kitchen there was a chrome-doored double-sized refrigerator. I opened it to see if it had been cleaned out of perishables, an indication that the residents planned to be away for a while. I didn't find any left-overs, but there was an open gallon of milk in the door and a fair amount of fresh fruits and vegetables in the crisper drawers. The residents probably hadn't gone too far. I noticed that on the bottom shelf there were five bottles of champagne lined up on their sides. I recognized the irregularly shaped dark glass bottles—Dom Pérignon, a hundred dollars a bottle. I helped myself to an orange and closed the refrigerator.

In the meantime Jedidiah checked out the walk-in pantry. It was well stocked with canned goods. Herrera's whole crew could hole up here for a couple of weeks with all this food. Someone in the house must have had quite a taste for Beluga caviar because they had more tins of it than they had tuna fish. Jedidiah found a box of herbal tea and put some water on to boil. We figured they could spare a couple of tea bags.

While I waited for the water to get hot, I wandered into the entertainment room, which was dominated by a large-screen projection TV and an overstuffed wraparound sofa. I checked out the rows of videotapes in the built-in bookshelves. The G-rated Disney movies were on the bottom shelves. The porn was on the top shelf. Ironically, both sections had a *Beauty and the Beast.* Not the same movie, though.

I don't watch a whole lot of television myself, and I'm not into porn. The way I see it, these kinds of diversions are just useless input that take up too much space in your brain. Don't get me wrong—I enjoy a good movie as much as the next person. I just can't see watching something mediocre or just plain bad simply to kill time. I'd rather read.

When I heard the kettle whistling, I went back to the kitchen where Jedidiah had set out two mugs for us. He poured the water over the tea bags, and we carried the mugs upstairs to the bedrooms.

There were two children's bedrooms off the upstairs hallway. I knew from Herrera's file that he had two boys and a girl. One room was all pink and purple with an army of stuffed animals and Barbie dolls scattered all over the place. The boys' room, which was larger, had two elaborate beds that looked like formula-one race cars. A dozen pictures of various baseball players were taped to the wall over one of the two desks. A bare-chested Bruce Lee hung over the other desk. The boys' room was much neater than the girl's.

The master bedroom came closer to the showy opulence I associated with drug money. A huge canopy bed with massive posts of some dark wood was the centerpiece of the room. It was cluttered with garish pillows in all colors and sizes, most of them with tassels. Two hulking bureaus made out of the same dark wood as the bedposts stood on opposite sides of the room like guard monsters. A 52-inch Sony television faced the bed. The rug had a rich deep pile and was the color of dried blood.

The master bath was dizzying. A checkerboard of cobalt-blue and white tiles covered every surface, including the ceiling, except for one wall, which was one big mirror. The double sinks, toilet, bidet, tub, and Jacuzzi were all in a lighter, contrasting blue. Herrera and his wife must have liked looking at themselves, I thought, because there was no way you could escape that mirror.

Jedidiah was in the walk-in closet shaking his head at the jam-packed racks of clothes. "This man is definitely living large," he said disapprovingly.

Mrs. Herrera must have had an Imelda Marcos complex because by my count she had about eighty pairs of shoes and I don't know how many dresses. Her designer jeans had all been dry-cleaned and pressed with sharp creases.

Herrera wasn't too far behind his wife in the shoe category. He had at least a dozen pairs of dressy Gucci and Ferragamo loafers. His passion, however, was apparently cowboy boots in all kinds of exotic leathers. I counted thirty-one pairs. He also had quite a few nice suits, as well as fifty or sixty short-sleeved silk shirts in all kinds of garish colors and patterns, paisley being the most conservative. Unbelievably, he even had a deep red one with lines of cocaine and little coke spoons printed all over it. I took it down off the rack to show Jedidiah. He just rolled his eyes.

We wandered back down to the kitchen, where we rinsed out our mugs with hot water and put them back in the cupboard. It was four-thirty in the morning.

"You want to get some rest?" I asked.

Jedidiah shrugged. "Sure."

Off the living room there was a hallway that led to a separate wing where there were two guest bedrooms and a separate bathroom. Both rooms had king-sized beds, and there was an assortment of men's clothing in both closets. I figured Herrera's bodyguards slept there.

Jedidiah picked the room closest to the living room and lay down under the bed. That way if he fell asleep, at least he'd be out of sight. He kept his headset on so I could wake him if necessary. I went into the living room and sat in the dark in one of the plush armchairs, moonlight beaming in through the patio windows. I had a good view of the backyard and the driveway, which were both colorless by the light of the moon. The chrome around the headlights of Herrera's Mercedes shone dully. Except for the passing red and green lights of an occasional airplane high in the sky, nothing moved.

I fought back a yawn and thought about watching some television but vetoed that idea. It would cast a glow that could be seen from outside, and I didn't want anything to look unusual. I thought about going back into the kitchen and checking out the refrigerator again, maybe helping myself to something better than an orange, but I knew I wasn't hungry, I was just bored. And tempted. Being in this house was like a kid getting locked in a candy store. Too many goodies.

All kinds of possibilities ran through my mind. I could go downstairs and fix myself a drink, play some pool, check out the pinball machine. I could try some of that caviar in the pantry. I could go back upstairs and check out those bureaus, see what Herrera kept hidden in his underwear drawer. I could check out the computer in the boys' room. I could go looking for a wall safe or a strongbox, maybe find out what Herrera had stashed here. I could do a lot of things. My brain started to itch just thinking about it.

But I resisted the temptations and kept my butt in that chair. I was not there to play. Herrera's riches were not my concern. I had no right indulging in his possessions even if they were ill-gotten gain. Bounty hunting doesn't have those kinds of perks. If I want something badly enough, I'll buy it for myself. I reminded myself that there was only one reason for my being there. My job was to take Herrera by surprise when he got home and bring him back to Newark. That was my concern—nothing else.

To fill the time, I did some meditation, taking advantage of the absolute quiet. It was a good opportunity to gather my energies and calm my spirit because I knew that later on I would need to be ready. When Herrera got home, the shit was gonna hit the fan.

I let my thoughts drift, hoping they'd drift away completely and leave my mind empty of all distractions, and before I realized it, dawn had sneaked up on me. The world outside was visible in shades of gray. The sun would be rising soon, giving color to the lush greenery in the backyard.

After a while I heard a sharp inhalation through the single earplug I was wearing. Jedidiah was waking up.

"Joshua," he croaked, then yawned loudly. "You want to get some rest?"

"In a while," I said. I wasn't tired now. In fact, after meditating I felt wide awake.

Jedidiah came wandering out into the living room, rubbing his face. "I need something to eat. You want something?"

I shook my head and went back to staring out the window. The palm trees blocked out the sun, but golden light came filtering through the fronds nonetheless. The sight of the world gradually coming to life was mesmerizing and wonderful. Suddenly the lawn sprinklers went on, sending rainbow mists through the sunlight. I checked my watch. It was 6:45 on the dot.

"Zora," I said into my headset mike, "you still there?"

"I'm here," she answered. "So where's Herrera?"

"We shall see," I said. "Hang tight."

Jedidiah came out of the kitchen, chewing a granola bar and carrying a glass of orange juice. He could have fixed himself a sumptuous breakfast, but he felt the way I did: take as little as possible and don't succumb to temptation. We weren't here to enjoy ourselves.

As it got on toward seven-thirty, I decided it was time to get out of that chair. The gardener might show up, and those large sliding glass doors made the living room a fishbowl. Jedidiah and I went upstairs and took up new positions. From the little girl's room Jedidiah could see the front of the property. I watched the rear from a window in the hallway. We were out of each other's sight, but the headsets kept us in contact.

The sun rose over the palms. I became fascinated with the specks of dust floating so peacefully through the sunlight beaming in through the window. The house was absolutely silent.

"You know any good jokes?" Jedidiah's voice suddenly came through my earpiece.

"Not really," I said.

"You hear the one about the drug dealer who didn't come home?"

I laughed despite myself, rubbing my face to stay alert. It was a quarter after nine, and now I was feeling a little sleepy.

"I take it back," Jedidiah said sharply. "Somebody's coming."

"You've got company," Zora said almost simultaneously.

Down in the driveway two cars suddenly came into view, a black Lincoln town car and a silver Ford Crown Victoria. The doors swung open, and a lot of people started piling out. I stepped back from the window so I wouldn't be seen. Jedidiah came up behind me.

I quickly scanned all the faces, looking for Herrera. There was a middle-aged woman with unnaturally dyed red hair corralling three cranky kids—two boys and a girl. This had to be Herrera's family. There were two older women as well—both squat and dark-haired but one dressed much better than the other. Herrera's mother or mother-in-law, I guessed, and the nanny, maybe. An assortment of men surrounded them protectively. The driver of the Lincoln was a young guy in a baggy black suit. Another young guy emerged from the passenger side wearing a T-shirt and jeans and carrying a matte black automatic in his left hand. Three more men came out of the Ford, all of them dressed for Miami Beach in colorful silk shirts and tan pleated pants. One was holding a sawed-off shotgun. None of the faces matched my photo of Herrera.

They started for the house, but the little girl was kicking up a fuss, screaming at her mother and throwing a tantrum over something. Mrs. Herrera was pleading with her in Spanish to stop the nonsense. This little family drama delayed the whole entourage. No one was going to enter the house before the lady of the house.

I moved quickly, tapping Jedidiah on the shoulder as I headed for the stairway. We rushed downstairs, ran to the guest wing, and slipped into the room where Jedidiah had taken his nap. I crawled under the bed. Jedidiah went into the closet. Fortunately, we were both carrying our backpacks. We knew from experience never to get separated from our gear and never to leave traces of our presence.

"You OK?" I whispered into my mike.

"Yeah," Jedidiah said. "There's a hatch that leads to a crawl space. I'm going in there."

"Stay put till you hear from me," I said.

"Right."

I could hear the mounting commotion of the new arrivals coming into the house. The little girl was still carrying on, and I could hear footsteps stampeding up the stairs. The boys were retreating to their room, I imagined. I heard voices in both Spanish and English, mostly female. It wasn't hard to catch the gist of what they were saying. The grandmother was complaining bitterly about the child's bratty behavior, and Mrs. Herrera was screaming at everybody else in frustration. I wasn't concerned about them, though. It was the men I was worried about. Where were they? What were they doing? And were they all armed?

I assessed our options, but they weren't promising. There were two windows in the room, but they both faced the backyard. If we tried climbing out, anybody in the living room might see us.

"So where's Herrera?" Jedidiah's hushed voice materialized in my ear like a thought of my own.

"He's not here," I whispered back. "Maybe he's coming by himself."

"Yeah, but when?"

"Don't know. Just have to sit tight."

Ever so quietly I moved on my back toward the edge of the bed, hoping to be able to hear better. The box frame was an inch from my nose. The women were still going at it, but I couldn't hear a single male voice. It was possible that the men were just being quiet, not wanting to get involved, or else the hysterical women were drowning out their conversation. I moved a little closer to the edge. If I could get to the door, maybe I could hear something intelligible.

I moved my leg out from under the bed and started to squeeze my body under the metal frame when suddenly I saw the bottom of the door fly open. I pulled my leg in quickly.

A brown leather flight bag dropped to the carpet. A pair of feet in oxblood leather pumps huffed into the room. The ankles were thick. I figured this was the grandmother. Mrs. Herrera was slender, and she'd been wearing white slacks. This woman had to be wearing a skirt from the amount of leg I could see, and the shoes looked too expensive for the nanny. The feet went directly to the closet and opened the door.

"What's going on?" Jedidiah whispered. "Who's this?"

"The old lady," I said, keeping it short. I was afraid she might hear me if I said any more.

Suddenly a second pair of feet whisked into the room, Mrs. Herrera in her white slacks. She started yammering at the grandmother as soon as she entered the room. It was all in spitfire Spanish, but from the tones of their voices I could tell the older woman was in a snit and Mrs. Herrera was trying to bully her into a reconciliation.

When they both finally calmed down, they sat on the bed and had a good heart-to-heart. I could see the depressions their weight made on the underside of the bed. They talked for at least a half-hour. I stayed perfectly still. Jedidiah and I ceased all communication.

Finally Mrs. Herrera stood up, and her white pants shushed out of the room. The older woman stayed and puttered around for a while, unpacking her bag and straightening up. Then she left, too, leaving the door open.

I waited a few minutes, then tentatively stuck my foot out again. I intended to get behind the door and listen. But when I heard a toilet flush nearby, I drew my foot back under the bed, like a turtle pulling in its head at the first sign of danger.

The old woman returned, and now she was closing the blinds. The room became dim, and under the bed it was dark. Suddenly there was a large depression in the middle of the box spring as she lay down on the bed. She hadn't seemed that heavy when I'd seen her in the driveway, but her depression seemed to consume a lot of my space. I checked my watch. It was only ten minutes after eleven, but she was already settling in for a nap. To calm her nerves, I assumed.

"How about a status report?" Jedidiah whispered in my ear.

But I didn't dare say a word. The room was perfectly still. The woman would have to be stone deaf not to hear me.

"Guess you can't talk," he said, and signed off. He knew that I was probably not answering him for a good reason. He also knew that if anything had gone seriously wrong, he'd have heard it where he was. The only thing for him to do was sit tight. Thankfully we both had the training and the discipline to do just that.

The minutes passed like drops of rain slowly coursing down a windowpane. I listened to the woman's breathing and monitored every movement she made. If she was indeed asleep, she was a restless sleeper. I listened for deep, rhythmic breathing, but every few minutes I'd hear a snort or a snuffle, and I'd imagine her bolting out of bed like a frightened cat if I accidentally tapped the bed frame with my foot. I'd heard how loudly she carried on before, so I knew she wouldn't be quiet if I woke her. The bodyguards would come running, and Jedidiah and I would be in the unfortunate position of having to defend ourselves from inside this one room. Yes, we could always take the woman hostage if it came to that, but terrorizing an innocent bystander went against my principles. Besides, that wouldn't get us Herrera, which was our whole purpose for being there.

There was nothing to do but wait for the woman to get out of bed and leave of her own accord. I decided to stop watching the clock and meditate to pass the time. I closed my eyes and arched my head back against the floor, arms at my sides, palms up. I cleared my mind of all extraneous concerns and concentrated on relaxing my body, one part at a time—feet, calves, thighs, butt, and so on until I was able to relax my scalp. Eventually I reached a state of restful self-awareness. It wasn't like sleeping because I knew where I was, but my body was in a suspended state of peace and replenishment.

Suddenly there was a knock on the door, and instantly my eyes were open. I lifted my head and saw a pair of scuffed Nikes standing in the doorway. "Grandma? Momma wants to know if you want to have lunch with us. We've been waiting for you."

I checked my watch. It was 1:25.

The springs above me squeaked as the old woman turned over. She groaned softly and sighed. "What did your momma make?" she asked in heavily accented English.

"Sandwiches," the boy replied.

"What kind?"

"I don't know. I'm having peanut butter and jelly."

The woman snorted her disapproval. "Close the door, Miguel. I'll be right there."

The boy closed the door, and the woman rolled out of bed. I could see her bare feet on the carpet. She slipped into her loafers, then went to the dresser with the mirror, stayed there for a minute, then left the room, closing the door behind her.

"Jed," I whispered into the mike as soon as she was gone.

"I'm here," he whispered back.

"You holding up OK?"

"Yeah, I'm OK. What happened?"

"The grandmother took a nap. She just left."

"I figured. I could hear her in here."

"I'm gonna leave my position and see what's going on out there."

"Good. Bring back something to eat," he joked.

"For sure," I said. "Caviar and champagne. Over and out."

I lay there for a moment visualizing the women and children having lunch at the big table in the kitchen. It was too hot to eat outside on the patio, and the dining room seemed too formal for peanut butter and jelly. I also visualized the men trawling the property like sharks in a big tank. I had to be careful. They could be anywhere.

Slowly and carefully I slid out from under the bed and went to the doorway. I didn't hear much, only the kids' voices. I went to the window and peered out through the blinds. The lawn shimmered in the midday sun, but other than that, nothing had changed out there. The Lincoln and the Ford were still in the driveway. I remembered the men who had gotten out of those cars—the driver in the baggy suit, the curly-haired guy in the T-shirt, the three *muchacho*s in their fancy silk shirts. I assumed that most if not all of them were armed. I moved to the edge of the window, straining to see if any new cars had arrived, hoping that Herrera had finally come home, but there were no new cars that I could see. I glanced at my watch again. We had been here ten hours, four of them spent in hiding. I wondered how much longer we could hold out.

"You want to stretch?" I whispered into my mike.

"Is it safe?" Jedidiah replied.

"It is for now. Come on out."

I went back to the door to stand guard as Jedidiah emerged from the closet, blinking and squinting as his eyes adjusted to the light. He arched his back, and I could hear it crack from where I stood. He'd sweated through his black T-shirt. "You think I could pee?" he asked in a whisper.

I'd thought about that myself. The problem was, the bathroom was out in the hallway.

"What do you think?" he asked.

"Take your pack," I said. "We'll go together." I found my backpack under the bed and put it on. We couldn't get separated; we'd be more effective in tandem.

We left the room and slipped down the hallway to the bathroom. Jedidiah relieved himself first while I went to the sink to get some water. I hadn't had anything to drink in hours, and this was no time to get dehydrated. When Jedidiah was finished, we switched places.

I was just zipping up, wondering whether I should flush or not, when the sound of brisk footsteps came down the hallway. Instinctively we both pulled our guns. The door was open an inch, so I peered through. A blur of motion passed me by. I opened the door a little more and saw the curly-haired man in the sleeveless T-shirt going into the other bedroom. He was the one I imagined would give us the most trouble. Of all the men who'd come that morning, he was the one who looked like a genuine drug thug.

I jerked my thumb back toward Grandma's room. Jedidiah quietly closed the lid on the toilet without flushing. Whoever found it would probably blame someone else for forgetting to do it. We moved quickly and went back to our former positions in the first bedroom—Jedidiah in the closet crawl space, me under the bed.

"You think he's taking a nap?" Jedidiah asked through my earpiece.

"Who knows?"

"Did he have a gun?"

"I didn't get a good look."

"I hope he's clean," Jedidiah said.

I hoped so, too. The curly-haired man's presence in that bedroom complicated matters. If we had to make our escape through the hallway, we'd have Curly at our backs. If he was armed and we were facing additional firepower from the living room, we'd be squeezed. It wouldn't be so bad if Curly was unarmed, but we had no way of knowing whether he was or not.

I stared up at the cotton ticking under the box spring and considered our situation. For the moment we were stuck. The man we had come for still hadn't shown up, and there was no guarantee that he would. Jedidiah and I couldn't hold out forever, so now I had to start considering our options for bailing out.

I decided to hold out a little while longer. We'd both just had some water, so our bodies were OK for now. I also had total faith in Jedidiah. He has an unbreakable spirit that carries him through the most difficult situations. The thing to do was to wait and see what developed. Planning strategies and counterstrategies would just clutter our minds at this point. We had to take whatever came and react to it appropriately in the moment that it happened. In the meantime I would continue to meditate.

Time became a circle with no beginning or end as I breathed deeply and completely, delving further and further into myself, seeking the inner reserves of my natural wisdom. I was calm and relaxed yet ever vigilant for signs of trouble. But the sudden commotion that came from the living room would have pulled me out of a coma.

"What's that?" Jedidiah said in my ear. It was so loud he could obviously hear it in the closet. It sounded like a party with raucous voices, laughter, and shouting.

"Stay there," I told Jedidiah. "I'll check it out."

I eased out from under the bed and went to the door to listen. It sounded like a big group of men. I didn't hear the kids, their mother, or the grandmother. I peeked down the hallway toward Curly's room. I wondered if he was still in there. I hadn't heard him come out.

I moved to the window and saw that there was a new car in the driveway, a silver Mercedes SL 500, the biggest one they make. Was Herrera finally home?

I went back to the door and listened intently to the cacophony of voices. I know a little Spanish, but even a native speaker would have had a hard time picking out anything intelligible from this jumble. I stayed there and listened intently, trying to isolate the voices. One of the male voices was high enough to override the general noise, and I could swear I heard him addressing someone as "Señor Herrera." I picked out Mrs. Herrera's voice. She was calling someone by name: "Carlos . . . Carlos."

"Papa's home from the office," I whispered into the mike.

"It's about time," Jedidiah said.

"Come on out and we'll say hi."

Jedidiah came out and stood with me by the door. He nodded toward Curly's room. "He still in there?"

I shrugged. "I think so. Unless he was very quiet when he came out." I checked my watch. It was after four. Curly was taking a pretty long nap if he was in there. "Let's go check out the party, but watch out for him." I nodded toward Curly's door.

We put on our backpacks and pulled our guns. I opened the door, and we stepped out into the hallway, walking lightly. The party grew louder as we moved toward the living room. I peered around the corner. The whole clan was gathered around the sofa opposite the painting of the Virgin Mary. Herrera looked just like his mug shot—a lined, deeply tanned face, grit-teeth smile, tiny dark eyes set too close together. He was wearing a white shirt open at the collar and pressed blue jeans. His arm was draped around his wife on his right. One of the silk-shirt boys was on his left.

The other silk shirts were on another sofa along with a new man, a grizzly-looking guy in his forties wearing faded jeans and a worn jean jacket. He looked like that cartoon character Taz the Tasmanian Devil—squat and hairy with a pronounced underbite. A big automatic was jammed into his belt. My guess was that this guy was Herrera's personal bodyguard. Curly was nowhere to be seen.

I signaled for Jedidiah to stay where he was. Herrera and his clan were drinking Heinekins; there were two six-packs on the coffee table. I figured we'd let them keep drinking and get a little looser before we made our move. Unfortunately, Taz was drinking Coke, which is what a good bodyguard should do when everyone else is getting drunk. But fortunately for us, he wasn't particularly watchful. Like everyone else in the room, he was focused on his boss. His eyes should have been scanning the premises for potential threats. Taz must have felt that it was safe there among his amigos.

I watched them drink and kick back while Jedidiah kept an eye out for Curly. I tried to assess the situation for what it was. Worst-case scenario, every man in the room was carrying a weapon. But in all likelihood, there probably weren't any more than two, possibly three guns in the room. But did Curly have that sawed-off shotgun with him in the bedroom? And what about the driver who'd chauffeured the Lincoln? Where was he?

Herrera and his men were well into their second beers now. There wasn't enough beer on the coffee table for a third round, and I had a feeling that the party might disperse if the beer ran out. Again I assessed our options. Most of the adult males were in one place right now, and the children and the older women were someplace else. This was as good as it was going to get. I caught Jedidiah's eye and nodded to him. It was time to make our move.

On my hand signal we moved together, stepping briskly into the room with guns leveled on both sofas.

"Freeze!" I shouted. "Hands up! Hands up!"

"Don't move, don't move, don't fucking move!" Jedidiah hollered.

We made a commotion of our own, sweeping into the living room fast and loud, showing our firepower. I went directly to Taz and took his gun. Everyone was dumbfounded, but Taz looked sick, his complexion suddenly yellow and waxy. I felt for him. He knew he'd screwed up, and now he was thinking about the consequences.

The man on the couch next to Herrera was on the verge of some kind of breakdown. He was shaking so badly it was as if he were his own personal earthquake. Herrera scowled at him and quickly scooted away from him on the sofa. Mrs. Herrera made a face and covered her mouth with her hand. It wasn't until the stink wafted over to me that I realized the man had shit his pants.

"No, please," the man pleaded. "Do not kill me. I have money. I will pay you more."

I was puzzled for a second. Then I realized that he must've thought Jedidiah and I were hit men sent from some rival drug gang. I shook my head no to correct his misconception, then pointed with my gun. "Him," I said, indicating Herrera. I looked Herrera in the eye, and he stared back defiantly. "You," I said. "It's time to go. Get up."

"Who are you?" Herrera snarled. "Who sent you?"

"You sent me," I said.

"What?"

"*You* sent me," I repeated. "If you hadn't done what you'd done, I wouldn't have to be here."

"You are a crazy man," he snapped. His English was clipped, his delivery ballistic.

"I have a warrant for your arrest," I said calmly. "You violated the conditions of your bail."

"Bail? What bail?"

"In New Jersey."

He glowered at Jedidiah and me, then turned his glare on the silk-shirt boys, who cringed under the heat. Stuff like this isn't supposed to happen to a drug lord. At least that's what Herrera thought.

Suddenly I heard Jedidiah shouting, "Drop it! Drop it or I'll drop you!" His arm was extended, gun pointed down the hallway that led to the guest wing.

I took a quick look down the hall and saw Curly in his stocking feet, his pants undone, looking like the proverbial deer in the headlights. The sawed-off shotgun was dangling from his index finger by the trigger guard.

Jedidiah rushed up to him, the muzzle of his gun coming within three feet of Curly's face. "Drop the gun or I'll kill you," he yelled.

The shotgun instantly hit the carpet with a thunk. Jedidiah is not someone most people want to argue with.

"Get out here," he shouted. "Come on, hurry up."

He hustled Curly into the living room and directed him to a seat on the arm of the couch next to the guy who'd messed his pants. Curly was so spooked he didn't seem to notice the smell.

"Stand up," I said to Herrera, but he just sat there scowling at me.

Jedidiah moved like a mad bull, going around to the back of the couch and jamming his gun into the back of Herrera's head. His wife shrieked. The grandmother stood at the top of the stairs and screamed.

The little girl was clutching her grandmother's skirt, crying hysterically.

Suddenly the kingpin didn't look so tough. He lifted his hands and, with a little prodding from Jedidiah, stood up and walked toward me. When he was away from the others, I turned him around, kicked out his knees, and got him down on his belly so I could cuff him behind his back. In the meantime Jedidiah instructed all the others to get on the floor facedown as well. He opened one of the panels of the sliding glass doors.

"Zora," I said into my mike, "come get us."

"I'll be right there," she said.

Jedidiah fetched Curly's shotgun and held it in his left hand, his .45 in his right, positioning himself in front of the open sliding doors so that he had a clear shot at everyone in the room. I got Herrera to his feet and marched him out onto the patio. He was cursing me up and down in Spanish, but I made sure he kept walking. Zora was just pulling the van into the driveway.

Zora had her .45 out and ready. She kept her eyes on the house as I escorted Herrera into the backseat. Once he was seated, I threw a chain around the handcuff chain and padlocked it to the front passenger seat. "Get comfortable," I said as I got in next to him. "It's gonna be a long ride."

He grumbled and cursed, yanking on the chain as if that would do any good. Jedidiah was backing across the patio, shouting at the people inside to be cool and stay put. As soon as he jumped in the passenger seat, Zora threw the van into reverse and started backing out of the driveway. Herrera looked longingly at his big Mercedes as we pulled away.

"I think it'll be a while before you drive that baby again," I said.

"Don't talk to me," Herrera snarled.

"Don't be so touchy," Jedidiah said, turning around in his seat.

As Zora backed out into the street and headed back the way we'd come, Herrera glared at me.

"You planning on giving me the evil eye all the way back to Jersey?" I asked.

"What else am I supposed to do? You said it yourself, it's a long way to go."

“You want a book?” I asked. I always keep plenty of reading material in my vehicles.

He made a sour face. “I never read nothing. Reading books is for pussies.”

Zora and I exchanged glances in the rearview mirror. Jedidiah just shook his head. A man who won’t allow himself to be enlightened is doomed to live in the dark.

“So what am I supposed to do?” Herrera demanded. “Look at the scenery? Why don’t you put on the radio at least?”

“Why don’t you try praying?” I said. “You’re gonna need it.”

Herrera didn’t answer me. He just looked away.

Herrera undoubtedly had plenty of underlings who would try to rescue him, so instead of going to one of the closer airports in Fort Lauderdale or Miami, we drove up to Tampa, where we had arranged to drop off the van, and caught a flight back to Newark from there. Late that night we delivered him to the Essex County Sheriff’s Department. He was held without bail and eventually convicted of drug trafficking. Currently he’s serving time at Trenton State Prison. He won’t be eligible for parole until he’s served a full twenty years—plenty of time to catch up on his reading.

12 The Gold-Plated .44

Criminal masterminds exist only in books, but there are still some very intelligent people out there working on the wrong side of the law. These people are less concerned with playing clever cat-and-mouse games with the police than they are with making money—lots of it. That's where real criminals concentrate their energies.

One notable exception, however, was a notorious drug dealer from Newark named Artemis Powell, who absolutely loved to taunt the authorities. When I first heard about him he had skipped out on a $100,000 bond and had been in the wind for the better part of a year, yet he continued to conduct drug business as usual in Newark. All the while he would taunt his bail bondsman, calling the man up on a regular basis and bragging that he would never be caught. The bondsman had tried two different bounty hunters, but neither one had even come close to capturing Powell.

When word got around that the second bounty hunter had given up, Powell put in another call to the bondsman. Powell challenged him to hire the "best bounty hunter in the world," and if that bounty hunter succeeded in capturing him, Powell would buy that man a gold-plated Desert Eagle .44 semiautomatic handgun. The bondsman told him to go to hell, but Powell just laughed and insisted that he was being straight up. Whoever brought him in would get the gold-plated gun—guaranteed.

The bondsman didn't take Powell's offer seriously, but he was worried about future business with the surety company that had written the bond. It had been almost a year since Powell missed his initial court date, and the presiding judge was pressuring the bondsman to produce Powell or pay the bail. (The wheels of justice turn slowly when it comes to recovering bail money. Judges will typically give bondsmen extra time to find absconders because they'd rather have the accused stand trial than have the money.) The surety company was also pressuring Powell's bondsman, demanding that he hire a "really good" bounty hunter because they weren't ready to write off $100,000 yet. On top of all that, word of Powell's golden-gun offer was spreading out on the street, which further humiliated the bondsman. Whenever anyone so much as mentioned Powell's name to him, he would literally shout and punch the walls.

I found out about Powell's offer in October 1991, a few days after Jedidiah, Zora, and I brought Carlos Herrera back from Florida. Instantly I became intrigued and called the bondsman, whom I had worked with before.

"I want the Powell case," I told him.

"Why?" he said bitterly. "You really think you can do better than those other guys?"

"Won't know till I try."

"What? You hard up for a gun? You really think you can win the gold one?"

"I don't care about the gun. I want to get *him*."

"Join the club."

"I'm serious. I think I can do it."

"That's what the other two guys said."

"Well, I'm not them."

"Yeah, I know," he said. "Your guys wear the masks and all that jazz."

"Yes, we're different, if that's what you mean."

"Well, I don't care if you wear dresses," the bondsman said, "as long as you bring him in."

"So does that mean you're going to give us a shot?"

There was silence on his end. I could hear him breathing. "All right," he finally said. "Knock yourself out. You can come by and pick up the paperwork this afternoon."

"Thank you," I said.

"Don't thank me yet."

That night I met up with four of the other Seekers—Job, Jedidiah, Jeremiah, and Rock—at one of our regular training sessions at the boxing gym we use. Before we got down to sparring in the ring, I told them about Powell and asked them to find out whatever they could about him. They had all heard of him, of course, but no one knew anything about his current whereabouts.

"From what I hear, he lives like a nomad," Jeremiah said. His gray sweats were soaked through; he had just skipped rope for twenty minutes without stopping. "Powell lives out on the street."

"But he must sleep somewhere," I said.

"No doubt he does," Rock said as he rotated his head on his shoulders, punching his boxing gloves into each other. "But nobody knows where."

"Then let's find out," I said. I was wearing red gloves, a sleeveless black T-shirt, and blue shorts. I had just gotten a little sweat going myself by working out on the speed bag. "Check with your contacts, see what they know."

"Yeah," Job said as he stretched his legs on the floor. "Powell's still selling dope, so someone must be seeing him."

Jedidiah was off to the side drilling body shots into a battered blue vinyl heavy bag, but he was still listening. "We'll find him," he said with a grunt as he landed a hard right. "Sooner or later Powell will show himself." Glove leather smacked into vinyl. "We'll find him." A punishing uppercut rocked the bag and rattled the springs holding it up. "All things unfold—"

"—as they should," the rest of us finished.

I grinned and nodded. I had no doubt that if there was information about Powell out on the street, we would uncover it.

Of course, information sometimes flows the other way as well. We had been working this case for only three days when I got a call on my cell phone at one in the morning. It was an early evening for me, and I had just gotten home. I was in the living room taking my boots off when the phone rang. I figured it was one of the other Seekers who was out working that night.

I picked it up before the second ring. "Joshua," I said.

"The man himself!"

I didn't recognize the voice. "Who's this?"

"Your obsession."

I didn't say anything. He had called me. Let him state his business or hang up.

"You there, Joshua Armstrong?" The caller's voice was dripping with mockery.

"I'm here."

"Don't you want to know who I am?"

"Who are you?"

"I'm your new ulcer, my friend. Artemis Powell."

"Well, well," I said. "You calling to turn yourself in?"

"No, no, no." He laughed. "But I bet you're wondering how I got your number."

"Somebody gave it to you." I tried not to sound alarmed, because I knew he was trying to rattle me.

"You been asking around about me."

"Exactly what is it you want?" I asked.

"Oh, I'm just calling to say hello and to let you know that you're wasting your time bothering with me."

"I don't think so."

"You're gonna *know* so, brother. You will regret ever getting involved with me."

"Is that a threat, Artemis?"

"Think of it as a fair warning."

"OK, I will. But I'm still gonna get you."

"Foolish man. And I thought you were supposed to be smarter than the others. I am sorely disappointed in you, Joshua Armstrong."

"I hope you got that gold-plated .44 ready for me."

He laughed again. "You're gonna wanna use a .44 on yourself when *I'm* through with you."

He hung up laughing. I stared at the cordless phone in my hand. Well, at least I knew he was out there. But the element of surprise was going to be tricky. He knew the Seekers were looking for him.

As I got ready for bed, I mentally outlined my strategy for finding Powell. First thing in the morning I'd call our information analyst, Mr. Baines, and give him everything I had on Powell—the old addresses, phone numbers, license plate numbers, and Social Security number. Very often Mr. Baines could spin gold out of straw, running down the smallest shred of information and cross-referencing it with the countless databases at his disposal to compile a fairly complete dossier, which could include the subject's most recent addresses, arrests, aliases, employers, medical records, bank accounts, type of vehicle he drives, and the last place he received a traffic ticket. Mr. Baines's services didn't come cheap, but they were well worth the expense.

There were also a couple of drug dealers I wanted to talk to, rivals of Powell's. There's no such thing as honor among thieves, and that's especially true among drug dealers. If Powell was doing good business—and from what I gathered, he was—then there had to be a competitor ready and willing to snatch his market share. That's why they call it the drug *business*.

As I climbed into bed, I could hear Powell's voice in my head. I visualized a smirk transforming the deadpan expression on his mug shot. He had a light-skinned complexion, lazy eyes, narrow nose, receding hairline, and dark goatee. He wore his hair long and Jeri-curled in the back. He was going to be worth catching, I thought as I drifted off to sleep. I wondered if he was really serious about that gold-plated .44 . . . .

The phone rang, jarring me out of a deep sleep. I reached for it on my bed table as I squinted at the alarm clock. It was 4:01 A.M.

"Joshua," I said, clearing my throat. "What's wrong?" My first thought was that a Seeker was in trouble.

"Did I wake you up? Sorry about that." It was Powell.

"What do you want?" I said.

"What do I want! I want you to know that I'm here, that's what I want. I'm here and you're there, and you don't know where in the hell I am. See, this is how it's gonna be. So why don't you just give up right now?"

"I haven't started yet," I said.

"You are *so* cool, Mr. Joshua Armstrong. All you Seekers are so cool. Wish I had me a little Mission Impossible team like you got."

"Is there a point you want to make?"

"Shit, yeah. I already told you. You are never gonna get any closer to me than you are right now."

"Will you be gift wrapping that .44 for me?"

Powell laughed. "You are one icy dude, Mr. Armstrong."

"Good night," I said, and hung up on him.

I turned down the ringer and stuck the phone under a pillow. If he called back, I didn't want him waking up the whole house.

As it turned out, Powell didn't call back that night, but I didn't get much sleep thinking about him. I kept playing out scenarios in my mind, dreaming up schemes to nab him. I watched the dawn materializing outside my bedroom window, trying to meditate and put it all into perspective. I didn't want this to get personal, even though Powell had stepped over the line by invading the sanctity of my home.

The next day I contacted all the connections I had who knew anything about the drug trade in Newark. They all knew who Powell was, and they knew his reputation for being a wild man. One former dealer named Corky, who had been one of my "clients" when he skipped out on his own bail several years earlier, met me at a bar. He told me that Powell loved living on the edge. He didn't use any of the local suppliers, and it was uncertain exactly where he got his dope, but he moved his product in defiance of the established hierarchy in town. He stayed on the move and hid in the shadows, often undercutting his competitors' prices and stealing their business.

"Joshua," Corky said, tipping back the last drops of a snifter of brandy, "if this son of a bitch was easy to find, you know somebody would've put a bullet in his head by now. He's making everybody look foolish. He should be dead, but he ain't. That must say something to you."

"Are you saying I can't find him?"

"Draw your own conclusions, my man." Corky studied his empty glass, then looked at me. "You're buying, ain't you?"

I nodded, and he ordered another brandy.

That night Mr. Baines got back to me, and he did not disappoint. He had come up with a lot of information—past addresses and phone numbers, relatives' names, an ex-wife, vehicles Powell had owned complete with their vehicle identification numbers, and the names of former employers. Mr. Baines had even discovered a prior conviction for possession in Texas that dated back nine years. Powell had been caught with less than a gram of hash, a misdemeanor for which he got a fine and a suspended sentence. Now my work was cut out for me. I had a lot of people to talk to.

But after a week of tracking down those leads, I found out just how smart Powell was. He'd severed his ties with just about everyone who had known him, relatives included. His parents had passed away years ago, and the best I could come up with was an aunt who had invited him to Thanksgiving dinner two years back. That was the last time she'd seen him. Past employers remembered him, but they had no idea what had become of him. His old neighbors had no recollection of him at all, which just indicated what an elusive character he was even back then. His ex-wife was living in Atlanta—she hadn't seen him in ten years, and she wanted to keep it that way.

The next Sunday night I was lying in bed staring up at the ceiling, hoping for an inspiration, some angle that I hadn't considered, but nothing was coming. Finally, after several hours, I was able to put it out of my mind and fall asleep.

Then the phone rang.

I sat up like a shot and snatched it off the night table. "Joshua," I said groggily. It was three-thirty. I'd been asleep for less than an hour.

"You getting any closer, Mr. Seeker?" Powell's mocking laugh again.

I whipped the covers off and got out of bed.

"You there, Mr. Seeker? I don't hear you."

"I'm here." I went to the window and looked out at the streetlight shining down on the empty pavement.

"I've been waiting for you to show up, man. You lose interest?"

"Nope."

"So are you closing in on me . . . as we speak?" He was howling, barely able to finish his sentence.

"When I show up, you will never know it's me."

"Oh, yeah? A sneak attack? Like in the movies?"

"Better," I said.

"Still think you can do it, huh? You're that confident? I like a man who's confident."

"I hope you're keeping that .44 cleaned and oiled. I don't want a rusty gun."

"Oh, don't worry about that. But I might have to use it first. On you." The mirth was gone from his voice. He was dead serious. "You take care of yourself, Mr. Joshua Seeker." He hung up.

I gripped the phone hard, wondering how long he intended to play Joker to my Batman. Once again I slept with the phone under my pillow.

The next morning I was in a foul mood when I got up, but lack of sleep was only partially to blame. Powell was getting to me. It wasn't the phone calls in the middle of the night as much as my desire to get him off the streets. He had my home phone number and he had no compunction about calling me. What if he also had my address? Would he come over and confront me? Corky had said that he was a wild man. Would he come gunning for me with that gold-plated .44? I couldn't say for sure, but there are all kinds of people in this world, and I didn't want to find out the hard way what kind Powell was.

As I sat at the kitchen table brooding over a cup of tea, I considered changing my phone number to keep him from calling in the middle of the night, but I didn't like that idea. That was a reactive strategy, and I always prefer to take proactive measures. But in this case I didn't know what proactive measures to take.

The mail had just arrived, and it was sitting on the table unopened. I noticed that the envelope on top was the phone bill. This was around the time when the phone company started offering caller ID to residential customers. It got me thinking. If I knew the number of the phone Powell was calling me from, I'd have a good idea where he hung out. Even if he called from different phones, a few pinpointed locations were better than what I had now. I tore open the envelope and found a flyer offering an array of new phone services, including caller ID. I called immediately, and by the end of the week I had a small white plastic box with an LED display attached to the phone in my den.

There were just two problems with this plan. For one thing, even if I had Powell's number, I wouldn't be able to jump in the car and find him. Once I got his number I'd have to get it to Mr. Baines, and it would take him at least a day to process it and get me an address. It wasn't going to be like the movies, where the cops can trace a call in a matter of minutes.

The second problem was Powell. He'd only called me three times in the course of nine days, and two of those were on the same night. If he didn't call again, this obviously wasn't going to work. I started sleeping on the couch in the den so I could intercept his call. Unfortunately, I didn't get as much sleep as I would have liked down there because I spent too much time staring at the ceiling waiting for him to call.

Three days later when he finally did call, I hadn't even gone to bed yet. It was eleven-thirty on a Monday night, early for him.

"So how's the search going, Mr. Seeker?" he said. "When can I expect to see you?"

"You'll be seeing me," I said. "Don't worry about that."

"You really think so, don't you?"

"I know so." I looked down at the LED window on the caller ID box. It was blank.

"You're wasting your time, Mr. Seeker. I'm telling you."

"Why don't you give yourself up? Make it easy on yourself."

Powell laughed.

"It'll save you the humiliation of my taking you down and hauling your ass to jail."

Still nothing on the caller ID box. I wondered if it was broken.

I could hear him snickering on the line. "'Seek and ye shall find'? Is that your motto, Mr. Seeker?" he asked.

"'All things unfold as they should.' That's my motto. If I am meant to find you, I will."

"What if you *ain't* meant to find me?"

"Then that's OK, too. Things happen for a reason."

"Do you always talk like a wise man, Mr. Seeker?"

Finally a phone number appeared in the window.

"Was there something specific you wanted to say to me?" I asked.

"No, just checking in to see how bad you're doing."

"OK, fine. Then you have a nice night." I hung up before he could say anything else.

I dialed Mr. Baines's number and got his voice mail. I left the phone number I'd just gotten off the box and asked that he get me an address. The next afternoon he called and told me that the number belonged to a pay phone in Harrison, New Jersey, which is just across the Passaic River from Newark. The street address didn't ring any bells with me, so I checked a map. I decided to take a ride over there to check it out personally.

It was the middle of the afternoon when I found the pay phone Powell had used. It was out in the open on a corner in an old warehouse district right near the river. The street itself was desolate. No trees, no grass, nothing—just slate sidewalks and red brick warehouse walls running the entire length of the block on both sides. About a dozen cars were parked on the street, and now and then a trailer truck would rumble by. It seemed like an odd place to make a call from. Anybody passing by would see Powell on the phone.

Of course, that worked the other way, too. At night there were probably no cars here at all, which meant he'd have a clear view of everything around him. No one could sneak up on him.

As I drove past the phone and turned onto the cobblestone road that ran along the river, I noticed that there was a small shantytown on the riverbank, maybe six or eight makeshift shacks sprouting up like an outcropping of mushrooms.

I came back that night at around nine o'clock. The streetlight over the phone placed it dead center in a large circle of light. Homeless people moved in the shadows, some of them making a racket pushing shopping carts full of cans and bottles over the cobblestones. I wondered if perhaps Powell was living over in that shantytown. He'd been operating freely for almost a year, and he'd eluded all his rivals in that time. Living like a homeless person would be a perfect cover for him. And how ironic—a drug dealer living in abject poverty. I stepped on the accelerator and drove on without slowing down as if I were just passing through. If Powell was around, I didn't want him making my vehicle.

A few nights later I got another call from him at three in the morning.

"Mr. Seeker, Mr. Seeker, I've been seeking your face, but I don't see you comin' 'round. What'sa matter? No luck?" He was still mocking me.

"Maybe I'm not trying yet."

"Oh, I know you're trying. You're trying hard. You're that kind of man."

"How do you know what kind of man I am?" I looked down at the window in the caller ID box. Nothing yet.

"Only a compulsive fool would go where others have failed before," he said.

"Very poetic," I said. A number appeared in the box. It was different from the last one.

"I could never be as poetic as you, O wise man." He started laughing again.

"So you wanna tell me where you are right now?" I asked.

"Naw, that wouldn't be any fun. You have to *find* me. Like hide-and-seek."

"Don't worry. I will."

"Well, I been waiting," he said. "How long am I supposed to wait?"

"You have a good night," I said. "Peace."

As soon as I hung up, I called Mr. Baines's voice mail and left the new number. The next afternoon he called me back with a new location. It was a pay phone outside Penn Station in Newark, which is about a ten-minute drive across the river from the first location. Penn Station is a pretty busy place, but a homeless man making a phone call from there at three in the morning wouldn't look out of place at all. Powell posing as a homeless man was starting to make perfect sense.

I never work on one case at a time, and as it happened, two other cases were suddenly ripe for the picking and in need of my attention. They were both in California—one in Los Angeles, the other in San Diego—and I could get them both in one trip, so the next morning I took a 6 A.M. flight out to L.A. I was gone for eight days.

When I got back, my answering machine was full of messages, including three from Artemis Powell. He seemed to miss me.

"Mr. Seeker, you there? Pick up, Mr. Seeker. I know you're there . . . ."

"Mr. Seeker, don't you love me anymore? I'm looking all over for your face, but I don't see you coming. Where are you, Mr. Seeker?"

"Where, oh, where has my Mr. Seeker gone to? You didn't give up, did you? I'm very disappointed in you if you did. I thought you never gave up. I don't give up, man. I got that piece all polished up nice and shiny for you, too."

The caller ID box had kept a log of the numbers that had called in. Powell had called from the pay phone in the warehouse district all three times. It was time for me to make my move.

I called Job and laid out what I had in mind. Since that pay phone was out in the open, we wouldn't be able to drive in and take Powell by surprise. I would have to go in on foot while Job hung back a few blocks away. We'd stay in constant communication with a hands-free communication system—earplug receiver and body mike transmitter.

I don't use elaborate disguises in my work, but when the situation dictates, I can put on a fairly convincing act. Knock-down drunk is one I do particularly well. A lazy tilt of the head, drooping eyelids, crumpled posture, and a stagger is all I need. Hopefully I'd blend right in with the skid-row scene down there.

Late the next night Job and I drove over to Harrison. I was dressed in my grubbiest jeans, the tattered field jacket and boots I use to do yardwork, and a stretched-out wool cap. Job parked the car in the shadows of a loading dock in the warehouse district two blocks from the pay phone. I got out and started walking along the river toward the shantytown, mimicking the walk of a man who's trying hard not to look drunk.

As I got closer to the shantytown, I could see dark silhouettes against the shimmering moonlit river, two figures just standing there in the high weeds. In the distance the shapes and lines of a steel train trestle reached across the water from one shore to the other, like mysterious geometry. I kept walking.

The pay phone came into view illuminated by the streetlight above. No one was anywhere near it, but there was some activity on the road. A wooden pallet was burning at the far curb with three homeless men huddled around it for warmth. They hadn't bothered to break the pallet apart to make a decent fire; they'd just set fire to it the way it was. I veered toward them but didn't make eye contact as I passed. They were talking, but they made no comment on my arrival. I kept going another twenty feet or so, then plopped down on the curb. Pulling out a pint bottle from my pocket, I unscrewed the cap with great deliberation and raised the bottle to my lips. It was a Four Roses whiskey bottle filled with green tea and a little honey. I sat there with my elbows on my knees, the bottle dangling from my fingertips, staring blankly at the pavement as if I were lost in my own hazy world.

Job's voice came through my earplug. "You see anything?"

"Nothing," I murmured.

"Anybody using the phone?"

"Not that I've seen."

"I called your answering machine," Job said. "He hasn't called tonight."

"No guarantee that he will."

"What do you want to do?" he asked.

"Hang out here for a while."

"OK. I'll be right here."

I took another swig of tea and stared out into the distance, making myself part of the scenery. After about forty-five minutes the pallet fire burned itself out and the three men disbanded. I was out there by myself for quite a while, but then at around two I heard movement in the weeds behind me. Out of the corner of my eye, I saw four homeless men—I wasn't sure if any of them were the same ones who'd been there before—carrying a fifty-five-gallon drum up from the riverbank. They set it down next to the cold remains of the fire, then started to kick and stomp on the charred boards, breaking what was left of the pallet apart and shoving the slats into the barrel along with torn-up pieces of cardboard. One of them struck a match, and pretty soon they had a roaring fire going, flames licking the air higher than their heads. I considered moving to a new spot to get out of its light, but the fire died down quickly so I stayed put.

I was getting stiff just sitting there, so I stood up and walked around in a vague circle, moving closer to the pay phone. After I got the circulation back in my legs, I crossed the road and took up a new position, leaning against a brick wall directly across from the phone. I stayed there for a while, then wandered back to my old seat on the curb. By now I'd been out there almost three hours.

"What do you think?" Job asked.

I muttered into my body mike, "Let's give it a little longer. He's called later than this."

"OK."

I pretended to be nodding off, letting my head bob and droop, then pulling it up with a jerk just before I'd tip forward. Of course, if I stayed out here much longer, I might not have to pretend. The fire in the barrel was dying down, and now only two men were hovering over it. The other two had disappeared into the weeds. I was very aware of the shantytown behind my back, wondering if Powell was in one of those shacks. The air had gotten chillier. I could see my breath. Would he show himself tonight?

The sound of a sputtering car engine gradually disturbed the quiet. I looked up and saw headlights jostling over the cobblestones. A baby blue Volkswagen Rabbit was coming this way. I stared into the headlights with belligerent curiosity, the same way any drunk would. The Volkswagen crossed over to the left side of the road and parked at the curb by the pay phone. I took a sip from my bottle and continued to stare at it. The two homeless men at the fire stared at the car, too.

No one came out right away. The driver just sat there. Was he surveying the scene, being cautious? Ten minutes passed before he finally came out.

A dark-haired man went directly from the car to the phone. He was wearing dirty khakis and a puffy navy-blue parka with duct tape covering the rips. I couldn't tell if it was Powell, even when he stood under the streetlight.

I climbed to my feet, feigning great difficulty, took a step forward, stopped, and wove in place for a few seconds. Then I lurched forward and zigzagged over toward the man at the pay phone. He was holding the receiver, feeding coins into the slot.

When I came up to his car, I just stared at it critically.

"Hey!" the man said. "What're you doing over there?"

I glared at him. "None of your business," I slurred.

"Just get away from there," he ordered.

"I'll do whatever the hell I damn please," I growled. I glared at the car for a few more seconds, then headed to my place against the brick wall on the opposite corner. As I passed the man I tried to get a better look at his face, but he was hunched forward, his face in shadow. He also had a thick full beard that covered his neck. Powell had a trim goatee in his mug shot.

I slid down the wall and sat on the sidewalk, sipping from my nearly empty bottle. The bearded man in the blue parka held the receiver to his ear as he punched out a number and then apparently got connected. I couldn't hear what he was saying because he was speaking softly. He made four short calls. But on the fifth call, he wasn't so circumspect.

"Ronald!" he yelled. "What the fuck're you doing, man? I've been waiting on you all week. . . . But when, my friend, when? . . . Don't give me that shit, motherfucker. I'll hurt you, you know I will."

From this end of the conversation, I surmised that Ronald owed the man money. The bearded man's wiseass voice and mocking laugh were awfully familiar. I was almost positive that this was Powell, but I wasn't one hundred percent sure because I'd only heard his voice on the phone, I'd never heard it live. I had to get a better look at his face.

I staggered to my feet and flung the empty whiskey bottle across the street and into the high weeds, snuffling and grunting as I did it. Wandering out into the middle of the street, I jammed my hands into my pockets as if I were cold and gripped the 9mm Glock in the right-hand pocket.

"Stand by," I muttered into the body mike. "I may have him. Start coming, but stay out of sight."

I stumbled toward the man, stopped short, then made a great show of straightening up and trying not to look drunk. The man was still on the phone shouting at Ronald, but he kept an eye on me. I wished he would turn around all the way and look at me so that I could see his face. I moved a little closer. He finished up his conversation and put his finger on the hook while he dug into his pocket for more change. When I was within ten feet of him, he suddenly turned around and assumed a threatening posture, gripping the receiver like a club.

"What do you want?" he snarled.

"You got a cigarette there, my man?" I asked, weaving where I stood, my hands in my pockets.

"No."

"Can you spare any change then? I need a smoke."

"Get the fuck outta here."

"Don't get tough with me, friend. I was in the army."

The man raised his chin, and the light from above revealed a smirking grin. His beard went all the way up to his cheekbones, but the long narrow nose and the lazy gaze were definitely Powell's.

"I don't care if you were a fuckin' Marine," Powell said. "I'll kick your ass if you don't get out of here. Now run."

I hunched my shoulders and snorted a laugh. "You don't mean that," I said, flashing a dopey smile. "All's I want is a quarter. Man, I know you got a quarter." I pretended to lose my balance and stumbled forward another step.

"Get the fuck away from me, man. I will hurt you."

"Don't hurt me, man. All's I want is some money. For a sandwich. I'm not gonna drink it. I swear." I stumbled backward a step, then forward two. Powell was about six feet away from me.

"Fuck you, man," he said. "Get the fuck outta—"

"No, fuck *you.*" I whipped out my gun and pointed it in his face. "Show me your hands. Get 'em up."

Powell's jaw went slack. "What the—"

The screech of tires distracted him as Job raced up to the scene, pulling to an abrupt stop under the streetlight. Job's window was down, and he was holding his Glock at arm's length, trained on Powell.

As Job got out of the car, I moved in on Powell, whose hands were up around his shoulders. "Down on the ground," I said, grabbing his coat and pushing him down. Keeping his cheek pressed to the sidewalk, I frisked him and cuffed him. Job stood over him, making sure Powell could see his gun. When Powell was secure, Job and I hauled him to his feet.

"What's the matter?" I said. "All of a sudden you got nothing to say? You used to talk pretty big on the phone."

Powell was shaking his head, confusion in his eyes. "Who . . . ?"

I got right in his face. "I'm the man who just won the gold-plated .44."

Job was laughing so hard his eyes were tearing.

"You're—"

"Joshua Armstrong," I finished for him. "I told you I'd find you."

He just stared at me in disbelief. No curses, no protests, no denials. He was totally dumbfounded.

Job and I got him into the car and delivered him to the county jail. A few days later we collected our fee from the bondsman, and Powell got a new court date. Given all the evidence the county prosecutor's office had against him, only a jury of idiots could possibly acquit him.

The next week I got a call from one of my cousins, Ice. "Joshua, I've got something for you. I'll stop by and drop it off this afternoon."

"What is it?" I asked.

"It's from Artemis Powell."

"No," I said. "Can't be."

"You'll see," Ice said. "Catch you later."

When Ice stopped by later that day, I met him at the door. He was holding out a zippered handgun pouch. "Powell's woman got the money to me and told me what to buy," he explained.

I unzipped the pouch, and there it was, a brand-new gold-plated Desert Eagle .44 semi-automatic handgun. It sparkled in my hand.

A folded piece of paper was also inside the pouch. It was a note. "A deal is a deal," it said. "You earned it." The note was unsigned.

As misguided as he was, Powell remained true to his word.

13 Bilil's Plea Bargain

As my Seeker family continued to mature both professionally and spiritually, my own family was just beginning. In 1992 I married my wife, Cindy, whom I had met earlier that same year. We exchanged vows in a traditional African ceremony, and not long after that, she became pregnant with the first of our two sons. With fatherhood on the horizon, I began to feel the joys and responsibilities of the next stage in my evolution. Now not only would I have to be a man, I would have to raise a man—two men, in fact—a difficult and daunting task given the number of males I had encountered who could not rightfully call themselves men.

While Cindy was pregnant, she preferred not to hear any of the details of my hunts and captures. (She still feels that way about my work today.) One case that I didn't tell her about was the hunt for Bilil Williams. I had discovered early on that in the real world everything is negotiable, and occasionally a fugitive will try to bargain with his bondsman. In this instance I was unexpectedly asked to broker a deal between a bondsman and his wayward client.

After word got out that the Seekers had successfully brought in the elusive Artemis Powell, a certain generally reputable bondsman—let's call him Tom Foster—called me up and asked if we could find a big-time drug dealer named Bilil Williams who had skipped out on a court date in Newark. Bilil was known for moving quantity in and around Newark, and it was no big secret that the police and the Essex County Prosecutors Office wanted him out of commission badly. He'd started in the business when he was in his teens, and now he had reached the ripe old age of twenty-nine, which in the drug trade made him a grand old man. Bilil was smart, and he had a remarkable gift for self-preservation. He wasn't flashy. He usually wore button-down blue shirts and khakis, and he drove a stripped-down Chevy sedan. If you saw him on the street, you'd swear he was a middle-class college boy. He'd never been charged with anything worse than personal possession, and that had only happened one time in his life. He had beaten the charge with no sweat. His caution was legendary. In my opinion he was just a hair shy of being paranoid, which is a good thing to be in the drug business.

Foster the bondsman gave me a file on Bilil that included all his known addresses. Unfortunately, Bilil hadn't been seen around Newark in months, and he had homes in New Jersey, New York City, South Carolina, Florida, and California. He could have been at any one of them, or he could have been somewhere else entirely. The outstanding bond was worth $75,000; our cut would be $7,500 if we found him in New Jersey, $15,000 if we picked him up out of state. But if we had to check out all of Bilil's locations, I figured this job would eat up so many man-hours we'd end up working for minimum wage. Still, I've always liked a challenge, and bringing in someone as notorious as Bilil could only enhance our growing reputation. Besides, Bilil had a close associate named Jerome Toussaint, who'd skipped out on his own bail six months earlier. Toussaint had been Bilil's chief enforcer, and he was facing a charge of attempted murder. His bond was worth $150,000, and we had that case, too, through another bondsman. If finding Bilil led us to Jerome, it would be well worth the effort.

Fortunately, the Seekers are constantly working the streets, keeping our ears to the ground and picking up as much intelligence as we can. We file away every little tidbit that comes our way, whether it pertains to a case we're working on or not. You never know when this information will be useful, and this was just the case with Bilil.

The Brown Derby is a bar in Elizabeth that I check in on from time to time. It's more than just a bar really. It's a place where plots are hatched and deals go down. At the door a bouncer frisks everyone who comes in for weapons. If anyone has a score to settle, they can do it outside. (This policy started when gang members got into the habit of stalking rival gang members in establishments like the Derby and opening fire just as their enemies were starting to kick back.)

Inside the Derby it's dark and smoky. The music is hip-hop, and the volume is loud. A large oval bar dominates the room. Inside the oval, women wearing either thong bikinis or negligees dance on the cleared-off end of a counter otherwise crammed with bottles of liquor. About a dozen dancers work there, but they only dance one at a time. When they aren't dancing, they're circulating around the room chatting up the customers. There's a small bedroom out back where, for a price, they will provide sexual services. An older gentleman sits at a table just inside the hallway that leads to the bedroom. He keeps track of what goes on in the bedroom and makes sure the girls take their turns when things get busy.

A few weeks before I got the warrant to apprehend Bilil, I happened to be in the Derby. It was a few days after New Year's, and it was business as usual there. The music was pumping, and a hefty girl in a pink baby-doll negligee was shaking her considerable booty behind the bar. She looked like an earthquake in progress. There's a little stage at one end of the wood-paneled room, but the dancers never use it. An artificial Christmas tree had been set up there, and underneath it was a sweatshirt and running-suit concession. Dozens of items were folded and arranged in neat rows in front of the tree. The most popular items were the sweatshirts with designer names emblazoned across the fronts—Tommy Hilfiger, Donna Karan, Calvin Klein. People in this neighborhood can't afford designer clothes—they just wear the names.

As usual I was working on a few different cases at the time, all of them local, and I was hoping to pick up some information about them—who these fugitives were hanging with, what they were doing for money, and most important, where they were living. Most of the people who frequent the Derby won't give you anything for free. That's why I'd gotten into the habit of keeping a roll of twenties in my shirt pocket to keep the wheels greased.

The people who work at the Derby know who I am and what I do for a living, and they respect me for that. Some of the things they do there are clearly illegal, but the staff doesn't want troublemakers in their place of business any more than anyone else does. So if I can clean up Dodge City for them once in a while, they're more than willing to relay things they might have overheard.

On that particular night I was talking to one of the bartenders when I noticed that one of the old girls was back in town, someone I thought had gotten out of the game. Her name was Shonda, a pretty girl in her early twenties with unusually large dark brown eyes. She looked a little pouty that night, which made me curious. Something seemed to be bothering her, and I'd come to learn that when people are upset, they usually want to talk.

"Shonda," I said, walking over to her, "how've you been, girl?" I gave her a hug, but she barely returned it. I looked her in the eye. "Something wrong?" I asked.

She sighed, and her pout turned into a frown. "Reece left me," she said as if that said it all. Reece was her man. Or at least that's how she saw it. From what I had seen, Reece had a lot of girlfriends. He was a punk who worked on the fringes of the drug trade, but he was good-looking and he had a lot of "gangsta" appeal, if there is such a thing. I had recently learned that the police were looking for him. He'd been out on bail on a minor drug charge and failed to make his initial court date.

"So what happened to Reece?" I asked Shonda, playing dumb with her.

"He moved to Georgia," she said.

"Where?"

"Someplace called Haddock."

"Haddock? Why'd he go there?"

"Bilil," she said.

"Bilil Williams?"

She nodded. "Reece's working for Bilil now," she said. "And when Bilil says move, you move. You know how that goes."

I certainly did. Bilil was Reece's entrée to the wide world of big-time drug dealing, which would mean serious money for Reece. If Bilil told Reece to strip naked and walk down Market Street in downtown

Newark backward on his hands at noon, Reece would ask how far.

"So what're they doing down in Georgia?" I asked.

"Bilil's hiding out down there. He's got some kind of legal troubles, I don't know. You gonna buy me a drink, Joshua?"

I bought her a drink, and we talked some more, but she was too depressed about losing Reece to talk about anything else. Since at the time I wasn't looking for either Reece or Bilil, I just filed away what she told me for future reference and moved on, working my way around the bar. I had no idea how valuable this little tidbit from Shonda was going to be until Tom Foster put me on Bilil's case a few weeks later.

As I read through Bilil's file, I started to piece together what had happened. The state had finally assembled a solid case against him, and he panicked. Unlike his fellow drug dealers, Bilil had very little experience with the courts, and he had never served time. My guess was that he got scared and ran. Based on the information I had gotten from Shonda, Bilil must have fled to Georgia right after he made bail. He could have afforded to post his own bail, but he must have intended to skip all along. Why forfeit his own money when he could use a bondsman's? Besides, if this was going to interrupt his business indefinitely, he wanted to hang on to as much of his cash and assets as he could. He must have taken Reece with him and probably a few more gangsta boys for protection. I figured they'd probably been down there for at least four or five weeks.

The next logical step was to go down to Haddock and see what I could find out firsthand. We had been planning a trip down to Georgia and the Carolinas to make a few pickups, so we simply added Haddock to our itinerary. When we arrived there, we found a respectable little community with about five thousand residents. Bilil had family there and had lived there as a boy. It was a place where he was comfortable, the kind of place that bail jumpers often think of as safe.

Since Bilil had a posse, I decided to take Job and Jedidiah with me. Usually the Seekers only work in pairs. If we do our homework, get all the information we need, and plan the mission carefully, we don't need more than two men to take down one. But I had a feeling this wasn't going to be one of our usual jobs.

We loaded up my Toyota Land Cruiser and brought enough food to last us for the better part of a week. We'd found that maintaining a good diet on the road was nearly impossible, so we filled up several large plastic tubs with fruits and vegetables. We rarely ate at diners and fast-food joints when we were home, so why switch to inferior fuel precisely when we needed peak performance?

We arrived in Haddock in the middle of a weekday afternoon. After we got settled at our motel, Job and Jedidiah went off to rent a second vehicle while I checked in with the local police chief, a bald man with wire-rim glasses who looked more like a preacher than a cop. I showed him the warrant I had on Bilil. The chief already knew Bilil's reputation, and he certainly didn't like having a major drug dealer in his community, but oddly enough, he'd never had cause to investigate Bilil or his men. Bilil apparently kept his nose clean in his hometown.

From the police station I went directly to Bilil's neighborhood and drove by his home. It was a nice house in a fairly new development. In keeping with Bilil's style, the neighborhood was just a little better than average but hardly ostentatious. It was the kind of place a bank manager or factory supervisor would live. The house had white vinyl siding and black shutters. The garage doors were closed, and there were no cars in the driveway. It didn't look as if anyone lived there—no lawn furniture, no bikes in the driveway, no garbage cans at the curb. I noticed that the mailbox was empty while all the other mailboxes on the street had letters and magazines sticking out of them.

I intended to check back after dark to see if there was any activity inside, but I already had a feeling there'd be nothing to see. Bilil wasn't stupid. He wasn't going to hang around any of his known addresses. He could be staying with relatives—if he had any relatives who'd put up his posse, too—or he might have rented a new place for himself, which was more likely. I could see we had our work cut out for us.

The next day we got started doing our homework, asking questions in Bilil's neighborhood, looking up his relatives, developing relationships with the locals, and visiting the bars where the players went. This is always a sensitive stage in any operation. We need information, but we can't let information about us get back to our target. We have to be careful about what we ask and who we ask. Generally it's best to keep the target inside a wide circle. In this case Bilil's wide circle was the entire town of Haddock. If we tried to enter his inner circle too soon—for instance, by trying to talk directly to members of his family—we'd run the risk of being found out—or worse.

At the end of our second day in Haddock, Job had tracked down addresses for Bilil's mother, aunt, and a male cousin who lived by himself. Jedidiah had found out from the mailman in Bilil's neighborhood that all the mail going to that address was being held at the post office. At a rib joint/strip club on the outskirts of town, I ordered a beer and talked to the bartender, who said that there were some brothers from up north who stopped by now and then. He complained about the rise of drugs in the community and how it was ruining the town. He suspected that these strangers could be dealers, but it was just a feeling, he had no hard facts. I showed him Bilil's photo, but he didn't recognize the face. But when I asked if one of them looked like a college kid, he said yes right away.

"The others look like a pretty bad bunch, but this one guy is all clean-cut and preppy-looking," the bartender said. "I remember because he seemed to be the leader of the whole crew, and that just seemed kinda peculiar to me."

I tipped the man generously and left.

Back at the motel that evening, Jedidiah, Job, and I divvied up our duties for the next day. Jedidiah would stake out Bilil's cousin's condo. Job and I would watch the post office to see if anyone from his crew picked up his mail. After dinner that night I decided to go back to the rib joint just in case Bilil had a hankering for ribs.

I went by myself, and once again I sat at the bar and ordered a beer. The bar had a cool, dark, subterranean feel. On a small stage near the entrance, a skinny stripper in a satin bikini and five-inch heels was dancing halfheartedly to a Fugees song, but since no one was paying any attention to her, she wasn't stripping. The bartender I'd talked to that afternoon was still on duty. I poured my beer into a mug and took it over to a corner table where I could see who came in the front door. I wasn't there long before a young man came over and stood in front of my view. His face was expressionless, but his eyes held a lot of nasty attitude. His hair was close-cropped with a part shaved into the right side.

He just stared at me, waiting for me to acknowledge him.

"Something you want?" I said to him.

He didn't answer me, but he took a seat.

I glanced over at the bartender, who was looking at me. He gave me a curt nod as if to say this guy was all right.

"So?" I said to the stranger.

"You looking for Bilil?" he said. I could tell from the way he talked that he was a local.

I just looked at the man. I wasn't going to say anything until I knew who he was and what he wanted.

"You here to arrest him or something?" he asked.

Maybe he thought I was there to carry out a hit on Bilil.

He tilted his head back and smiled like a shark, showing his front teeth. "I might be able to offer you some help," he said. "If you want it."

"Who are you?"

He pinched his nose and laughed. "Call me Charles."

I seriously doubted that was his real name.

"You a cop?" he asked. His face was dead serious again. "Course, you wouldn't tell me the truth if you were."

"I'm not a cop," I said.

"Whatever." He didn't believe me. "There's this old hotel a couple of miles south of here," he said. "The Mayfair. You ought to check it out. It's a nice place. Lot of people from up north stay there." He stood up to go.

"You wouldn't be in the same business as Bilil, would you?" I asked.

He smiled down at me. "I don't know. What's Bilil do for a living?"

"You wouldn't be, like, a rival of his?"

"Naw. I don't know what you're talking about." He walked back to the bar where a snifter of brandy was waiting for him. He scooped it up and headed down three steps to the pool room, ignoring the stripper as he passed.

Charles was either a rival drug dealer who wanted to eliminate a competitor or he worked for Bilil and this was a setup. I had no way of knowing which.

I went back to the motel and discussed it with Job and Jedidiah. We all agreed that a setup was a definite possibility. Bilil's lack of experience with the law might lead him to believe that he could pull some crazy shit like an ambush at a backwater hotel. But Charles being a rival drug dealer seemed equally plausible. Still, we weren't going to take any chances. We decided that Job and I would go to the Mayfair Hotel immediately to check it out.

The Mayfair turned out to be a rather stately old place with white columns and a porch full of rocking chairs set on a hill overlooking a stream. It was on a country road surrounded by farmland, facing a cow pasture. The hotel had three floors, but the parking lot out back was nearly empty when we pulled in at around 8:30 P.M.

We sat in the car for a few minutes and surveyed the scene, looking for signs of an impending ambush. There were no trees or high bushes near the Mayfair, and the roof was steeply sloped. I didn't see any convenient hiding places for gunmen. Outside, the hotel seemed pretty safe, so we decided to go in and check the rates. We were both dressed casually in sports shirts and khakis, like a couple of tourists. The lobby was in keeping with the exterior of the hotel—old and homey, the rugs gently worn, the antique furniture polished to a fine gloss. As we ambled in, we did a quick visual sweep without being obvious about it.

Hell of a place for a shootout, I thought. We were both carrying identical Glock 9s.

The desk clerk was a short, stocky man in his thirties. His pressed white shirt was immaculate, top button buttoned, tie all the way up. His hands were as clean as a surgeon's.

"Gentlemen, may I help you?" he asked as we crossed the lobby.

"Yes," I said. "Do you have any rooms available? We need two doubles for the rest of this week, leaving Sunday."

He was already tapping out keys on his computer before I'd even finished my question. "Yes, indeed, sir. You're in luck. We have two rooms left."

"Great," I said. "What are your rates?"

"Ninety-five dollars a day, continental breakfast included."

I nodded and looked at Job. "My cousin recommended this place," I said to the clerk. "He said it's very quiet out here."

A knowing grin slowly spread across the clerk's face. "Your cousin wouldn't be Mr. Williams, would it? From New Jersey?"

I put on a surprised smile. "You mean Bilil?"

"Yes. I believe that's what his friends call him."

"You know Bilil?"

"Well . . . of course. He's staying here. He and his friends."

"No kidding," I said. My smile slowly faded. Job walked behind the desk and stood right next to the man.

"Excuse me, sir," he started to say to Job, but I cut him off.

"No, excuse *me.*" I went into my pocket, pulled out my bail enforcement agent ID, and held it in front of his face. "We have a warrant for Bilil Williams's arrest. We hope that you'll help us. It's your choice, of course, but if you choose *not* to help us, we will be compelled to contact the local authorities and let them question you in connection with harboring a fugitive."

Suddenly the clerk didn't look well. He was between a rock and a hard place, and he knew it. "I . . . I'd like to help you, but I don't know how."

"Is Bilil here now?"

"No. He went out late this afternoon. Hasn't been back."

"How many people are staying here with him?"

"Four other men."

"Are they here?"

"No. They all left together with Mr. Williams."

"Do you know when they'll be back?"

"No. They come and go at odd hours. Sometimes they stay out all day and come back late at night. Sometimes they don't leave their rooms at all. They stay on the phone all day."

"If they were to come back today, about what time would that be?"

"I have no idea. As I said, they keep odd hours."

I left him with Job while I took another look around the lobby. It wasn't very big, but I noticed that there was a small alcove with a couch and two armchairs. It was lined with books and tucked away in a corner. I walked back toward the desk and checked to see if someone coming in the front door could see into the alcove. It was hardly noticeable at all.

I pointed at the clerk's telephone. "Do you have an intercom buzzer on that phone?" I asked the clerk.

He looked puzzled. "Yes."

"Press it."

"But—"

"Just press it. I want to hear what it sounds like."

He did as I asked. The buzz was nice and loud. "Press it three times fast," I said. "One, two, three."

He was confused, but he did it anyway. I nodded, satisfied that we'd be able to hear it back in the alcove. "OK," I said to the clerk. "When Bilil comes in, I want you to hit that buzzer three times, like you just did. We'll be waiting back in the reading room."

"And don't try to warn Bilil that we're here," Job added grimly.

"Oh, no. Of course not," the clerk said. "I understand."

"I hope so," Job said. He started toward the reading room.

"And one more thing," I said, looking the clerk in the eye. "Act natural. You look too nervous."

"I'm OK," he said. "I'll be fine."

"Good. Then there won't be any problem."

"No. None."

I headed toward the alcove.

"Sir," he said, stopping me.

"What?"

"Could you try to be careful with the antiques? When you arrest him, I mean."

"Don't worry about the antiques," I said. "They'll be fine."

I joined Job in the reading room. He'd already pushed the two armchairs against the wall in a place where we wouldn't be seen. We both found books that looked interesting and settled in for a long wait, which is exactly what it turned out to be. As time passed, we heard guests coming in and going out, and we eavesdropped on all the clerk's phone conversations. Every half-hour or so one of us would go out for a bathroom break or a drink of water. It wasn't that we needed it as much as we wanted to keep our presence fresh in the clerk's mind in case he started getting ideas. The clerk began to look a little less nervous than he had when we first arrived, but I could see that he was still afraid of us.

At ten-thirty Job and I were in our seats. He was absorbed in his book, but I was looking out the window, staring at the night sky over the treetops. I was beginning to wonder if Bilil had gotten hinky and abandoned this location.

Unless this really was a setup, I thought. But if it was, what was Bilil waiting for?

My rambling thoughts were suddenly interrupted by the high whining scream of engines. It was coming from outside. Suddenly the intercom at the front desk buzzed three times. The racket outside abruptly died down. The intercom buzzed again, three times fast. Job put down his book and looked at me.

I stood up and looked out the window at the parking lot in back. In the glare of the floodlights, two men in leather jackets and helmets were just getting off their motorcycles, Japanese speed bikes—one red, the other purple. The men pulled off their helmets as they walked toward the hotel, revealing their faces. It was Bilil and Shonda's old boyfriend Reece. I was surprised to see Bilil with such a flashy ride.

"Well, look who's here," Job said under his breath.

We stood back from the window so they wouldn't see us. They were coming in the back way. Bilil and Reece would have to pass through the lobby to get to the stairs that led up to their rooms. The Mayfair didn't have an elevator.

I went to the front desk. The clerk's eyes were bugging out of his head. "Just be cool," I said to him quietly. "It'll all be over in a few seconds. Just make like we're having a nice little conversation. And smile." I had my gun in my hand down by my side.

Job hung back and stayed out of sight in the reading room.

I heard the back door open and close. Bilil and Reece came strutting through the lobby, their footsteps heavy on the large oriental rug. They were coming toward the front desk, heading for the staircase. I took a deep breath and waited . . . waited . . . waited for the right moment. Then just as they were about to pass me, I whipped around and extended my gun hand, pointing it at Bilil's head. Bilil froze and looked to his associate. Reece was reaching into his leather jacket.

"Don't do it," Job warned in a low growl. He was standing right behind Reece, the muzzle of his Glock buried in Reece's scalp. Reece didn't move a muscle.

"Down on the floor facedown, hands above your heads," I shouted. "Both of you."

Reece hesitated for only a moment before he got down on his belly. But Bilil didn't move. He just stared at me, his expression gradually changing as it went through a series of emotions—shock, anger, humiliation, rage—finally settling on a look of grim understanding.

"You got me," he said flatly. "So who sent you?"

"You did," I said.

"What do you mean?"

"*You* sent us here."

He just looked at me, waiting for me to explain.

Reece was down on the floor, wriggling around like a fish on the deck as Job knelt on the small of his back and cuffed him. "I'm sorry, Bilil," Reece kept saying. "I'm sorry, man. I'm really sorry."

Bilil ignored him and stayed focused on me. "You here to do me or what?"

I shook my head. "We're taking you back to Jersey. There's a judge in Newark who wants to see you."

"Oh . . . ." He started nodding as he began to understand. "I see."

I tossed my handcuffs to Job. He got behind Bilil and grabbed one of his wrists.

"Hold on, hold on," Bilil said. "Let's talk about this."

I caught Job's eye. He was as wary of Bilil as I was. Something wasn't right. Bilil was much too calm. "What do we have to talk about?" I asked him.

"A lot," he said.

Bilil wanted to go to a diner to talk, but I didn't like that idea. He was acting as if the warrant for his arrest was just some little misunderstanding and that we could work it out over a cup of coffee. He was smooth, but Job and I had dealt with smooth characters before. I insisted that he be cuffed—in the front so that he could have his coffee, but chained to Reece's cuffs. Instead of going to a diner, I drove to the nearest McDonald's, intending to order at the drive-through. Job sat in the back with Reece and Bilil. Reece was trying to look mean and angry, but I could see that he was nervous. He had gangsta style, but I wondered how much real gangsta experience he had. Bilil, on the other hand, seemed totally unfazed. He was definitely up to something.

I stopped the car at the big plastic Ronald McDonald and rolled down my window. "Two coffees," I said into the microphone in Ronald's throat. "One tea and—" I looked back at Job, who just shook his head. "That's all. Two coffees and one tea—with honey if you've got it."

Ronald repeated my order in a tinny female voice, and I drove on to the pickup window. A young woman handed me a white paper bag. I paid her, then pulled the Land Cruiser around and found an isolated parking space at the rear of the lot.

"So what do you want to talk about?" I said, handing Bilil his coffee.

The chain connecting his handcuffs to Reece's rattled as he took the coffee. He carefully pried open the lid and balanced the cup on his knee as he opened two packets of sugar and two creamers, stirring them in as if he had all the time in the world. He didn't answer my question until he'd blown over the surface of the hot brew and taken his first sip. "You're working for Foster?" he asked.

I nodded.

"And how much is the bond on me? Seventy-five?"

I nodded again.

Bilil took another sip.

I poured honey into my tea from a little clear plastic container and stirred it in with a plastic swizzle stick. Bilil was trying to be cool, but I wasn't impressed. Whatever was on his mind didn't really matter. I had him in custody, so like it or not he was going back to New Jersey.

Reece slurped his coffee loudly but avoided eye contact with anyone, including Bilil, who was sitting in the middle. Reece was exuding extreme attitude, like a hunk of smelly cheese, but no one was paying attention.

Bilil started talking, but it was as if he were talking to himself, thinking out loud. "Seventy-five means what? Seventy-five *hundred* if you take me in?"

"Fifteen thousand," I corrected.

“So what’s that?” he said. “That’s nothing.”

“You won’t be going home alone,” I said. “I’ve got a couple of other pickups to make down here.”

“Even so,” he said. “It still ain’t much for taking me in.” He sipped his coffee. “How about this? Foster’s got the deed on this little house I got in Newark. It ain’t worth shit. He can have it. I’ll kick in another twenty for him and thirty for you on top of that. Just let us go. That sound fair?”

Job arched his eyebrows. It wasn’t uncommon for fugitives to try to bribe bounty hunters, but I’d never seen a fugitive who treated it like a business transaction. Bilil was so bloodless you would have thought he was talking about pork-belly futures rather than his own freedom.

“I’m talking cash,” Bilil said. “I’ve got it, all of it. No waiting.”

I kept stirring my tea, staring at his eyes in the rearview mirror. I had no doubt that he had the money. Losing a house and fifty grand was nothing to him, just the cost of doing business.

“I know you don’t trust me,” Bilil said with a sly smile, “but I also know you’re working for Foster, and you have an obligation to at least present my offer to him.”

He was right about that. We’re not cops; we work for the bail bondsmen who give us our assignments. So whether this offer was serious or not, we had to at least tell Foster about it.

“Use my cell if you want,” Bilil said, nodding at Job, who’d taken the phone when he’d frisked Bilil.

“I’ll use my own,” I said, pulling it out. I dialed Foster’s direct line and stepped outside the Land Cruiser for privacy.

It rang twice. “Tom Foster,” he answered.

“You sitting down?” I said.

“Where the hell is this place?” Jedidiah asked for the third time since we’d started out. I was driving the Land Cruiser down a two-lane county road. Bilil was in the backseat with Jedidiah. Job and Reece were behind us in the rental car. On both sides of the road, flat farmland stretched all the way out to the edges of the woods.

“Keep going. It’s not too far from here,” Bilil said. We’d left Haddock at about eleven-thirty after hooking up with Jedidiah.

Jedidiah caught my eye in the rearview mirror, and I could tell from his face that he wasn't comfortable with this situation. To be honest, I was a little uneasy myself and so was Job, but we were working for Tom Foster, and he'd made his decision—go for the money. I didn't know it at the time, but Foster's business wasn't doing so well and he was in desperate need of cash.

We drove another twenty miles, Bilil giving me directions. A tense silence filled the interior of the Land Cruiser. It was interrupted only by Bilil's terse instructions: "Turn right here. . . . Left. . . . Stay straight." The farmland gradually gave way to woods, and eventually, except for an occasional run-down hillbilly shack, that's all there was. The paved road abruptly ended and turned into a dirt road. The sound of gravel pelting my wheel wells peppered my thoughts. Tree limbs met above the road, blocking out the night sky. I switched on my high beams. There was no moon that night. The world beyond my headlights was a black void.

"Take this right," Bilil said.

I didn't see a place to turn—it was all woods—so I slowed down to a crawl. Then I saw what he was talking about. It was no more than a path, just two tire tracks running through the undergrowth. The tracks hadn't seen much traffic, and I suspected that it wouldn't take long for the ferns to reclaim it completely if it went unused. If Bilil hadn't been there to point it out, I would never have found it.

"Take this as far as it goes, then park. We'll have to walk the rest of the way in."

I couldn't see Jedidiah's expression, but I could just imagine what he was thinking because I was thinking the same thing: What the hell are we getting into?

But Bilil must've picked up on our vibe. "A man in my position has to protect himself," he explained.

"Me, too," I said, and stopped the car in the middle of the path. I opened my door to get out. "What're you doing?" Bilil asked.

I stared into the glare of Job's headlights and signaled for him to come over.

I got back into the Land Cruiser. Job walked up to the driver's side and leaned on the door. "What's up?"

“You take the Land Cruiser. Jed and I will take the other car. Drive Bilil out to some secluded spot and be sure to wear the intercom. If anything happens to us, you bring Bilil home in a body bag.”

Job looked at Bilil and nodded.

“Hey, wait a minute,” Bilil protested.

“No, *you* wait a minute,” I interrupted. “If this is a setup, say so now.”

“This ain’t no setup. I got the money in a cabin. Out in those woods.” He pointed with his chin.

“Great. Then you got nothing to worry about.”

I got out of the Land Cruiser and went into the trunk to collect the equipment we’d need, then carried it over to the rental car. When Reece saw Jedidiah and me getting in with him, he cut me a look that could’ve drawn blood. “What the fuck is this?” he grumbled.

“Change in plans. You’re gonna be our guide.”

“Wha’?”

“Relax,” Jedidiah said. “We’ll tell you when you can start thinking.”

I backed the rental car out into the road to let the Land Cruiser out. Then, as Job headed down the road the way we’d come, I pulled back in and followed the path. The rental car bounced over the ruts and humps, the springs complaining bitterly the whole way. I couldn’t drive very fast for fear of breaking an axle. It was at least fifteen minutes before the path came to a dead end at a small clearing. Tire tracks in the soft dirt indicated that other vehicles had parked here before, but the clearing was empty now.

Jedidiah looked at Reece. “Now what?”

“We walk,” Reece said. “Do I still need these?” He held up his handcuffed wrists.

“Oh, yes,” I said.

Reece gave me a dead-faced stare.

Jedidiah escorted him out of the car while I popped the trunk and unpacked the two duffels that held the equipment. Jedidiah and I were already carrying 9mm Glock handguns with extra clips, but I took out a few more clips just in case. We each put on body armor, which is lightweight and covers more of the torso than a standard-issue police bullet-proof vest. I handed Jedidiah a shotgun and pulled out two air tasers, small metal boxes the size of cigarette packs that can send a jolt of electricity through the air and knock a man down ten feet away. I also pulled out two monocular night scope headsets, which contained a built-in intercom system. Jedidiah, Job, and I would stay in constant contact with one another. When Jedidiah and I put the headsets on, we looked like high-tech pirates.

"What're those things for?" Reece asked. He seemed a little nervous all of a sudden.

"Don't worry about it," I said. He was eyeing the shotgun cradled in Jedidiah's arm. "Here," I said, putting a flashlight in his hand. "You lead the way."

"What about the cuffs, man?" he asked again.

I just grinned at him. "Show me the money."

Jedidiah started to laugh.

"It ain't funny," Reece said with a scowl. "I'm being serious here."

"So are we." I put my face up to his and stared at him with my uncovered eye. I wasn't kidding around now, and he knew it. "No surprises," I said. "You understand what I'm saying?"

Reece didn't say anything, but he understood. He turned, pointed with his flashlight beam, and started walking through a patch of knee-high ferns. We followed him—me right behind, Jedidiah bringing up the rear. I had my Glock out; Jedidiah was ready with the shotgun.

At the end of the patch of ferns there was a narrow path. It wound around the trees, presenting new obstacles every few feet—teetering rocks, tangles of roots that grabbed at our toes, mud puddles too big to walk around.

"It ain't far from here," Reece said.

I didn't answer him. I was more interested in listening to what was going on around me. The woods were so thick that even with the night-vision scope I couldn't see more than fifteen feet in front of me. An owl was hooting somewhere above us. I wondered if he saw something that we didn't.

As we kept walking, the woods just got thicker. "Where are you taking us?" I asked Reece. "I don't see a cabin."

"We ain't there yet," Reece said. "It's so far out nobody can find it. But it's there."

"Don't bullshit me, Reece."

"I ain't bullshittin' you," Reece insisted. But I didn't like his tone of voice. Something wasn't right. I could feel it.

A deep voice suddenly boomed out of the darkness. *"Don't move, motherfucker!"*

I didn't bother trying to locate it through the scope. I just grabbed Reece by the face and pulled him to my chest, jamming the barrel of my 9mm into his neck. "Who's there? Show yourself or I'll shoot him."

"Do what he says," Reece shouted in panic. "This motherfucker ain't fooling."

Suddenly three figures materialized out of the woods like ghosts. Two of them were carrying assault rifles. The third was pointing a TEC–9 automatic pistol at my head. I didn't recognize any of their faces, but I assumed this was the rest of Bilil's posse.

Jedidiah had moved off to the side. He had the shotgun leveled at the three intruders.

I couldn't believe it. It was a genuine Mexican standoff. And I'd thought this shit only happened in the movies.

"Let him go," the TEC–9 said.

I ignored him and spoke into Reece's ear. "What's this all about?"

"I dunno, man. I dunno nothin'." He was giving me attitude even though I had a gun jammed in his neck.

"Bilil never intended to give us that money, did he?" I said.

Reece didn't answer.

"Joshua, Joshua, what's going on?" Job's voice was in my ear.

"I said let him go," the TEC–9 bellowed, but I didn't budge. They thought they had the drop on us, but the way I saw it, we were holding most of the cards. Yes, they had more firepower than we did—the automatic pistol and the assault rifles had more rounds in their clips than our handguns—but we had Reece. We also had our night scopes, and we were wearing body armor. On top of all that, we had the shotgun. One blast would spray buckshot out in a swath that would hit all three of them. The only thing that worried me was them panicking and starting a crazy-ass firefight where they just shot at everything and anything until their clips were empty.

"Joshua!" Job said. *"Joshua!"*

"Things are a little funky on this end," I told him through the headset mike. "Stand by with that body bag."

"Let him go, motherfucker." Mr. TEC–9 was getting testy.

"Job," I said. "Call my cell and put Bilil on." I said it loud enough for everyone to hear. "The phone's in my side pocket, left side. I'm gonna take it out now, so just be cool."

"What the fuck?" one of the assault rifles said.

I waited for it to start ringing before I pulled it out of my pocket. I pressed the answer button with my thumb. "Bilil," I said, putting it to my face.

"Yeah, I'm here."

"You fucked up, my friend."

"You kill anybody yet?"

"Not yet. I was thinking maybe you should be the first."

"Yeah, your man here is dying to do it. He's holding this big-ass piece right in my face."

"You're pretty slick, Bilil. Let me guess. Your boys have standing orders to shoot anybody who comes down this path. That's why you brought us this way, right?"

Bilil didn't answer.

"So what're we gonna do?" I said. "Spill some blood?"

"Naw, man," Bilil said. "Don't have to do that. You can have the money."

"Oh, yeah? I'm supposed to believe you now?"

"You can't blame a man for trying to save some money."

"Don't bullshit me, Bilil."

"Lemme talk to Jerome. I'll fix it."

Jerome? I thought. *Jerome Toussaint?* I had hoped Bilil would lead me to Jerome, but I'd never imagined it would come down like this.

I looked at the three men in front of me, forcing myself to keep a neutral expression. "Which one of you is Jerome?"

"Me," the TEC–9 said.

"Here." I tossed him the cell. "Talk to Bilil."

Jerome caught the phone. "Yeah?" he said into it.

"What's going on?" Bilil asked him. I could hear his end of the conversation through the intercom.

“It’s not good, man,” Jerome said.

“Yeah, I figured. These brothers are ice cold.”

“What do we do?” Jerome asked.

Bilil didn’t answer right away. He was thinking it over—as if there was anything to think about with Job holding a gun to his head. “Give ’em the fuckin’ money,” he finally said in disgust.

“Just give it to ’em?”

“Yeah, don’t worry about it.”

Fifty thousand wasn’t enough to spill blood over, not when it was Bilil’s blood. But Bilil was obviously a cheapskate, and like everyone else in the world, he didn’t like to lose. I wasn’t ruling out the possibility that Bilil had just given Jerome some kind of secret code word that would trigger Plan B, whatever that was.

Jerome tossed the phone back to me. I put it to my free ear, but Bilil had already hung up. “Job,” I said into the mike, “when I say ‘Do it,’ just shoot him. You understand?”

“Home in a body bag,” he confirmed with grave conviction.

“Throw your guns away,” I said to the posse. “Otherwise Bilil gets it.”

No one made a move. A moment turned into a very tense minute. Then Jerome tossed his pistol into the ferns. Reluctantly the other two threw their assault rifles into the brush.

“Very good,” I said. “Now where’s the money, Jerome?”

He cocked his head back. “This way.”

“You first,” I said. “All of you.”

The two other gangstas looked to Jerome for their orders. He shrugged as if it didn’t matter anymore, then started walking down the path. They followed him.

“Shoulder to shoulder,” Jedidiah shouted, moving up behind them with the shotgun leveled on their backs. “I want to see all of you.”

“Go,” I said to Reece, shoving him away. “Run.” He started running back the way we’d come. He was handcuffed and unarmed, so I wasn’t worried about him. Besides, we had enough to contend with without having to deal with him, too.

We walked for ten minutes in silence, but it was hard to tell how far we had gone because it was slow going in the dark. Finally I spotted a kerosene lantern burning in the distance. Through the night scope I was able to make out the outline of a small shack. As we got closer, I saw that there was a road on the other side of the shack, about thirty yards off, which just confirmed my guess. Bilil had brought us the long way through the woods so that his posse could ambush us. Anyone who approached the shack from the path through the woods was automatically marked for execution—no orders were necessary.

When we got to the shack, I went in alone with Jerome while Jedidiah held the other two at bay outside with the shotgun. By the light of the lantern I got a better look at Jerome's face and compared it with my memory of Jerome Toussaint's mug shot—dark complexion, long horse face, sleepy eyes. Yes, I was almost certain this was him.

The interior of the cabin was sparsely furnished, but there was one plush armchair. Bilil's seat, I assumed. The shack had a tin roof and wood plank walls, the wood gray with age. The place had the feel of a boys' clubhouse.

Jerome went to the kitchenette, reached up over the cabinets, and pulled down a gray metal strongbox. I watched him carefully, thinking there could be a weapon inside.

"Dump it out on the table," I said. "All of it."

But when Jerome turned the strongbox upside down, only money poured out. Untidy packets of old bills held together with rubber bands. He picked out ten packets and handed them to me.

I shook my head. "Count it. Out loud."

Jerome rolled his eyes and sighed loudly, but he did as I asked, taking off the rubber bands and laying out the bills one at a time as he counted. It took him about twenty minutes to get to fifty thousand. He put the rubber bands back on and pushed all ten packets across the table toward me.

"OK?" he asked with attitude.

"Fine." I picked up the packets and stuffed them into my jacket, then pointed toward the door with my gun. "Go outside."

As we came outside, one of the gangstas said, "You got your money. Just let us go now."

I shook my head. "Let's take a walk first."

"Wha'?"

"We're going back the way we came," I said, pointing with my gun. "Everybody."

They hesitated, but Jedidiah stepped forward with the shotgun and got them moving. We walked back through the woods, heading toward our car. When we got to the darkest part, where the treetops blocked out the sky completely, I told them to stop. "OK," I said, "throw your flashlights away. *Far* away."

"What're you, crazy?"

"Throw them away."

They hesitated, but they did it. I could hear the flashlights rustling the distant underbrush.

"OK, you're free," I said. "Except you." I took Jerome by the wrist and handcuffed him behind his back.

"Why you taking me?" he protested.

"Because if your friends here try some kind of retaliation, we kill you first." I said it loud enough for everyone to hear. I decided not to tell him that I knew who he was. Not yet. "Now move," I said as I steered him down the path.

With the night scopes we were able to move quickly. Jerome wasn't exactly comfortable trotting through the pitch black, sandwiched between me and Jedidiah, but he did it. We got back to our car, and Jedidiah got into the backseat with Jerome. I motioned with my eyes to Jedidiah, who knew exactly what I wanted. He pulled out another set of handcuffs and cuffed Jerome to the door handle.

"What the hell you doing, man?" Jerome complained.

"Taking you in," I said. "You're wanted in New Jersey."

"Naw, man. That ain't me. You got the wrong brother."

As I turned the car around and drove back along the path to the unpaved road, Jerome continued to protest, but I tuned him out. I knew he was the one.

"Job?" I said into the intercom.

"I'm here."

"Hang on to Bilil and meet us at the place where you rented the car. We're leaving right away."

"I hear you."

On the way back I swung past the Mayfair Hotel and found Reece in the parking lot, still in cuffs, trying to start his purple motorcycle. Jedidiah hauled him off the bike and threw him in the backseat with Jerome. His bail bond wasn't very big, but I knew that his grandmother had put up the money by herself, so I figured I'd do her a service by bringing him in.

We went back to the motel to pick up our clothes, transferred our prisoners—Bilil included—to the Land Cruiser, dropped off the rental car, then headed for home. The next day I delivered Bilil, Jerome, and Reece to the Essex County jail, then went over to Tom Foster's office to give him his twenty grand, which he was very happy to have. The money covered his expenses on Bilil's case, and now he didn't have to make up a story for the surety company.

Bilil was convicted and sentenced to a two-year term. I'm hoping that our paths will cross again someday, and maybe next time the charges against him will be serious enough to demand a healthy six-figure bail and a long stint in prison if he's convicted. He'll have a tough time trying to buy his way out of trouble a second time because I won't be listening.

14 Family Values

About six months after our adventure in Haddock, a bail bondsman gave me an unusual assignment: pick up an entire family—father, mother, brother, and sister. Their name was Kozlowski, but they had been known to use several aliases. They were all in the burglary business. Eugene, the father, had been a burglar all his life and had taught his trade to his children. Both son and daughter had gone to trade school to hone their skills. Shawn, the son, was an expert welder; his sister, Sandy, specialized in disarming alarms. Sondra, their mother, was their fence; she stayed home and worked the phone, selling off the merchandise that the rest of the family stole. When I got the case, the Kozlowski family also happened to be the target of a New Jersey State Police task force.

The Kozlowskis were a precision team. Usually they broke into retail businesses and restaurants, but occasionally they'd do private homes in wealthy neighborhoods. Their modus operandi went something like this: Sandy, who was small and skinny, would disable the alarm. At restaurants she would gain access by greasing her body and squeezing through the kitchen exhaust vent. Once the alarms were disconnected, Eugene would case the place, locating the valuables. If there was a safe—and there usually was—Shawn would get to work with an acetylene torch. Once they knew what they basically had in terms of loot, Eugene would put in a call to Sondra, who would then get to work finding buyers for the merchandise, everything from jewelry to handguns. Sometimes Sondra would have buyers lined up before the merchandise actually left the premises, and the rest of the family would deliver the stuff directly from the heist.

A year and a half before I got the case, the Kozlowskis had skipped out on a court date in Bergen County, New Jersey. They'd been caught fencing stolen jewelry to an undercover police operation in Teaneck. The jewelry had come from a break-in that occurred in Alpine, the exclusive community on the Hudson River where Eddie Murphy, among others, has a home. A year and a half is a long time to be in the wind. Other bounty hunters had tried and failed to find them, and the trail had gone cold. The Kozlowskis apparently lived like gypsies, never staying in one place for very long, always picking up stakes as soon as they'd made a score.

Despite the cold trail, I decided to give it a shot anyway and started putting out feelers for people who might have had some contact with them. It took me a while, but I was eventually introduced to a fence who had worked with them in the past. This fence, whose name was Manny, told me about another fence named Mordecai, who had a warehouse in the Bronx. Mordecai was not your average fence. Rather than buying whatever swag came in the door, he commissioned freelance burglars to steal specific high-ticket items—anything from diamond earrings to Mercedes-Benzes. According to Manny, the Kozlowskis were now working almost exclusively with Mordecai.

I checked with one of my contacts in the Bronx who knew all about Mordecai's operation. He knew where Mordecai's warehouse was located, and he even knew when Mordecai did most of his business—late afternoons and early evenings on weekdays. This made sense because it was the time of day when the police changed shifts. Cops going off duty don't go out of their way to make arrests unless they absolutely have to, and the cops going on aren't always up to speed at the beginning of their shift. Also, rush-hour traffic in New York is insane and therefore a good cover for illegal activities. And since most professional break-ins happen during the day, when people are at work, Mordecai's hours were perfect for fresh deliveries.

I took a ride up to the Bronx and scoped out Mordecai's warehouse. It was in an industrial district that pretty much emptied out by 5 P.M. Though I wanted to park and stake out the place, I didn't do that. Mordecai and his patrons were savvy criminals who would undoubtedly keep an eye out for unfamiliar vehicles that lingered too long.

Up the street there was a little bar with neon beer signs cluttering the tiny front windows—Bud, Miller, Killian's, Beck's, Rolling Rock. It was the kind of dark, smoky place where you could get a beer and a shot, but you'd be pushing your luck if you tried ordering a mixed drink. I decided to go in and check out the place.

I ordered a beer at the bar and took in the scene through the mirror behind the bottles. A few working stiffs were sitting at the bar with me. Two of them were drinking alone; the other two were apparently friends. I eavesdropped on their conversation. They were griping about some other guy, apparently their boss.

Tables lined the wall opposite the bar and stretched all the way to the back, where a jukebox sat between the entrances to two short hallways. One hallway led to the rest rooms; the other to the back door. The jukebox was an old Wurlitzer, the kind that has brightly lit yellow tubes of bubbling water outlining the face.

The bartender was a fifty-something pug-faced Hispanic bantamweight with a thick Ricky Ricardo accent. I asked him if the jukebox was a genuine Wurlitzer.

He just shrugged as he rinsed glasses in the sink under the bar. "Hector bought it. He loves that thing."

"Who's Hector?" I asked.

"The boss. He owns this place."

"Did he get it from . . . ?" I nodded in the direction of Mordecai's warehouse. I wanted to give the impression that I was intimate with Mordecai's operation.

The bartender shrugged. "I guess so. Hector gets everything over there." He rolled his eyes toward the warehouse.

I sipped my beer and nodded. "Yeah, I heard they get good stuff sometimes. But not always."

The bartender raised his eyebrows and leaned in close. "You just tell them what you want," he whispered confidentially, "they'll get it for you." He was nodding with great consumer confidence.

"Yeah, I know a guy who did that once," I said, "but he didn't get what he wanted."

"What did he want?"

"Rolexes. Some special model, I don't know. Whatever it was, they didn't get it for him."

"I am very surprised," the bartender said. "They usually get you what you want."

"Yeah, that's what this friend of mine thought. But the people they sent out didn't get the right watches. He said they must've been the wrong people for the job."

"Yeah?"

"Yeah. He even knew a place where the watches he wanted were, but it was—you know—a hard place to get into."

"And the people they sent couldn't do it?"

I shrugged. "I guess not."

"Who'd they send? You know?"

I shook my head. "My friend said he wanted this family to do the job. A father and a daughter and a son, I think he said. He said they were supposed to be good."

The bartender nodded, again with great confidence. "They *are* good. I have heard of them, but I don't know their name."

I shrugged. "Me neither."

"You know who would know? Hector. You know Hector?"

I shook my head. "I just started working around here," I said.

"He's not around tonight," the bartender said. "But he's here most nights. He knows about that family. I will bet you."

I nodded and shrugged, acting as if it really didn't matter to me. One thing I didn't want was to sound too anxious. That would look suspicious. If this bartender mentioned to someone that I had been asking a lot of questions about the Kozlowskis, it could get back to them, and if they were as cautious as they seemed to be, they'd move on right away. Since I now had the name of someone who knew about them, I decided to leave things alone for the night.

I asked Job to go to the bar three nights later, hoping that he could strike up a conversation with Hector. Job made sure that the bartender I'd talked to didn't overhear his conversation with Hector. Too many people asking about the Kozlowskis could cause suspicion. Job got into a discussion with Hector and another patron about whether the Yankees should move out of the Bronx. It turned out Hector had a bit of a drinking problem, so it wasn't too hard to get him off one topic and onto another. In the course of conversation Job implied that he'd done a few break-ins in his time and was looking to start up again. Hector kept drinking steadily, and the more he drank, the more he talked. One topic led to another, and by the end of the night Job had gotten two solid pieces of information out of Hector: the Kozlowskis were currently fencing stolen goods through Mordecai, and they were living somewhere in Connecticut.

It would have been silly to run a trace on them with this little information because undoubtedly the Kozlowskis weren't using that name. But at least now I had a start. Over the next two weeks, I had several of the Seekers drive to Mordecai's at various times to photograph any cars with Connecticut license plates parked in the area. At the end of two weeks we had twenty-six Connecticut license numbers. I ran them all and came up with twenty-six names and addresses.

All the names were males, so I had to consider the possibility that one of these men was either Eugene the father or Shawn the son. Eugene was forty-nine and Shawn was twenty-eight, so I eliminated anyone over the age of fifty-five. I assumed that Eugene would probably lie about his age to get a new license, but he wouldn't make himself that much older than he really was. Besides names and addresses, I also had the heights, weights, hair color, and eye color of all the owners of those vehicles. Since I knew that Eugene and his son were both around six feet tall, I eliminated the seventeen men on the list who were under five-foot-ten. This left me with nine possibles. It was time to hit the road.

Going out alone, I started with the men who lived closest to home. The first one was in Stamford. He lived in a condo, which I watched for a day and a half. In that time I saw a middle-aged Black man go out in the morning and come back at the end of the day. Obviously this wasn't Eugene, so I moved on.

The next two were in the Norwalk area. One address was in a white middle-class neighborhood. As soon as I spotted a young white woman with two small children coming out of the house and piling into a minivan, I eliminated that one. The woman was too old to be Sandy and too young to be Sondra.

The other address was in a racially mixed blue-collar neighborhood of older attached homes. I watched this house for two days and saw absolutely nothing. No one went in or came out. I struck up a conversation with a neighbor who was out walking his dog. I told him that I used to live in the neighborhood and that I was brought up in the house I was checking out. The man told me that the Bedford family lived there now, but they were away visiting Mrs. Bedford's niece in Pennsylvania. I started to think that this could be the Kozlowskis until he mentioned that the Bedfords had no children of their own and that they treated this niece like a daughter. I moved on.

My next stop was the New Haven area. I had two addresses to check out there. The first one was a house in West Haven where, I quickly discovered, a Black family lived. The other address was in an average-looking suburban development where all the houses looked alike. It was the kind of place where I couldn't park and watch without being noticed. The house was modest-looking, with gray aluminum siding and white trim. There were no signs of anyone living there. Every time I drove by, the house seemed to be empty. It took me two whole days of drive-by surveillance before I finally spotted the man who lived there. He was just coming home, getting out of his car. I got a good look at him, and it definitely wasn't Eugene, so I kept on driving.

The sixth man on my list lived farther upstate in Waterbury in a green shingled house on a tree-lined street full of older homes—a nice neighborhood from the look of it. Most of the driveways were short and could accommodate only one car, so there were lots of cars parked out on the street, which was perfect for me. I parked my car halfway down the block and settled in with my zoom-lens camera. A man sitting in a parked car peering through a pair of binoculars looks too suspicious, so I prefer to use a camera with a long-range zoom lens. An added advantage over binoculars is that I can photograph my targets if necessary.

I was there less than two hours when a woman emerged from the house. She went out to the curb and brought in the garbage cans. I studied her face through the zoom lens. It was Sondra Kozlowski, I was convinced. She was a little heavier and had longer hair than she'd had in the photo I had of her, but it was definitely her. I was grinning as I held the camera to my face. I had finally found the nest.

But where were the rest of them? I didn't want to risk going in to make an arrest with only Sondra at home. Even though I did have a warrant for her arrest,compared with the charges that Eugene and the kids were facing, she was small potatoes. The charge against her was based on an outstanding parking ticket that the police had linked to a burglary. Their theory was that she had waited outside in the getaway car while the family did the job.

I decided to stick around a while longer to see if anyone else showed his or her face. Later that afternoon Sondra left the house and came back an hour and a half later with two grocery bags. This was curious. It didn't seem like enough food for a family of four, unless she was the type who went to the market more than once a week.

I sat in my car and watched the house until after midnight, and still there was no sign of the other Kozlowskis. I came back the next morning, and at around ten I spotted Shawn pulling up to the curb in a brown Nissan Maxima. When he got out of the car, he looked tired and disheveled, as if he'd been up all night. Maybe with a girlfriend, I thought. Or maybe doing a break-in. He went inside and didn't come out for the rest of the day. There was still no sign of Eugene or Sandy.

I had other work to attend to back in Jersey, so I left Waterbury that evening and came back a week later. Again I found a parking space about half a block away, and within two and a half hours I had spotted the mother, son, and daughter each separately going in or coming out of the house. But it still wasn't enough for me to attempt an arrest. I was determined to catch the *whole* family, including Eugene, so I decided to bide my time. It was two weeks before Christmas. People were out shopping like mad, and usually thieves are out stealing like mad, looking for the most portable high-ticket items they can find, mainly jewelry. I figured the Kozlowskis would be out doing their thing and thus hard to apprehend all together, but if I waited a little while, I might stand a better chance. I needed a time when people are typically at home, which usually keeps burglars away.

It was a no-brainer, really. I decided to come back on Christmas Day.

I returned to the Kozlowskis' neighborhood with Rock and Jedidiah just before dawn on Christmas morning. We let ourselves into the house, quickly checked to make sure no one else was staying over, then got down to business. We synchronized our actions and woke up the Kozlowskis simultaneously. Rock went to Shawn's room, Jedidiah took Sandy, and I took the parents. I don't know if visions of sugarplums were dancing in their heads, but these people certainly didn't expect their first sight on Christmas morn to be a masked face looming over the bed.

When I woke up the parents, Sondra screamed. Eugene sat up like a shot and couldn't stop fluttering his eyelids. He was so shook up he couldn't speak. Unfortunately, women never seem to have that problem.

"What the hell you doing in my bedroom?" Sondra shrieked. "Who are you? Get out, get out!"

"Sorry to disturb you," I said, "but we have to go someplace."

"What?!" The shrillness in her voice could've shattered glass. "What're you talking about?"

"Get out of bed, please."

"No! Get out!"

But Eugene, who'd gotten his blinking problem under control, was wearing a long sad face. He realized what was going on, and he looked up at me with a resigned expression. "Jersey?" he asked.

I nodded. "The whole family."

"Yeah, I know." He groaned, throwing back the covers and getting out of bed. He was wearing striped pajama bottoms and a T-shirt. His wife was wearing a long powder-blue nightshirt. She stopped shrieking as the weight of reality started to bear down on her. Her eyes were brimming.

I told the couple to put some clothes on and come with me. I didn't have my gun out, but my jacket was open, and they could see that it was there. In the meantime, Jedidiah had escorted a sobbing Sandy down to the living room in accordance with our prearranged plan. Rock, Jedidiah, and I had agreed to get the Kozlowskis out of bed and assemble them downstairs. Poor Shawn had made the mistake of trying to resist Rock. I heard the tussle through the bedroom wall. It was very short, sort of like a Ken doll taking on GI Joe—no contest.

I cuffed both Eugene and Sondra and led them downstairs. Sandy and Shawn were sitting on the couch, also cuffed, with Jedidiah and Rock standing over them. I told the parents to have a seat while I checked Sandy's cuffs to make sure they were on tight enough. She was a skinny little thing, and I wouldn't have been surprised if she'd added "escape artist" to her résumé.

Shawn was glowering at me, insisting on running his mouth, even with Rock's hand wrapped around the back of his neck. Sandy's face was streaked with tears. But it wasn't the fact that she was being arrested that upset her. It was the shock of being dragged out of her own bed by a large masked man.

I nodded toward the front door, and Jedidiah and Rock took the kids out to our car. When they were gone, I pulled out the handcuff keys and removed Sondra's cuffs.

Eugene furrowed his brow. "What're you doing?"

I ignored him and spoke directly to Sondra. "Your family is most likely going to prison," I said. "They're gonna need someone to come home to when they get out. If they don't have anyone, you won't have much of a family left. You understand what I'm saying?"

She just shook her head in confusion.

"I'm giving you a pass," I said. "I'll tell the bondsman I couldn't find you. The bond on you isn't that much anyway, so he'll just take the loss. But you be there for your family when they need you. Do you understand?"

She didn't say a word, but she didn't look as confused as she had before. I helped Eugene to his feet. "Time to go," I said.

He looked down at his wife, then looked me in the eye. "Thank you," he said quietly. "I appreciate it."

I just nodded and led him outside. We had to get going. There was another pickup I wanted to do in Connecticut before the day was out. I don't think Eugene fully comprehended my motivation for sparing his wife. Serving justice is one thing, but I could see what would happen to these people if they all went to prison. Following the letter of the law would not promote their evolution, and without the hope of evolution, in five years these people would be right back where they were now—stealing, fencing, and waiting for a predawn wake-up call from the bounty hunter who happened to catch their next warrant.

In my adult life, I've always tried to make time for meditation in one form or another, but as I furthered my study of ancient Egyptian philosophy, my method of meditation began to evolve and encompass more than achieving my own inner peace. In 1993 I set up a prayer table in my home, which I still use today.

It's a low bench somewhat like a coffee table with three short stools in front of it. The seats of the stools are covered in dark kente cloth. The table contains several articles that help me meditate: white candles, a Masai spear, seashells, an incense bowl, an Egyptian scarab encased in glass, a glass of water, and a small notebook. Burning candles and incense helps me focus. The spear symbolizes the warrior spirit. The glass of water represents the ocean, and the shells remind me that all life springs from the ocean. The scarab represents change. When I meditate, I stare at the candles and visualize what changes I'd like to see in myself, my family, my friends, and the world. I write down my thoughts on the pad.

My sons, who are now in elementary school, meditate with me at least once a week. Instead of exploring inner thought, which is what I do when I'm alone, we talk. We ask each other how our days went and if there's something we want to discuss. It's a quiet, respectful time, a time of communication and bonding. Part of our ritual is remembering our ancestors. The boys will ask me to tell them about relatives who have passed on, some of them people I've only heard about from my parents. I tell them everything I know about the particular ancestor we've chosen to discuss, and then we write down that person's name in the notebook. The boys enjoy seeing the list grow week after week. It's our way of passing on our heritage and keeping the ancestors alive in us. The last thing we do when we meditate is take the glass of water outside into the backyard. We recite the names of the ancestors we've talked about so far, adding the new one to our list, and after each name is said, we pour out a little of the water onto the grass and say *"Ashay,"* which means "respect."

It's a simple ceremony but a valuable one. It shows us where we came from and where we're going. It shows that we are not alone in the world, that we are part of a procession of souls leading back to the beginning of life. It makes us stronger and gives us hope.

In the fall of 1993, when my oldest son was just an infant, I was sitting at the prayer table meditating by myself when the telephone rang. I let the answering machine in the next room pick it up, but as soon as I heard the troubled voice on the other end I ran to get it. It was one of my aunts, and she was in tears.

"Gloria's car is gone," she said through her sobs. "Tyrone took it, and we can't find him."

No family is immune from trouble and heartbreak, mine included. I got my aunt to calm down enough to tell me that her son—my cousin Tyrone—had taken off with his sister Gloria's brand-new car, a metallic-blue Honda Prelude. Gloria had only had the car a couple of months, and Tyrone had been "borrowing" it without asking ever since she brought it home. But now he'd been gone for more than a week, and Gloria needed her car to get to work. My aunt asked me if I'd find him before he got into some real trouble.

I asked her what she meant by "real trouble."

She didn't say anything, but I could feel the worry and tension through the phone. "Tyrone used to be such a good boy," she finally said with deep regret in her voice. I had a feeling she was saying this to herself.

I was thirty-six at the time, and Tyrone is about ten years younger than I am. I hadn't seen much of him since he was in high school, but I knew that after he graduated, he'd started running with a bad crew. I'd just assumed he'd grown out of that. I asked my aunt to tell me what the real problem was, but she was having a hard time forming the words, as if saying it would make it even more real than it already was. I told her that if she wanted me to help, she couldn't hide the truth from me. Finally she told me. Tyrone was dealing drugs and getting high himself. She said he was in a downward spiral that was going to become a tailspin if something didn't change pretty soon. I agreed to go look for Tyrone and get the car back.

I knew a few members of the crew Tyrone used to run with, so I paid a visit to one of them, a young man named Dewayne who had provided me with some solid information in the past. Dewayne was not a hard-core member of the crew, and when I found him in front of his mother's house changing the oil in her car, I could see that he was teetering on the edge of change. He definitely had the potential to evolve, but he was having a hard time letting go of his old friends.

I asked him if he knew what Tyrone was up to, and he immediately pleaded ignorance. As he worked on the car, I kept pressing my case, and finally he broke down and told me something I could use. According to Dewayne, Tyrone had a serious girlfriend named Janiece Banks who lived in Irvington. If anybody knew where Tyrone was, it would be Janiece, he said.

I took a ride over to Irvington and found Janiece at her job. She worked behind the cash register at a small record shop that specialized in hip-hop music.

"I need to find my cousin Tyrone," I said to her, raising my voice over the thug music blasting through the speakers mounted on the wall. I was appealing to her as a concerned family member, not as a bounty hunter.

She just looked at me, giving me a large dose of ghetto attitude. It was a pose that went with the music. Janiece was tiny, and she almost disappeared in her baggy jeans and hooded sweatshirt, but she had the kind of pretty I-don't-need-you face that can stop a man cold.

I explained to her that Tyrone's sister was going to tell the police her car had been stolen if she didn't get it back soon. If that happened, and the police found him with the car, he'd be charged with grand theft auto.

"Ain't nobody gonna find Tyrone," she said with snide confidence.

"Really. I wouldn't bet on it."

"He ain't even in New Jersey. They won't find him."

"So where is he?" I asked.

She puckered her lips and shook her head.

“I’m not gonna turn him in,” I said. “I just want to talk to him.”

She shrugged.

“You want him to get arrested?” I asked. “If he goes to prison, he won’t be *your* honey no more. Tyrone’s got a nice face. Those old cons will be all over him.”

That broke her cool a bit. Her eyebrows twitched. She waited for me to say more, but I didn’t. I wanted that image to sink in—her man with another man.

She pouted. “Tyrone told me not to tell nobody where he is.”

“That’s not gonna help him.”

“I promised.”

“Then he’s gonna get arrested.”

“Not if his sister don’t call the po-lice on him.”

“She won’t listen,” I said. “Her head’s as hard as his.”

Janiece’s pout turned into a deep frown. I could tell she was thinking hard. After a minute she lifted her eyes and looked at me. “You say you just want to talk to him?”

“That’s all.”

“I’ll give you a phone number.” She wrote down a number on a scrap of paper. She knew it by heart.

I glanced at it and saw that it had a 202 area code. Washington, D.C.

“Is this his home phone?” I asked.

“No.” That’s all she said, and I decided not to press her. Not right then.

I thanked her for her help and left the store. When I got back to my car, I called Mr. Baines, my information analyst, and asked him to run the number. An hour later he called me back. The number belonged to a pay phone outside a Wawa convenience store on Massachusetts Avenue in the southeast section of Washington.

I decided not to bother calling Tyrone. Better to pay him a visit, I thought. I found a set of D.C. plates in my basement collection and put them on my Land Cruiser, and that afternoon I drove down there by myself. I didn’t want to bring any of the other Seekers with me. This was a family matter.

As soon as I got into town, I found the Wawa and checked it out from across the street. There were three pay phones in a row on the brick wall outside the store. No one was hanging out there, and Gloria's light metallic-blue Honda wasn't parked anywhere in the area. I pulled my vehicle into the Wawa's parking lot and backed into a space where I could watch the front of the store. Then I put on a hooded sweatshirt and went inside to buy a container of orange juice. The place was empty except for the clerk, a plump lady with a shock of short braids covering her head. She was wearing a purple T-shirt with HAVE A NICE DAY written across the front in spangles. I wondered if she knew Tyrone.

I went outside and scanned the pay phones as I pretended to be looking for change to make a call. The one on the far right matched the phone number Janiece had given me. I went back to my car, drank my orange juice, and watched the store. The sun was starting to set; it was almost six o'clock.

The sky gradually turned dark and the streetlights flickered on. Cars came and went, people running in for cigarettes, milk, newspapers, chips, sandwiches, whatever. I sat there for three hours, just watching, but by nine o'clock neither Tyrone nor his sister's light blue Honda had shown up. Of course, in the drug trade this was still early, so I settled in, prepared to wait all night if I had to. I sank low in my seat and put my head back, surveying the scene through half-closed eyes. I wasn't sleepy, but I wanted to rest up in case this turned into a long night.

More people came and went. Vehicles pulled in and pulled out—cars, pickups, vans, even a couple of Honda Preludes—but not the one I was looking for. At around ten-thirty, a group of young men gathered in front of the store. There were four of them, and they were all wearing baggy jeans and loose-fitting jackets. They appeared to be in their late teens, maybe early twenties, a little younger than Tyrone. They seemed to be waiting for someone. I watched them as they hovered around the pay phones, smoking and joking, intimidating some of the customers with their aggressive presence.

At twenty to eleven a light blue Honda Prelude pulled into the lot and parked alongside the building. No one got out, but the young men quickly gathered around the driver's side window. Thirty seconds later they skulked back to the car they'd come in and drove off. I didn't have to see the merchandise to know that it was a drug buy.

I was practically facing the Honda broadside, so I had to strain my eyes to make out the license plate number. I couldn't make out the whole number, but it was a tan plate with black lettering, the Jersey colors. It began GBF, same as my cousin Gloria's plate number. That was good enough for me, but unfortunately I couldn't see through the glare on the Honda's windows to be sure that the driver was Tyrone. I had to wait for him to come out to make a positive identification.

A dark green minivan drove into the lot and pulled up alongside the Honda, blocking my view. No one got out of the van, but I could see the driver very well. It was a young white girl—blond, college age. There were other kids in the van with her. Tyrone was making another sale.

This was going to go on all night if I didn't do something about it, and the longer Tyrone hung out here, the more likely it was the cops would bust him. After the van left, I took out my cell and dialed the number of the pay phone. I could hear it ringing outside my window. It was out of sync with the ring that was coming through the cell.

The driver of the Honda quickly got out and ran to the phone. As soon as he turned the corner and stepped into the bright lights in front of the Wawa, I saw his face clearly. It was Tyrone.

I got out of the Jeep, pocketed my cell, and pulled out my air taser. I pulled down the brim of my cap and walked briskly but didn't run.

Tyrone was at the pay phone. "Hello? Hello?" he kept repeating. I hadn't hung up on my end, so he wasn't hearing a dial tone. "Hello?" He slammed it back on the hook. "Motherfucker," he grumbled as he headed back toward his car.

I timed my steps so that we met at the corner of the building just as he was moving out of the bright lights. I took him by surprise, shoved him hard and kept shoving until he was up against his sister's car. He crashed onto the hood but quickly bounced back, reaching into his jacket pocket. "Take this, mother—"

It was then that he saw the air taser in my hand, already trained on his face. I could tell by his expression that he knew what it was, and it was less than three feet from his nose. Only an idiot or a fool would test his luck against a taser at this range. Initially Tyrone was angry and dumbfounded, but when he finally recognized me, his face suddenly changed. A con man's smile replaced the vengeful sneer.

"Joshua?" he said. "Josh, it's me. Tyrone."

I shook my head slowly. "No. This is not you." I was sitting on my anger.

"C'mon, man, we're cousins," he said. "How can you point that thing at your own blood? What's this all about?"

"It's about you turning yourself around."

"What? I don't know what you're talking about."

"Give me the gun," I said, holding my hand out.

"C'mon, Josh. Just tell me what's wrong. I'm not one of those criminals you have to hunt down."

I was losing my patience with his bullshit. "Give me the gun," I repeated.

"I don't have no gun, Josh."

But I was already on the move, grabbing his jacket, turning him around, and slamming him against the hood. With the prongs of the taser jammed into the soft spot behind his ear, I went into his pocket and took the gun myself. It was a chrome-plated .380 semi-automatic. I checked his other pocket and came up with a fistful of small glass vials with bright red plastic stoppers and white chunks inside. Crack. I dug through that pocket until I found them all. He had more than thirty of them.

"Josh, it ain't what you think—"

"It's *exactly* what I think," I said as I patted him down. In his front right-hand pants pocket, he had a wad of dollar bills folded in half. They seemed to be all twenties. When I counted them out later, it turned out to be almost $3,000.

I put the cash in my own pocket. "I'm giving this to your mother for all the trouble you caused her," I said.

"Hey, Josh, that ain't all mine."

"Shut up." I grabbed him by the collar and marched him over to a sewer drain at the edge of the parking lot. I dropped the crack vials onto the pavement, stomped on them, then kicked whatever was left into the sewer.

"Josh, no! You don't understand."

I ignored him and popped the clip on his .380. I emptied the bullets into the sewer, too, then dropped the clip and stomped on it until it was too misshapen to fit into the gun. I kicked it into the sewer, then tossed the gun in after it. A loud *plunk* echoed back up as the hunk of metal hit water.

"Aw, man," Tyrone complained, "I paid a lot for that."

I turned him around and marched him back to the Honda.

"What're you gonna do now?" he griped. "Handcuff me? Arrest me like those other people you pick up all the time?"

I slammed him into the passenger side of the Honda. "You are going to drive this car home tonight and give it back to your sister. And you are going to apologize to her and to your mom."

"Josh, I can't do that—"

"Don't say you can't. You can and you will. You are going to face up to this like a man. And don't try to run because I'll catch you, and then I *will* treat you like a criminal. Now get in the car."

Tyrone was nearly in tears. "But, Josh, you don't understand. There are things I got to do here."

"There's just one thing you have do. Drive this car back."

"OK, OK," he said, "just let me go inside and pee."

I shook my head. "Hold it until you get home."

"But—"

"Get in."

He could see that I wasn't fooling around. Perhaps I was a little harder on him than I might have been with a stranger, but I think he deserved it. He was family, and he should have known better. And I think my harsh treatment did some good. He drove his sister's car home that night with me following behind. He may have stopped to pee along the way—I don't know, I lost track of him somewhere in Delaware—but my aunt told me that the car was back in the driveway with the keys on the kitchen table in time for his sister to take it to work the next morning. Tyrone did the right thing, and I didn't have to stay on his tail the whole way for him to do it. When I finally got past my anger, I was proud of him.

I see him around the neighborhood from time to time, and he's holding down a job now. His mother and sister haven't complained to me about him, so I assume he's straightening himself out.

Almost everyone is capable of evolution. It's just that some people need guides to lead them, while others need guides to shove them from behind. I had men like Kanya McGee and Leo Osten to serve as my guides, and I was now learning that part of the process of my own evolution was to serve as a guide to others. In Tyrone's case, I like to think that I was his guide from behind.

15 You Can Run . . .

We've had cases in which time was of the essence and a fugitive had to be found fast. One case in particular sticks out in my mind: the Seekers were given just one weekend to track down and apprehend a fugitive.

This time, as in the Peter Hawkins bomb threat case, we were asked for assistance by the police. A nearby town had just built a new holding facility, which contained a jail that was supposed to be state-of-the-art—video surveillance system, computer-controlled electronic locks, spanking new cells with stainless-steel toilets, the whole deal. The building had been open for business for only a few weeks when I happened to be bringing in a fugitive one afternoon. The captain saw me coming in and asked me to stop by his office before I left. He said he wanted to discuss something with me.

In his office the captain told me that they'd been having some problems with the new facility. At the wake-up bed check that morning, a guard had discovered that one of the detainees was missing. The centrally controlled electronic locks had malfunctioned, and the prisoner had escaped.

The captain's tone turned grave. "Joshua," he said, lowering his chin, "I hate to say this, but we need your help."

I had known the captain for many years, but like most of the police brass I'd dealt with, he'd always been patronizingly dismissive about the Seekers' abilities. "Ground balls," he'd always say, referring to the kind of fugitive we captured. "You guys get the easy ones. I mean, how hard can it be to pick up a junkie?"

I let that comment pass. Every fugitive I'd ever picked up was potentially dangerous, and I think the captain knew that. But I didn't pick a fight with him because that's not my way. Besides, the police in this town were better than most in terms of giving us room to operate, and I didn't want a senseless argument to damage that relationship. I figured, let the man believe what he wants to believe.

But now that the captain was actually asking for my help, I was having a hard time not gloating. "So why's this guy so important?" I asked. "What is he, a serial killer?"

"No, no, no. Nothing like that," the captain said. "He's a runner for a dealer in town. His name's Nick Carpanza. We picked him up holding a brick of hash."

"Doesn't exactly sound like Al Capone."

"He could get there if he lives that long. A real nasty little shit."

"Why is he so important to you?" I asked.

The captain took a deep breath. "The new building is scheduled to be dedicated on Monday morning. It will be very embarrassing if this gets out. The taxpayers spent an awful lot of money for a jail that's supposed to be able to hold John Gotti, and this little punk Carpanza slips out without anybody seeing."

"You sound like you're the one who's gonna take the heat."

"I am," the captain said. "The chief's out of town till Monday. I've been in charge all week, so it happened on my watch. It would make me very happy if we could get Carpanza back before the dedication. If you know what I mean."

"Oh, I understand," I said. I could really have busted his balls at this point, but I didn't. He was already sweating it out, so there was no need.

"I can make you a copy of everything we have on Carpanza. Do you think you can find him before, say, seven o'clock Monday morning?"

"Most definitely," I said.

"Don't bullshit me, Joshua. This is serious."

"I'm always serious," I said. "The question is, are *you* serious?"

"What do you mean?"

Before I agreed to anything, we had to negotiate our fee. I calculated the probable amount of bail the court would have set for Carpanza's release if he had gone that route, took 10 percent of that, and doubled it for the rush order. "Plus expenses," I concluded.

The captain balked, his long, grim face turning grimmer. "I don't know if I can approve that much," he said. He let his words hang there, waiting for me to make a counteroffer.

"Well," I said, "good luck finding him. Nice talking to you." I started to get up.

"Hang on, hang on," he said. "Everything's negotiable. Let's talk."

"Not much to talk about," I said. "How much did that lockup cost you? A couple of million? I'm sure you can fix whatever's wrong with it, but what you'll never be able to fix is the public perception that it's a useless piece of crap if people find out that Nick Carpanza escaped. Am I right?"

"You're absolutely right. One hundred percent. But—"

"So when you think about it," I continued, cutting him off, "my fee is very modest compared to the damage this situation will cause if it's not rectified."

The captain was silent. He just stared at me.

"You don't agree?" I asked.

"You're right, you're right," he grumbled.

"So do you want me to take the case or not?"

He sighed in resignation. "Yes, I want you to take the case. Just make sure you get him back here before Monday morning. The earlier the better."

"We'll do our very best."

"No. Do better than that. Bring this kid in. Or else I don't want to see you or your crew in this town anymore."

Like all government workers, the captain was worried about his own ass first. He was protecting his job and his precious pension. But that was OK with me. It's a strange and wonderful world, and on occasion I'd seen good results come from inferior motives.

The captain had a copy of Nick Carpanza's file made for me. I looked it over, but it held no revelations. Nick was nineteen. He had a few arrests for drug possession, but never in enough quantity to earn him a stiff sentence, and one conviction the previous year for grand theft auto. He'd spent four months at a "boot camp" facility for youthful first offenders, which interested me more than his criminal record. He was six-foot-one, 187 pounds. If he was still fit from boot camp, he might give us a run for our money.

I stared at his mug shot. A sullen young man with a lot of attitude stared back at me from under heavy brows. I could just imagine what was going on inside his head. Chip on his shoulder, mad at the world. He thinks he's bad, but he wants to graduate to something bigger, something he's worthy of, like moving dope in weight or hiring kids to steal cars on order. Nick Carpanza wants to grow up to be somebody. Too bad all the somebodies who ever impressed him were gangsters.

I called Jedidiah right away and explained the situation. I decided that he and I would start the search on our own. We'd never had all seven Seekers working on the same case together, but if it came down to that, I'd call the others in as needed.

Jedidiah had his own contacts in this area, so I thought it best if he did some exploring on his own. I'd go the usual route, starting with a visit to Nick's last known address, which was his mother's apartment, working it from there. Jedidiah and I agreed to stay in touch via our cell phones.

Nick's mother's name was Anita Jackson. His Italian-American father had run off a long time ago, and his mother had since gotten remarried to a man named Jackson. Her apartment was in the projects, four identical ten-story brick buildings separated by bald little lawns marked off with chains on short metal posts. The report on Nick didn't say anything about him having any siblings. If his mother had small children, I figured she'd probably be home caring for them. If not, she was most likely out working.

I took the elevator up to the seventh floor. The interior of the elevator was stainless steel, dented from overuse, the shine dull from having graffiti scrubbed off it so many times. The seventh-floor hallway was empty, but I could hear music playing behind walls, and a variety of cooking smells seeped out from under the doorways. I knocked on the door to apartment 7C, unsnapping the security strap on my holster just in case Nick was in there. He had no history of violent behavior, but that didn't mean anything. He was young, he'd been through the system, and he was on the run. A man in his situation will take desperate measures to protect his tenuous hold on freedom.

The door opened as far as the chain would allow, but at first I didn't seen anyone there. Then I looked down. A little girl no more than ten years old was staring up at me. She had the kind of innocent eyes that could peer right through to your soul. She was wearing pink sweatpants and a red sweatshirt.

I peeked into the apartment, but all I could see was a wall. "Is your momma home?" I asked the little girl.

She shook her head.

I thought about asking if her brother Nick was home but instantly rejected that approach. If he was in there, I didn't want to get into it with his little sister present. Not only could she get hurt, it wouldn't be healthy for her to see her brother getting arrested.

"Where's your momma? At work?"

But the little girl disappeared. A second later another child appeared in the gap in the door, this one a little older. "I'm looking for your momma," I said to her. "Can you tell me where I can find her?"

This girl was bolder than her sister. "Momma said not to answer the door to strangers."

"Your momma's absolutely right," I said. It was almost four o'clock in the afternoon. I assumed they'd just gotten home from school and usually took care of themselves until their mother got off work. "If your momma's not home, I'm not going to disturb you. But I do have something important I have to talk to her about. If you just tell me where she works, I'll go talk to her there."

The girl narrowed her eyes and gave me a suspicious look. "Burger King," she said defiantly.

"Which Burger King?" I asked. I knew of at least three within a few miles of there.

"The one on the corner," she said as if I were an idiot. She nodded toward it with her head as if she could see it through the walls. I assumed that meant the closest Burger King, the one two blocks away.

"Thank you very much," I said.

She watched me through the crack as I headed back down the hallway toward the elevators.

When I arrived at the Burger King, I parked in the back and watched for a while. I knew that if I went in and asked to talk to Nick's mother, I probably wouldn't get what I wanted. For one thing, it might get her in trouble with her boss. Fast-food places run like assembly lines, and one worker taking an unscheduled break could upset the whole operation. She'd never open up to me if I put her job in jeopardy.

There was another reason I didn't want to confront her inside. If I asked her about things she didn't want to hear with an audience eavesdropping, she'd surely get defensive. Logically, what person in the world would discuss her child's problems with the law in front of her boss and coworkers?

To get what I wanted, I had to talk to her alone, but I had no idea when her shift had started, and I didn't have a lot of time to spare. My hope was that she'd come out for a break in the lull just before the dinner rush. At a quarter of five, two Black women came out the back door and immediately lit up cigarettes. They were both wearing Burger King uniforms, both in their late thirties, I guessed.

I got out of my car and walked toward them. Neither one paid much attention to me, assuming that I was a customer on my way inside.

"Excuse me," I said to them. "I'm looking for Anita Jackson."

They both went silent. One stared at me with attitude; the other looked away. But they didn't have to say a thing. The one staring me down had the same soulful eyes as the little girl back at the apartment.

"Anita?" I said to her. "I have to talk to you."

"About what?" she said. "Who are you?"

I looked at the other woman. "In private would be best," I said. "It's about your son."

But the other woman was already wandering away.

Anita Jackson's brows were furrowed. She was indignant. "What son you talking about?" she snapped. "Who are you?"

I told her who I was and what I did, and that raised her temperature from simmer to boil. "You leave my boy alone," she screamed. "You hear me?"

I cut her off before she got hysterical. "Nick is in big trouble," I said firmly. "He escaped from jail, and the cops are out looking for him. They're mad. If they find him, they may hurt him. If I find him, I won't hurt him. I'll just bring him back."

Anita was struggling to focus her anger on me, but tears were spilling out of her big eyes. She knew I was making sense, but she just wanted all of this to go away. The situation was beyond denial, however, and it was my job to make her face reality. As I had learned in the Hawkins case, cops do not like being messed with. In their minds Nick Carpanza had humiliated them, and it wouldn't be unheard of if they treated themselves to some "street justice" while they were bringing him in. It's amazing how many people have "accidents" that involve head trauma and ruptured organs when they're put under arrest.

"Help me find your son before they do," I said gently. "I promise you I won't hurt him. And once he's back in jail, they won't either." I explained that the jail was new and the building was going to be dedicated on Monday. There would be too many outsiders in the building for the cops to try anything with Nick. They wouldn't want visiting dignitaries and reporters to see someone in their lockup who had obviously been beaten. But I gave Anita the name of a good bail bondsman and strongly suggested that she make bail for Nick as soon as he was arraigned. There was no telling what might happen *after* the dedication.

Anita was understandably torn. I was a total stranger to her—why should she listen to me? But what I was saying made sense to her. She knew that Nick could suffer a terrible beating from the police; it seemed that no week went by without a story in the paper about a suspect dying in police custody under questionable circumstances.

She avoided looking me in the eye, but I just waited until she did. "Help me find him," I urged. "It's the only good option he has right now."

Anita covered her mouth and looked at the ground, still trying to sort this all out in her mind. I bent my knees and moved into her line of vision. It was important that she look me in the eye. I wanted her to trust me.

Finally she let out a long pitiful sigh that rattled her chest and made her shiver. "He has a cousin in Newark—his name is Jerome Cook, but his friends call him Forty. He and a bunch of other boys have a place on Pennington Street. Nick hangs out with him a lot."

I asked her if she knew the street number or Forty's phone number, but she said she didn't. Nick never told her much about his friends or his activities on the street. I thanked her for her help and asked for a phone number where I could reach her so I could keep her informed. She gave me her home and work numbers.

As I walked back to my car, I pulled out my cell phone and called directory assistance. "For Newark," I said. "Do you have a number for Jerome Cook on Pennington Street?"

"Please hold for that number," the operator said. A recording gave me the phone number.

I thought about dialing it and using some ruse to get the address then decided not to. With so little time to find Nick, I didn't want to disturb the nest in case he was there. An odd phone call might get him nervous, and he'd probably take off, which would make our job even harder. Instead, I decided to use Mr. Baines. He could get the address through his contacts with the phone company.

It was after five. Mr. Baines doesn't keep nine-to-five hours, but it was Friday, and there was a chance he might not be there. I dialed his number and got his voice mail. I left a message and told him that I needed the address that went with Jerome Cook's phone number. I said this was a rush so a prompt reply would be greatly appreciated.

I then called Jedidiah to find out what he was up to. "How's it going?" I asked.

"Nick's got a girlfriend," he said. "She's having his baby."

"Really. You talk to her yet?"

"I'm trying to find her," he said. "Her name's Tina, but no one wants to give up her last name."

Finding this Tina could be a bull's-eye or just a big waste of time, depending on what Nick was like. If he didn't give a damn about her or their child, Tina probably wouldn't know anything about where he was. But if he did care about Tina, he'd most likely be in contact with her. Nick's mother seemed like a decent woman, and he had two younger sisters. My hope was that he had a little more respect for women than the average nineteen-year-old in his situation. If Jedidiah could find Tina, she just might know where Nick was. Whether she would tell us before Monday morning was another story, but we'd deal with that when and if the time came.

I headed home to have dinner. It was too early to check out the scene on Pennington Street—I wanted to wait until after dark for that—and since I would probably be gone for the entire weekend, I wanted to spend some time with my family. My job sometimes takes me away from home for weeks on end, but I always make time for them. It's important for my sons to know that their father is there for them. I could only assume that Nick's father hadn't been there for him when he was growing up.

At about nine o'clock I headed back out to continue the search. I hadn't heard back from Mr. Baines, so all I could do was cruise up and down Pennington Street, keeping my eyes open and hoping I might spot something. One section of Pennington Street is a known drug haven. The apartment buildings on the adjoining blocks contain a mix of working poor families and individuals caught up in the maniacal drug cycle—dealing, stealing, and using.

I double-parked at the end of the busiest block of Pennington Street and took in the scene. There was a lot of activity. Cars were constantly coming down the block and stopping at different addresses. Street dealers came out from behind the stoops, and deals were made through open passenger windows. Coke, smack, pot, whatever you needed. The street was dark because the streetlights had been shot out so many times, the city didn't bother to repair them anymore. The dealers preferred the darkest parts of the block where the only source of light was the headlights. For the most part I could see only silhouettes and fleeting glimpses of faces. For all I knew I was looking right at Forty. Or even Nick if he was stupid enough to show his face.

I took out my monocular night-vision scope and slowly scanned the street looking for someone who could be Nick, based on the photo and description I had. Unfortunately, there were too many young men out there who fit Nick's description, and if I went out and started questioning them one by one, they'd scatter like cockroaches, thinking I was a cop. A few might even try to take me on, even if they did think I was a cop. It was Friday night and business was brisk. Like all good salesmen, they'd fight to protect their territory.

I kept wishing my cell phone would ring. I wanted that address from Mr. Baines. If chasing down Forty was a dead end, I wanted to find out sooner rather than later.

As I surveyed the block, I noticed that there was a liquor store on the corner across the intersection. Unless I was very wrong, Forty's nickname must've referred to his taste for malt liquor, brands like Colt 45 and Olde English, which came in forty-ounce bottles. I decided to go over and see if he was a regular customer.

The store was called Brookside Liquors, and the interior was typical of places that stayed open late in bad neighborhoods. When you walked in, there were no wares that a customer could actually handle. Everything was behind a wall of counter-to-ceiling bulletproof Plexiglas. A man on the other side worked the window. You told him what you wanted, passed your money through a slot, and he sent your order and your change through a drawer in the counter.

I walked up to the window and leaned into the perforated holes in the Plexiglas. "You seen Forty?" I said. "He said he'd be here."

"Forty? What brand?" the man said.

"No, I don't want a forty. I'm looking for a brother named Forty. You know who I'm talking about?"

"What brand forty?" The man was frowning at me. He was a squat middle-aged Black man, but his English was minimal. From the look of him, he might have been African. Nigerian maybe.

A customer came in, and the man suddenly became very agitated. "What brand forty? What brand?" he demanded. "I have other customer."

Understandably he didn't want a lot of people congregating inside the store. That could mean trouble, and he didn't want any.

"You don't understand," I said, speaking slowly. "I'm looking for a brother *named* Forty. Do you know him?"

The clerk scowled at me and waved me away from the window. "Get out. Please get out," he said. He wanted me to disappear.

I was about to plead my case once more when the customer who'd just come in came up behind me.

"You buy me one, and I'll take you to Forty."

I turned around and faced a man in a tattered green parka. He didn't exactly look like a homeless person, but he was well on his way. His hair was OK, but he hadn't shaved in a while. His smell wasn't repulsive, but it was definitely funky. He flashed a toothy smile at me, worked his eyebrows up and down, and gave me a look like a dog begging at the table.

"You know Forty?" I asked.

"I certainly do," he said.

"You know where I can find him?"

"I certainly do."

I waited for him to say something more, but he just looked at me. "You planning on telling me where Forty is?"

"I certainly am." He rolled his eyes toward the big cooler behind the Plexiglas.

I turned to the cashier. "Let me have a bottle of Colt." I pulled out a five-dollar bill and slipped it into the slot. The cashier sent the malt liquor and my change through the drawer.

I showed my new friend the bottle, but I didn't give it to him. He was practically drooling for it.

"What's your name?" I asked.

"Ernest."

"Ernest what?"

"Ernest Hoyt."

"So where am I gonna find Forty, Ernest?"

"East Orange. At a house party."

"Tonight?"

"That's right."

"You jiving me, Ernest?"

"I certainly am not."

"What's the address?"

"I do not know."

"What part of East Orange?"

"Near that college over there?"

"Upsala College?"

"Yes, sir. That's the one."

"Who's throwing this house party?"

"Girl named Bunny. Bunny Williams."

"How come you're not there?"

Ernest frowned. "Ain't got no car. And it costs money to get in."

"I see." I handed him the bottle of Colt 45. He took it gratefully. He was going to have his own party all by himself.

I went back to my car and headed for East Orange, a city that borders on Newark. It took me about twenty minutes to get to the mostly empty campus of Upsala College, which had gone bankrupt the previous year. The area around the college was a mix of big old homes and redbrick apartment buildings that had been quite exclusive when I was a kid but had since succumbed to creeping urban blight. The Garden State Parkway was just a few blocks away, and the neighborhood on the other side of the parkway was more crowded, the streets lined with two-family wood-frame houses separated by no more than three or four feet. I started cruising the streets, looking for signs of a raucous house party. I didn't bother checking the phone book for a Bunny Williams. It was a good bet that she didn't have her phone listed under the name Bunny, and the book had pages and pages of people named Williams. Without her real name, Mr. Baines wouldn't be able to do much for me either.

After going up and down streets for more than an hour, I finally located a three-story brick apartment building where lots of young people were coming and going, a good number of them clearly intoxicated. Cars were double-parked all down the block. I found a space for my car three blocks away and walked back to the building, following the crowd up to the second floor, where a very large young man was stationed at the door. He was wearing khaki pants and a black polo shirt and holding a fistful of dollar bills.

I noticed that the couple in front of me paid twenty dollars apiece to get in, so I had a twenty ready as I came up to the big man. "Forty get here yet?" I asked.

He looked at me suspiciously and didn't take my money.

"Bunny said he was gonna be here." I started to put my money away, but the big man reached out for it and added it to his roll.

"Don't know nothing about no Forty," he said. "You can go ask Bunny yourself."

I stepped inside where the music was blaring, the thump of the bass line rattling the bottles and plastic cups that had been set down on the table in the hallway. The place was packed with people, most of them in their twenties. Some were dancing, but most were just milling around.

I checked out all the rooms before I talked to anyone. A plastic garbage can full of ice and beer stood in the middle of the kitchen. The counters were jammed with bags of chips and pizza boxes.

In one of the bedrooms, young people were smoking blunts, cigar-size marijuana joints. A woman in bell-bottom jeans and a skimpy halter top was sitting on the bureau, talking loud and ruling the roost. I wondered if this was Bunny.

The second bedroom was pretty dark, and there were a lot of bodies writhing on the bed and on the floor. I hoped Forty wasn't one of them. If he was, I'd have to wait around for the orgy to break up, which could take hours.

I went into the kitchen and helped myself to a beer. I pretended to peruse the junk food while I checked out the faces. Nick Carpanza could very well be here. This was his crowd, so he'd feel comfortable here.

A hefty young woman in an ankle-length skirt and ridiculously high platform shoes was picking at a piece of chocolate cake on a paper plate, tearing off chunks with her long copper-colored fingernails.

I smiled at her and got her attention before I said anything. She smiled back as she chewed. I went over to her and said hello. She just giggled.

"You know Forty?" I asked her.

"Who?"

"Forty Cook." Since I had no idea what Forty looked like, I could only hope that he wasn't standing right next to me.

"Yeah, I know him," the woman said. She wasn't smiling so much now that she knew it wasn't her I was interested in.

"You seen him tonight?"

She shook her head. "He's supposed to be coming by later with some weed."

"Yeah, I know," I said. She had just presented me with my cover story: I was here to buy some weed from Forty. Ernest had sent me. "Damn," I said. "Forty told me he was gonna be here by now."

"A friend of his got into some kind of trouble with the police. I heard Forty's helping him out."

"You mean Nick?" I said.

She just shrugged. "I don't know who he is."

"I hope Forty comes soon." I grumbled for effect and wandered away. I drifted through the apartment one more time, then left. There was no sense sticking around. If Forty showed up with Nick, I'd never be able to take him with all their homeboys hanging around. And with all that party noise, the cops were bound to come by sooner or later, and I didn't want to be on the premises with all that smoking in the bedroom. I decided to watch from outside instead. I went back to my car and drove around the block, circling back to Bunny's apartment building. Without too much trouble I was able to find a parking space with a good view of the front door. Fortunately, the entrance was well lit, so I could get a pretty good look at the faces coming and going.

I sat in my car and watched from around 10 P.M. until 2 A.M. A lot more people showed up in that time, and the party got even wilder. I hadn't seen anyone who looked like Nick going in, so I went back inside and made another stab at finding Forty. The big man who'd been working the door was gone. The music was deafening now, and everyone was high. The ones who weren't mellow on weed were just plain drunk. I picked out a few people who looked somewhat coherent and discreetly asked about Forty. I found two guys sharing a bottle of wine who knew him, but they swore he hadn't been there that night.

I went back to my car and decided to watch a little while longer since new people were still arriving. By four o'clock things had died down considerably, and there was still no sign of Nick. I could just imagine what it looked like up in that apartment—a battlefield after the battle with people passed out everywhere. I tilted my seat back and decided to get some rest myself. I had a feeling I was going to need it.

16 . . . But You Can't Hide

I was fast asleep when vibrations in my chest suddenly woke me up. The sun was up, and my windows were fogged over. I reached into my pocket and pulled out my cell phone. I glanced at my wristwatch as I answered it. It was almost six-thirty.

"Yeah," I said into the phone.

"Good morning." I immediately recognized Mr. Baines's voice.

"How're you feeling?" I asked, rubbing my eyes.

"Fine," he said. "I got something for you."

"Good, good." Hearing that perked me right up. "Tell me."

"I traced that phone number you gave me. The address is 1567 Broad Street, apartment four. It's registered under the name Jerome Cook."

I jotted down the address on a scrap of paper. "Beautiful," I said.

"You need anything else?" he asked.

"Not right now, but maybe later today."

"I'll be here if you need me."

"Great," I said. "Peace."

"You, too," he said, then hung up.

I started up the car and headed back to Newark. I was pretty sure this address was right around the corner from Pennington Street where

I'd been last night. Nick's mother was right about the area; she just didn't know the exact address—unless she'd been holding out on me.

But that didn't matter now. If I hurried, I'd still have time to catch Forty off guard. As I drove down Central Avenue, I thought about how I should approach him. If he was helping Nick hide out, I had a feeling he wasn't going to listen to reason. To him I was no better than a cop, so it would be useless to plead my case to him the way I had with Nick's mother. But if Nick was with him in his apartment, there wouldn't be much opportunity for discussion. They'd either run or fight, which meant no time for talk.

By the time I got to Forty's building, I'd decided that the direct approach would be a big mistake. True, the clock was ticking on this assignment, but that was no reason to start getting stupid. It was almost 7 A.M., too late to take anyone by surprise. I parked the car in the alley behind the building and reached for my zoom-lens camera under the seat.

Fifteen sixty-seven Broad Street was a beautiful three-story brownstone, but like all the others in this neighborhood, it was in need of some serious repairs. It was the kind of building that usually had only one apartment per floor. Cook's apartment was number 4, which would be the top floor if the basement apartment was number 1. I hung the camera around my neck and climbed onto the roof of my Land Cruiser, which gave me a leg up onto the flat roof of the garages that lined the alley. I crossed the roof and went over to a splintered timber telephone pole that was set behind one of the garages. I pulled on a pair of leather gloves and climbed the pole until I was about as high as the top floor of Cook's building. Using the camera, I scanned the apartment windows.

There were three windows on each floor, two large ones and a smaller one in the middle. A curtain was drawn across the small window, which I assumed was the bathroom. The shade was up in the room on the right. I could see the lower half of a double bed. The sheets were messed, but no one was in the bed. The window on the left had no shades or curtains. It was the kitchen. Someone was sitting at the table.

I adjusted the focus and saw that it was a young woman. She was wearing a blue plaid flannel shirt that was way too big for her, staring into space as she sipped from a yellow mug.

Who was she? I wondered. Forty's woman? It looked like she'd spent the night alone unless Forty was in the bathroom or somewhere else in the apartment. I studied her face, looking for an emotion that might give me a clue to who she was and what she was doing there. I was hoping she'd look worried or jittery, a possible indication that she was in there with a wanted man, but her face was blank, caught in that unmotivated state before the caffeine kicks in.

Suddenly I felt my cell phone vibrating again. I put down the camera and pulled out the cell. "Yeah?"

"It's me—Jed." Jedidiah.

"How you feeling?" I said. "You got something?"

"I'm in Plainfield," he said. "I found Tina's big sister, Georgette. She's at her apartment here with some guy named Jerome Cook—"

"Forty!"

"What?"

"Jerome Cook's street name is Forty. I'm at his place in Newark, looking at his woman right now. Must be a real player, this Forty."

"Ain't much to look at. I've seen him."

"Maybe he's *got* forty," I said. "He spend the night with Georgette?"

"Looks that way," Jedidiah said. "You want me to go in and talk to him?"

"Wait till I get there. If he leaves, follow him. He's tight with Nick, and he might be helping him."

Jedidiah gave me the address where Forty and Georgette were. "I'll call you if anything happens."

"Twenty minutes," I said.

I climbed down the pole, got back into my car, and headed for Plainfield. As I drove I reached into a paper bag on the floor in the backseat, found a PowerBar and a banana, and had breakfast.

I found the address Jedidiah had given me and spotted his car right away. He was parked across the street, sitting behind the wheel, slouched down with his head against the headrest. He looked as if he was sleeping, but I knew he wasn't. Jedidiah is rock solid. In all the years I've known him, he has never fallen down on the job.

I pulled up next to his car and caught his eye. We didn't bother rolling down our windows. I pointed at the apartment building with my eyes. Jedidiah nodded. He understood what I wanted.

As I was parking my car, Jedidiah got out of his and took care of the building's front door, unlocking it with a strip of plastic. He led the way up to Georgette's apartment, which was on the second floor. We listened at the door for a few minutes. We heard music but no voices. I assumed that Forty and Georgette were still in bed, but I don't like to make assumptions. That's a good way to get your head blown off.

I nodded toward the wall beside the door and looked at Jedidiah's waist where he kept his gun. He knew what I wanted him to do: hug the wall and have his gun ready. Forty was a dealer, so he probably carried a weapon.

I knocked on the door.

No answer.

I knocked harder.

This time I heard footsteps shuffling toward the door. "What do you want?" a sleepy woman's voice asked.

"Georgette?" I said. "I have to talk to you."

"Who are you?" She sounded annoyed.

There was a peephole in the door, so she could see that I was a stranger. "It's about your sister Tina. It's important."

"Huh? What about my sis—"

Another voice suddenly butted in, gruff and belligerent. "Who the fuck're you? What do you want?" This had to be Forty.

"Tina's in trouble," I said. "I need to talk to Georgette."

The dead bolt clacked, and the door swung open. My eyes immediately went to the man's hands, then to the woman's, to see if they were holding anything. They weren't, but the man was wearing baggy jeans and no shirt. He could easily have a small-caliber pistol in his pocket.

"I said what do you want?" Forty was all set to get in my face, but his glance was suddenly diverted when he noticed Jedidiah standing next to me. Jedidiah has the kind of demeanor that flattens attitude very quickly. He was holding his gun behind his leg.

Forty made a sour face. "Man, what is this? I didn't do nothing."

Georgette was clutching her bathrobe. "He's been with me all night. I swear."

They assumed that we were cops. The alibis came pouring out before anyone made an accusation, which was typical. I didn't confirm or correct their assumption.

"I'm not looking for *you,*" I said to Forty. I shifted my gaze to Georgette. "I need to find Tina."

"What for?" Forty demanded.

I ignored him and concentrated on Georgette. I had a feeling she was going to tell me more than he ever would. Jedidiah could deal with him.

"Can we come in?" I asked her.

Forty said no, but she nodded and waved us into the kitchen. There were full plates on the table—scrambled eggs, bacon, and coffee. We had interrupted their morning-after breakfast. I wondered how much Forty's other woman had enjoyed her breakfast back in Newark.

Georgette sat down at her place and offered us seats. I took one, then Forty reluctantly took his. Jedidiah preferred to stand. Georgette was a pretty woman with high cheekbones and almond-shaped eyes. Forty was scrawny and shifty-looking with a mess of short dreads on top of his head.

"I'm not gonna bullshit either of you," I said, maintaining eye contact with Georgette. "I need to find Nick, and if Tina's hiding him, or even if she just knows where he is, then she's gonna be in trouble with the law." I explained who I was and why it would be better for me to find Nick than the police.

"Don't tell this man nothing," Forty said. He was adamant, bouncing up and down in his seat. I had hoped he'd gotten the message—*anyone* hiding Nick would be in trouble, including him. But he wasn't picking up on that.

Georgette looked distressed, but she followed his advice and clammed up.

I turned in my seat and looked Forty in the eye. "Aiding and abetting. You know what that means? That's what the cops are gonna get all of you on. You, Georgette, and maybe even Tina—"

"But Tina's just a kid," Georgette blurted out. She was on the verge of tears, but a hard glance from Forty shut her up.

"The cops are very pissed off," I said. "Nick made them look like fools. The longer he stays in the wind, the worse it's gonna get for everybody. They're gonna be looking for blood."

But Forty was a hard-ass dude. He slouched in his chair, crossed his arms, and looked away. He was *not* going to cooperate.

"Well, go on and finish eating," I said, "'cause we're not leaving." I crossed my arms the same way.

"What're you talking about?" Forty snarled. "I'll call the cops."

"Do it," I said. "And I'll tell 'em how tight you are with Nick."

He scowled at me, but he didn't have an answer for that.

"Baby," Georgette said to him, "maybe we should—"

"No," he snapped. "Maybe we should do nothing."

"Fine with us," I said. "We'll do nothing with you."

And that's just what we did, nothing. We just sat in that kitchen and stared at each other from breakfast till lunchtime. But the way I figured, leaning on these two was worth our time. Even if they didn't know exactly where Nick was, they both had knowledge that could lead us to him. Better to hammer the walnuts I had now than to go out looking for some that might not taste any better.

Periodically Forty would sneer at us, but we just let him have his way. Georgette eventually took a shower, and they both got dressed. Forty threatened to leave, and I told him that was fine but one of us would follow him. He huffed and puffed and stormed around the apartment, but he didn't leave.

I deliberately didn't look at my watch the whole time, but there was a clock on the kitchen wall. At one o'clock I mentally calculated the time we had left to find Nick. We had to get him back to the jail before seven on Monday morning. Any later than that and anyone could see us bringing him in. That gave us thirty-one hours to find him.

"I have to go see my momma," Georgette suddenly announced. She'd been sitting at the kitchen table flipping through a magazine. "Momma's expecting me."

"Perfect," I said. "I want to meet your momma. Maybe she'll tell me where Tina is."

"No!" she screamed. "You can't ask her that." Tears suddenly sprang from Georgette's eyes.

"Why can't I ask her that?" I said.

"Momma don't like Nick. She *hates* him. She gets all upset when anybody just says his name."

"Why?"

"Because she don't like him."

"Why? What'd he do to Tina?"

"Nothing." Georgette wouldn't look at me, and Forty was making bug eyes at her from across the table.

"What did Nick do to Tina?" I persisted. "Is it because he got her pregnant?"

Georgette fell apart then. She was like a smashed fish tank, tears and wails gushing all over the place. I'd obviously hit a nerve.

Forty was holding his forehead, cursing under his breath.

Jedidiah spoke up, softly but firmly. "I know where your mother lives, Georgette. You want us to go see her?"

Georgette tried to say no, but she was blubbering so hard she could only shake her head.

"Hey, man, listen to me," Forty said, dropping the hard-guy routine and suddenly sounding reasonable. "If their mother finds out, she's gonna make Tina get an abortion, and Tina don't want to do that. She wants the baby. Nick, man, he's messed up, but he loves her. He just wants to do the right thing."

"He should've thought about that when he got her pregnant," I said.

"Yeah, man, but you don't understand—"

I raised my finger and interrupted him. "Here's what you and Georgette don't understand. If Tina's hiding Nick, or if a cop just asks her where he is and she lies, she can be charged with a crime. Now it would be a real shame if she had to have that baby in prison."

A pitiful wail burst out of Georgette. "Nooooo! That can't happen. Not to my little sister."

I took her hand. "Then help us find Nick. Tell me where I can find Tina."

"Don't tell him," Forty warned.

But Georgette was waving him off. "She's staying with some girlfriends in Union. You promise not to hurt her?"

"Georgette!" Forty said, raising his voice.

"We will not hurt your sister," I said to Georgette. "You have my word on that."

Georgette picked up a ballpoint pen that was lying on the table and wrote down an address on the corner of a magazine. Forty tried to stop her, but Jedidiah grabbed him by the shoulder and sat him back down. Georgette ripped off the address and handed it to me.

"Don't hurt my sister," she repeated. "Please!"

"Don't worry," I assured her. I turned to Jedidiah. "Stay with Forty till you hear from me. We don't want him warning Nick."

Jedidiah nodded.

Forty protested, but even he knew he was just making noise. He and Jedidiah were going to be buddies for at least the rest of the day.

I left the happy trio and drove to the address in Union that Georgette had given me. It was a two-family house. Tina's girlfriends lived on the second floor. I rang the doorbell, but I didn't have a lot of hope that Tina would still be there. It was Saturday afternoon. She was probably out, maybe with Nick. No one answered the door, so I rang the bell again.

I peered through the small window in the door. It was covered by a sheer curtain, but I could make out a figure coming down the stairs, a woman in dark blue warm-up pants and a big denim overshirt. She peeled back the curtain and looked at me for a long time, sizing me up. She seemed to be about seventeen, maybe younger. Very pretty, with almond-shaped eyes just like Georgette's.

"Tina?" I said, risking that it was her. "I need to talk to you."

She didn't answer. She just stared at me.

I explained who I was through the door and gave her all the reasons she should help me find Nick before the police did. "Your baby's gonna need a father," I told her. "If Nick goes back and he's convicted, he'll be out in three years max. If he stays on the run, he's gonna get himself into a lot more trouble. You know that. He'll get himself killed on the street, or he'll end up in prison for a long, long stretch. Either way he won't ever be with you and the baby."

She just stared at me.

"Are you hungry, Tina? Let me buy you a decent meal. For the baby." I told her I'd already talked to Georgette, and I promised not to hurt her.

But Tina didn't budge. Those almond eyes didn't blink.

I had only one card left. "If you won't talk to me, I'm gonna have to go talk to your mother, see what she knows about Nick. I'm gonna have to tell her about—"

Before I could finish, she unlocked the dead bolt and opened the door. "Don't tell my mother." She said it flatly, not pleading, not threatening. "Momma's sick. Her heart can't take it."

"She's got a heart condition?"

Tina nodded, her eyes still boring into me.

"Will you help me?" I asked. "If you do, I won't have to bother your mother."

She turned and headed up the stairs. I followed her up to an apartment. The front room was the living room. Blankets and a pillow were in a tangle on the couch. This must be where Tina slept last night. Maybe with Nick. She plopped down on one end of the couch and clutched the pillow to her stomach as if she was practicing having a pregnant belly.

"How do you know it'll just be three years?" she asked in a sullen mumble.

"I know about things like that. If he hasn't done anything else wrong and he behaves in prison, it'll be about three years more or less."

"So how old will my baby be when he gets out?"

"How many months pregnant are you?"

She shrugged. "I just found out."

I assumed three months, then figured it would take a few months for Nick's case to come to trial. "About two and half," I said.

"Babies don't remember stuff when they're that young, do they?"

I shook my head. "What's the first thing you remember?"

"Kindergarten."

"There you go."

"So my baby won't know her daddy was in prison."

"Not unless you tell her."

Tina just shook her head. She wanted to have a normal family. I wondered if perhaps she wanted to improve on her own family situation. She sat there staring at the floor, doing some hard thinking. I gave her all the time she needed. There was nothing I could say that would sway her. She had to come around on her own. I took a seat and waited.

After a long while she came out of her trance. "Three years, you said."

I nodded. "Could be more, could be less. But the longer he stays out there, the worse it's gonna be. For him, for you, and for the baby."

She stared down at the carpet again as she processed this bit of information. "If he goes to prison, can he get into some kind of program?" she asked.

"What kind of program?"

"Rehab."

"Is he an addict?"

"No."

"Then why does he need rehab?"

"He likes to get high. Not all the time, but whenever he's with Forty they always do something. If he got away from Forty and got into a program, maybe he wouldn't do that stuff no more."

"I can talk to some people," I said. I suspected that Tina was in denial about Nick's drug use. If he was getting high with Forty, he was probably more than just a casual user. For Tina and the baby's sake, I hoped he hadn't been sharing needles with anyone.

"You promise to get him into a program?" She looked me straight in the eye.

"No promises, but I'll do what I can."

She hugged the pillow tighter and stared down at the carpet again. I held my tongue and waited. She seemed to be more level-headed than Georgette, and I was impressed with her. Threats and con jobs wouldn't work with her. This was a negotiation, and she was going for the best deal she could get.

"Nick's in Newark," she finally said.

"Where in Newark?"

She shook her head. "I was only there once. It's an apartment over a Chinese take-out place near Clinton Avenue but not *on* Clinton Avenue. It's like one block over."

"What's the name of the restaurant?"

She shrugged. "I dunno. I wasn't paying attention to that."

"Whose apartment is it?"

"Some friend of his. He didn't tell me who."

"Anything else you can tell me?"

She shrugged again. "I was only there once. It was at night."

"Does Nick have a car?"

"No."

"Does he have a gun?"

She looked down and shook her head. I knew better than to take her word on this one.

I pulled out my cell phone and started making calls to some of the other Seekers. Tina needed a baby-sitter to keep her from calling Nick, so I called Zora, who promised to come right over. Tina was tough, but I still felt it would be better to have a woman looking after her rather than one of the other Seekers. While we waited for Zora, I called Job and asked him to get a map and a phone book to locate all the Chinese take-out places off Clinton Avenue. I promised to meet him at his place to help as soon as I could. Clinton Avenue is a major thoroughfare in Newark, so this was going to take some time.

Zora showed up at Tina's a half-hour later. I filled her in on what was going on, then headed straight to Job's house. He was at the kitchen table, a map and two phone books spread out in front of him, writing down the names and addresses of all the Chinese restaurants that fit our criterion. He'd already found thirteen places.

"And I'm not through yet," he said. "Gonna need a lot more Seekers than we got to stake out all these places."

I scanned the list. "Maybe we can narrow this down a little."

As I studied the list, I put in a call to Jedidiah. "How's it going over there with Forty and Georgette?" I asked.

"Boring. We're just looking at each other."

"Listen," I said, "Nick's girlfriend told me he's staying in Newark at some friend's apartment. It's over a Chinese restaurant somewhere off Clinton Avenue. Any idea who that friend might be?"

"Hmmm . . . Let me see." Jedidiah lowered his voice because Forty must've been within earshot. "Forty's tight with two other brothers, Carlos Dixon and Shawn Brooks. Brooks has a place on Bigelow. That's a block off Clinton, right?"

"Yeah, but is it over a Chinese restaurant?"

"I don't know. I didn't check the place out myself. It was just on my list of possible locations."

"Do you have a street number?"

"Sorry. I got this on the street. Usually don't get the specifics that way."

"For sure," I said. "But this is good. We're getting closer."

"You need me now?"

"Not yet. You just keep Forty and Georgette off the phone. Try calling Rock when you need to be relieved."

"Got it."

I put the cell back in my pocket and told Job what Jedidiah had just told me about Shawn Brooks. I checked the phone book for a Shawn Brooks, but there were no listings under that name on Bigelow Street. This didn't surprise me. The phone was probably in someone else's name. Job, in the meantime, used the Yellow Pages and the map to narrow down his list of Chinese restaurants. He found two strong possibilities—China Delight, which was on Bigelow, and Lotus Garden, which was on a side street between Bigelow and Clinton. I had passed by Lotus Garden before, and even though the address wasn't on Bigelow, it looked as if it was because it was on a corner.

"Well," Job said. "I guess I know where we're going."

I checked my watch. It was almost nine o'clock. Saturday night isn't the best time to go bounty hunting. People don't have a Saturday night routine. Either they go out or they invite friends to come over. Breaking into an empty apartment would be useless, and walking into a roomful of homies smoking weed or crack or whatever wouldn't be very smart either. If we tried to take Nick away from his friends, it could turn into a pitched battle. But time was running out, so we had to do something.

"Take your car," I said to Job, "and go check out Lotus Garden. Just watch the place for a while. I'll take China Delight. Call me if you see anything."

Job was already on his feet putting on his jacket. "You got it," he said.

As I went out to my car, I kept thinking we'd better be getting close. If this turned out to be a dead end, I wasn't sure what approach to take next. Naturally, if we didn't get him, we didn't get him, but I was caught up in the challenge now. The way I saw it, the Seekers' reputation was on the line.

I drove to China Delight, which was on a relatively quiet block. It was between a bodega and an empty storefront. All three stores were in the same redbrick building, which had two floors of apartments above. The entrance to the apartments was between China Delight and the empty storefront. I parked my car across the street and went in to check the names on the buzzers in the vestibule. As I suspected, there was no Brooks listed. In fact, there was no one listed. People in the inner city tend not to advertise their whereabouts.

I tried the inner door, which of course was locked. But it wasn't the best lock on the market, and I knew I could get in pretty easily with a strip of plastic.

I then went back to my car and got comfortable. I had a feeling it was going to be a long night, just me and the stereo. Rock called me at around ten to let me know that he was taking over for Jedidiah at Georgette's place, and I called Zora to make sure everything was OK with Tina. Unfortunately, neither Forty nor Georgette nor Tina had given up any more information about Nick. Forty had surprised me. I'd thought that after a while he'd do anything to get rid of Jedidiah, even rat on his friend.

Job called in at around eleven-thirty. He was about half a mile away, staking out the apartments above the Lotus Garden restaurant, doing exactly what I was doing. He said that the restaurant was pretty busy and a few people had come in and out of the building but no young men who fit Nick's description.

Well, at least Job had something to look at, I thought. China Delight was dead. It hardly looked open. Except for an old man walking his dog, no one had come out of the apartments.

By one o'clock, lack of sleep was beginning to catch up with me. I ejected the cassette I had been listening to—a meditative flute, chimes, and drum ensemble—and stuck in a Thelonious Monk tape. The music was just quirky enough to keep me awake without jarring my calm.

Time seemed to stop. Its movement was imperceptible until I checked my watch, which I tried to avoid as much as I could. Clock-watching only engenders impatience, which is the enemy of good surveillance. I've found that the best way to endure a stakeout is to think of it as meditation. It is what it is; it has no set beginning, middle, or end.

By three-fifteen, there was almost no traffic at all on the street, and by four a light fog had settled over the city, which gave the night a surreal glow. Memories of old black-and-white horror movies drifted through my thoughts—vampires, the Wolfman, Jack the Ripper stalking the streets of London.

My eyes were drooping, I wanted to sleep so badly, but I was determined to stick it out at least until five. Five in the morning is usually the quietest time of day. Wherever Nick was, he'd most likely be fast asleep at that hour and not on the move. If nothing else happened here, I figured I could catch an hour between five and six.

I struggled to keep my eyes focused on the front door to the apartments, but I was really looking forward to five o'clock. Part of me hoped that Nick wouldn't show so that I could get some rest.

But then at four thirty-five, a car came down the street, a red Pontiac Grand Am. I slumped down farther in my seat and shut off the tape player. The car pulled up in front of China Delight, which had closed at midnight. A tall, lanky young man in a dark blue parka got out on the passenger side. He leaned in and said something to the driver, then slammed the door shut. The Pontiac drove off and made a right at the next corner.

The young man stumbled and weaved on the sidewalk, then stopped and stood still as if trying to get his bearings. I had already pulled out my monocular night scope and was putting it on. Through the scope the young man's face was suddenly illuminated in green. I could see he was having trouble keeping his eyes open. I studied his face for a moment, then looked at the photo the police had given me. The light fog blurred the night-scope image somewhat, but it looked like a pretty close match. Instantly I was wide awake.

Nick was heading for the front door. He was in bad shape, but it would be foolish to think I could take advantage of him in this condition. If he had a gun—and I assumed he did—the drugs had probably made him more paranoid than he already was, and they had also lowered his inhibitions. He might be slow, but he wouldn't hesitate to shoot if he perceived me as a danger, which he probably would if I tried approaching him.

But if he made it inside the building, that would present other problems. I'd have to pinpoint which apartment was his, and there was always the possibility that he wasn't staying alone.

If I'd been able to take him safely on the sidewalk, I would have risked it, but now he was in the vestibule. I'd have to run to get to him before he got inside, and if I did that, I might as well shout out that I was there to arrest him. What I did instead was get out of the car very quietly and wait until he was inside, then I ran across the street and used my strip of plastic to unlock the door. I opened it a slit and peeked in. Nick was slowly trudging up the stairway, scraping the wall as he went.

I went inside but hung back, keeping my distance from him. When he finally made it to the second floor, I quickly climbed the steps and peered down the hallway to see which apartment was his. He stopped at the second door on the left, an apartment that faced the rear of the building. He stood at the door, searching through all his pockets for the key, and when he finally found it, it took him forever to get it into the lock.

When he was finally inside, I rushed to the door and listened. Light seeped out from under the door. I could hear him stumbling and bumping into things. Something crashed to the floor, but I didn't hear any voices, no one telling him to shut up. It was a pretty good bet that he was in there alone.

I headed back down the hallway and went halfway down the steps where I could make a phone call without waking anyone. I dialed Job's number.

"I found him," I said softly. "As soon as you get over here, we'll take him. I'll meet you at the front door."

"Be right there," Job said.

Ten minutes later I met Job in the vestibule and explained the situation. "Nick just got in and he's wasted," I said. "Let's wait till he falls asleep, then we'll go in and take him."

Job nodded. "The usual."

"You got it."

We went upstairs and stood by his door listening for sounds of activity. There were none, but we waited almost half an hour before we made a move. At ten after five, I pulled out a set of lock picks on a key ring and got to work on the lock. It was a fairly good lock, so it took me a few minutes to get it open. In the meantime, Job stood guard with his hand on his gun just in case the light clicks and scratching noises I was making woke Nick.

With my hand on the doorknob, I nodded to Job, and we both pulled up our masks. I pulled out my gun, opened the door, and we stepped inside quietly but quickly. I closed the door to keep the hallway light from spilling in. We stood in the dark for a few moments until our eyes adjusted. It seemed to be a small apartment. A dull glow from the floodlights outside in the alley leaked in through the kitchen. The bathroom was straight ahead. The closed door to my left had to be the bedroom, I figured.

I nodded for Job to check the kitchen while I peeked into the bathroom. There were no other doors that I could see. Job returned, shaking his head. Nothing to be concerned about in there.

We went back to the closed door off the hallway, both of us with our guns pointed up. I pushed the door open slowly. The shade on the window was up, and a square of streetlight crossed the mattress on the floor. Nick was on his back on top of the covers. His shoes and shirt were off, but his socks and pants were still on. I took another step in, Job right behind me. I was reaching for the light switch when suddenly a phone rang.

Instinctively Job and I pointed our weapons at Nick, expecting him to wake up. Job found the light switch, and a naked bulb on the ceiling flashed on, illuminating the whole room in harsh, unforgiving light.

The phone rang again. It was on the floor on the other side of the mattress.

Nick didn't move.

It rang a third time.

We held our positions, waiting.

It rang a fourth time and a fifth and a sixth and a seventh. On the eighth ring, whoever was calling gave up. Nick hadn't budged. I stared down at him, wondering if he was dead.

Job checked his neck for a pulse. "The boy's alive," he said, but he sounded doubtful. He went through Nick's pockets until he found a wallet. The driver's license inside confirmed that this was indeed Nick Carpanza.

But it was the track marks on Nick's arms that told the real tale.

From the comatose way he was passed out, I assumed he was a heroin fiend. Even though Tina had downplayed the extent of her boyfriend's drug use, she had been determined that he get into a rehab program in prison. Now I knew why.

I got down on one knee and started slapping Nick's cheeks, trying to wake him up. He moaned and rolled his head to the side, but it was no use. He was in another land.

"Let's get him on his feet," I said to Job.

We each took an arm and dragged him up. He was as floppy as a balloon full of Jell-O. I wrapped his shoes in the shirt that was on the floor, and we carried him out into the hallway. Job held him up against a wall as I locked the door. Then we took him outside.

We poured him into the backseat of my car, and I cuffed him to the door handle just in case he woke up, though it didn't seem likely that would happen for some time.

"I'll take him back," I said to Job as I shut the back door. "Call Zora and Rock and tell them they can go home. You get some sleep and I'll see you tonight."

Job nodded. As he started to turn away, I called to him.

"Thanks," I said.

He smiled. "No problem."

Job went back to his car, and I drove off toward the new holding facility. Night turned into a moist gray dawn as I drove down Routes 1 and 9. Spears of sunlight were just coming over the horizon as I pulled into the parking lot of the new municipal building.

Nick hadn't made a peep since we'd put him in the backseat, and he was only slightly more awake when I dragged him out. I tried to make him stand up, but it was no use, so I put him over my shoulder and carried him in. The desk sergeant raised his eyebrows over his cup of coffee when he saw us. I bent my knees and set Nick down on a wooden bench across from the front desk. He slumped over onto the seat like a rag doll.

"This is Nick Carpanza," I said to the sergeant, a barrel-chested Black man. "He's the one who escaped from here on Friday."

"Is he dead?" the sergeant asked.

I shook my head. "High."

"Are you that bounty hunter Joshua?"

"Uh-huh."

"You in a hurry?"

I shook my head and took a seat next to Nick.

The sergeant picked up his phone and made a call. After he hung up, he looked over at me. "The captain says he'll be here in twenty minutes. He wants to congratulate you himself."

"Fine," I said.

"Can I get you anything? Coffee? A soda?"

"No thanks," I said. "You want me to take this guy down to the lockup?"

"That's OK," he said, picking up the phone again. "We'll take care of it."

A few minutes later two uniformed cops came out and carried Nick away. I settled into my seat, propped my head on my fist, and closed my eyes. I was dead tired.

"Joshua, you're a wonder."

My eyes shot open. I had dozed off. The captain was standing over me, wearing a navy-blue blazer and a red tie. He looked as if he was dressed for church.

"Thank you," he said, lowering his voice even though the desk sergeant was the only other person around. "You saved our asses."

I stood up and stretched. "I enjoy a challenge," I said.

"Send me a bill and we'll cut you a check right away."

"Sure, no problem," I said. "Now, can I ask you to do *me* a favor?"

"Anything."

"Two things actually. One, don't let your men rough up Nick, and two, put in a recommendation to the prosecutor that Nick get into a program when he's sentenced."

The captain looked disgruntled.

"Look, I had to make some promises in order to get him. And I live up to my promises. Anyway, those aren't big things I'm asking for. You can do it."

"I'll do what I can," he said.

"Do more," I persisted. "For me."

Gradually his face relaxed, and he started to nod. "OK. Don't worry about it."

I grinned at him. "After all, Captain, you never know when you may need our services again."

He grinned back. "Never, I hope."

"Yeah, but it would be awfully sad if you ever put up the Bat Light and Batman didn't come."

The captain chose not to comment on that. "Go get some sleep, Joshua. You look tired."

"I am." We said good-bye, and I left the municipal building. From there I went straight home to bed.

Nick was sentenced and served two and two-thirds years with time off for good behavior. He entered a rehab program in prison, and from what I've heard, he was clean when he was released. I don't know where he is today, but I hope he hooked up with Tina and their baby. For most cons, rehabilitation is a myth, but I have seen it happen. Nick's life will probably never be a fairy tale, but perhaps it hasn't turned out to be a horror story either. I'm always hopeful.

17 Facing Death and Winning

Bounty hunting is a dangerous profession. Fugitives can be violent and unpredictable, and chasing them down can present all kinds of hazards. If you don't learn how to reduce the odds of retaliation and injury, you won't be in the business for very long. The life of a successful bounty hunter is an endless series of calculated risks, with the emphasis on calculation, not risk. If you do things the smart way, you will survive and thrive. But if your philosophy is firepower first, brain power later, then you're playing a low-odds, high-stakes game with your own life on the table. I learned an important lesson in this regard early one morning on the streets of Philadelphia a few months after we captured Nick Carpanza. It was the day I faced death and won.

All the Seekers are well trained in street tactics and strategies for outwitting fugitives. We study police manuals that detail methods and procedures for subduing and securing suspects, entering unfamiliar territory, approaching someone in a vehicle, using a variety of weapons, and handling hostile crowds. We read ancient texts that deal with the art of war. I would say that a Seeker does as much preparation for bounty hunting as a Navy SEAL or an Army Ranger does for combat.

The only difference is that the military trains for the battlefield, while we train for the streets.

This kind of training is invaluable for what we do, but it's not everything. You can give a man the knowledge, but if he doesn't have the right frame of mind, he'll never be able to use that knowledge properly. In fact, I'd go so far as to say that when things get real, mental preparation is more crucial than physical training. If the mind is not ready to act, even the best-trained person in the world will not survive.

When the Seekers go out on a job, we carry a lot of equipment—guns, mace, restraints, scopes, binoculars, all kinds of things—but that's not what keeps us from getting killed out there. The greatest asset we have is so simple and basic, most people overlook it—the ability to breathe. In stressful situations, people tend to stop breathing. When you're standing eyeball to eyeball with a hardened felon who's determined to shoot it out with you rather than go back into the system, you need a clear head and inner calm so that you can truly see what's going on. If you're excited, and your heart's thumping, and you're struggling for air, I guarantee that you're not seeing the situation for what it truly is.

In the summer of 1996 the Seekers started looking for a man named Albert Hines who had missed several court dates in Newark. He was out on bail on a grand theft auto charge, but over the years he'd been arrested for a variety of offenses and had done some time in New York on an armed robbery conviction. In one way he was a textbook career criminal, but what made him somewhat different was that he had severed all ties with his family and old friends and just drifted from place to place, living from one scam to the next. No one seemed to know him very well, and the file I had gotten from his bail bondsman was pitifully short on information.

I ran a check on his prison records and managed to track down a man named Nathaniel Grady who had been Hines's cellmate for a while at Attica Prison in upstate New York. I caught up with Grady at the box factory on Long Island where he worked. I waited until lunchtime and approached him as he was eating a big sandwich at a picnic table set up on a strip of grass between the factory and the parking lot.

Like most ex-cons, he immediately went on the defensive when I introduced myself and said I wanted to ask him about his stint in prison.

He thought I was someone from the system aiming to haul him back in. But when I told him I was interested in Albert Hines, his face relaxed a bit. I explained that I had to find Hines and that any leads he could give me would be greatly appreciated. I had a few twenties in my shirt pocket just in case his wheels needed greasing.

Grady stroked his bushy beard as he thought it over for a minute. "Very difficult man, that Mr. Hines," he finally said, tucking his chin in and looking at me from under his eyebrows. His voice was very low.

"How do you mean he was difficult?" I asked.

"Not friendly. Hardly said a word. Made everybody nervous. A very hard man . . . It showed in his face."

"Doesn't sound like you two talked very much."

Grady frowned and shook his head. "Only when he was in the mood. And that wasn't very often."

"Do you know if he had any family or close friends or girlfriends maybe? Anybody like that?"

"Albert never said anything about family. I just figured he was hatched from an egg, like an alligator."

"No women on the outside?"

"Yeah, he did have this one woman. That was the only time he ever opened up and talked, whenever he got a letter from her. He used to say that she was the only person in the world who ever gave a shit about him. I think he really loved her from the way he talked."

"You remember her name?"

"Parker was her last name. . . . Denise Parker, I think. Yeah, I'm pretty sure that was her name—Denise. She lived in Philadelphia. The Germantown section. I always remembered that because my grandmother was from Germantown."

"You remember anything else about Hines?"

Grady shook his head. "Prison is something I try to forget."

I thanked him for his help and got up to leave.

"If you find him, don't bother giving him my regards," Grady said as I walked across the grass.

I checked the Philadelphia phone book at my local library and found a Denise Parker who lived on Wayne Avenue, a main thoroughfare that runs through Germantown. I took down the phone number and passed it on to Mr. Baines, who was able to construct a general profile of Denise Parker. She was thirty-two years old, had never been married, and worked for an insurance company in Center City, Philadelphia.

I took a ride down to Philly and found the high-rise office building where she worked. My plan was to ask her directly about Hines to see how she would react. Maybe Hines had mistreated her, and she wanted to get back at him. On the other hand, maybe she was protecting him, and if I sensed that, I'd trail her in the hope that she'd lead me to him. Unfortunately, she wasn't in the office the day I showed up. I struck up a friendly conversation with the receptionist, who told me that they hadn't been seeing much of Denise around the office lately. Phone calls kept interrupting us, but the receptionist, whose name was Beverly, was very flirty and chatty, and I think she enjoyed talking to anyone who would listen to her for more than ten seconds.

Beverly told me that Denise had been taking a lot of sick days in order to spend time with her boyfriend who was in the army and had just gotten back from a long-term assignment in the Persian Gulf. It was a perfectly plausible story, but I wondered if perhaps Denise's soldier boy was really Albert Hines.

I drove to Germantown and staked out Denise's apartment building. It was a nice eight-story brick building in a borderline area between a residential section of large old private homes and the beginning of the ghetto. I parked across the street and settled in to watch the front door, and to my amazement within two hours I saw Hines coming out of the building arm-in-arm with an attractive woman who fit Denise Parker's description.

I used the telephoto lens on my camera to get a closer look at him. He was about average height—compact and muscular. My guess was that he had gotten into weight lifting in prison. He was wearing a baseball cap, but it was obvious from the lack of hair around his ears that his head was shaved. I thought I caught the glint of a diamond stud in one ear. His expression was neutral, but I could easily imagine that face wearing the mean expression in Hines's mug shot—jaw set, nostrils flared, eyes cold and angry.

If it had been nighttime, I might have tried to take Hines then and there, but it was midafternoon, and lots of kids were hanging out in front of the building. Dawn would obviously be the best time to snatch him. I called Jedidiah in Elizabeth and asked him to drive down and meet me at 1 A.M. at an all-night diner on Roosevelt Boulevard a few miles from Denise Parker's place. I figured we could sneak into the apartment in the wee hours and take Hines by surprise in bed. I asked Jedidiah to pick up my cousin Ice and bring him along for the experience. Ice was in his late twenties and at the time trying to become a Seeker. Having spent some time in the navy, Ice was thorough and precise in everything he did. He's a very articulate man and has the kind of edgy personality that often gets results out on the street.

At one o'clock I was in a booth by the front window of the diner, taking my time with an omelet and a cup of tea, when a black Mercury Grand Marquis with New Jersey plates pulled into the parking lot. Jedidiah emerged from the driver's side as Ice got out on the passenger's side. I watched Ice, how he walked, what was in his eyes. He had a natural aptitude for bounty hunting, but he needed a lot more experience. I figured it was time he met a real hard case like Hines.

I caught Jedidiah's eye as soon as he walked in. He nodded and headed for my booth with Ice bringing up the rear. We all shook hands, and they ordered food. After the waitress brought them their orders, I laid out the situation for them. My plan was to hang out until 4 A.M., then enter Denise Parker's building and take Hines by surprise. Jedidiah would go up the fire escape in the rear while I went in through the front door. Ice would hang back and wait at the bottom of the fire escape to provide backup if it was needed. Jedidiah asked a few questions, but this was a pretty standard scenario for us. We had made arrests this way many times before. Ice quietly soaked up what we were saying. He wasn't scared, but this was all relatively new to him.

After we finished eating, we went back to our cars to get a little rest, though I had a feeling that Ice was too wired to rest. We drove to a supermarket and parked side by side at the edge of the parking lot out of the glare of the overhead lights. Jedidiah's car was a rental. I had my Land Cruiser loaded with all my equipment.

At four o'clock I looked over at Jedidiah slumped behind the wheel of the Grand Marquis. He was already looking at me. We exchanged nods and started our engines. I put my car into gear and led the way to Denise Parker's building. When we got there, Jedidiah and Ice drove down the narrow alley behind the building while I parked on the street out front.

The Seekers always try to get as much information as possible about a fugitive and his situation before we attempt an arrest, but this was one time when a case of mistaken identity changed the whole nature of the mission. It so happened that there was another fugitive from the law living in Denise Parker's building, a man named Marques Gilliam who was wanted on an outstanding warrant in Baltimore. He was living on the second floor with his new wife.

Gilliam had a nasty temper and a reputation for getting into brawls over the least little thing. I found out later that early that night he'd tangled with a man named Tony McDaniel at a local bar because he'd thought McDaniel was eyeing his wife. The two men got into a heated argument, but the bouncer made them take it outside. Once they were out on the sidewalk, they really got into it, and it didn't take long for Gilliam's temper to get way out of hand. He wrestled McDaniel to the ground, sat on his back, and smashed his head against the concrete a few times too many. When the ambulance finally arrived, McDaniel was out cold, had a fractured skull, and was bleeding profusely.

Gilliam quickly collected his wife, intent on making himself scarce before the police showed up, but before he left, one of the bar patrons warned him to watch his back because McDaniel had a mean son of a bitch for a brother and a few close cousins who didn't take crap from anyone. Gilliam, who hadn't bothered to find out who Tony was before he cracked his skull open, had heard of the McDaniels. From what he knew of them, they would definitely come gunning for him. No doubt about it.

Gilliam and his wife made it home, but he was really worried now. Knowing that the McDaniels clan would be out looking for him, he couldn't fall asleep. He knew he'd done some serious damage to Tony's face and head and might even have killed him. According to the statement his wife gave to the police, Gilliam had been pacing around his living room when I pulled up in front of his building. When he spotted me, he thought I was Tony McDaniel's brother. It just so happened that

I bore a passing resemblance to the man he'd sent to the hospital, so to Gilliam that was a logical assumption. He quickly threw a bullet-proof vest over his T-shirt, grabbed his .45, and came running downstairs, dead set on getting me before I got him.

I was sitting behind the wheel of the Land Cruiser, wearing the headset communications system, waiting to hear from Jedidiah that he and Ice were in place and ready to go. Jedidiah's voice crackled in my ear. "We're OK on this end," he said.

"OK. Ten minutes from now," I said. I had cased the building and checked the locks that afternoon after Albert Hines and Denise Parker had left. Ten minutes was all I'd need to get into the building and pick the lock on Denise's apartment door. If it all went according to plan, Jedidiah would be coming through the window as I walked in the door.

"Ten minutes," Jedidiah confirmed. "Over and out."

My headphones went silent. The street outside my windshield was totally empty, not even a stray cat anywhere in sight. It could have been an oil painting it was so still out there. I reached for the door handle and threw the door open, feeling my inside pocket with my other hand to make sure I had my lock picks, when suddenly out of nowhere a gunshot blast shattered the window and rattled the door in my hand. Instinctively I ducked below the window level. A second shot rocked the whole vehicle, followed by another and another. It felt like a rhino ramming into the door panel.

Instantly my heart was pounding like crazy, my gaze bouncing all over the place as I tried to figure out where the hell these shots were coming from. I was stretched out across both front seats, trying to stay as low as I could, but the shift console prevented me from lying on the floor. Two spent rounds were lying on the mat under the brake pedal. My breathing was ragged, my heartbeat careening out of control. I kept thinking this was it. I'd had a good run, but my luck had finally run out. My time had come.

Now over the years I've had a lot of training in both the martial arts and practical street techniques, and one thing all my instructors have stressed repeatedly is the importance of breathing. When you're under attack, the dance of life and death tries to suck you into its chaos. Time changes and takes on a different dimension. It becomes interminably slow while at the same time feeling like a rocket thundering through the stratosphere. As I lay on those seats listening to the blood throb in my ears, waiting for the next blast, I knew that in order to survive I had to pull myself back into the now and take control of time. I had to regain my center and calm down, and the only way to do that was to control my breathing. So I trusted my training, and instead of immediately pulling my weapon, I stopped to exhale all the air out of my lungs. Then I breathed in through my nose, taking a long deep breath. Immediately I started to feel more settled. I could think clearly now.

From the way the windows had broken, I took an educated guess that my attacker was firing at the driver's side from behind the Land Cruiser at an angle. I reached between the seats, feeling for the shotgun on the floor under the passenger's seat.

The gunman, who I thought was Albert Hines, kept firing. I lost count of the number of rounds. I was more focused on my breathing, forcing myself to keep taking deep even breaths. Suddenly the firing stopped. I waited a few seconds, then peered over the seat. My attacker was standing in the middle of the street fussing with his gun. It had apparently jammed on him.

Now it was my turn.

I didn't rush, but I also didn't hesitate. I sat up, pointed the shotgun out the open door, took aim, then fired one shot. I paused for a moment to take aim again, then fired another. Gilliam hit the ground and didn't shoot back, but I figured he could have been playing possum. I quickly hopped into the backseat, where the closed back door provided at least some mental protection as I reloaded the shotgun. When I was ready, I poked my head up and scanned the street, but no one was there. Gilliam was gone.

By this time Ice and Jedidiah had come running, having heard the gunshots. But Gilliam was nowhere to be found. We checked the entire area and combed the building floor by floor, but Gilliam had disappeared. Later, when the police canvassed the scene, they found blood on the pavement and torn pieces of Gilliam's cheap Korean-made body armor. I had definitely hit him. Amazingly I had escaped without a scratch. My vehicle, however, was in need of some major bodywork.

Later that week we caught Albert Hines at another location in

Philadelphia, but Gilliam managed to get out of town before a manhunt could be organized. He was caught by the police a month later in Connecticut. One side of his face was perforated with pellet wounds, and he had only one eye. He was taken into custody and transported back to Philadelphia where he was tried and convicted of attempted murder.

This was the only time in my entire career that I've ever had to discharge my weapon during an arrest. But if I hadn't known to breathe, I would never have had the chance to do anything. Breathing dispelled the fear of dying and showed me what I had to do. That's how I faced death and won.

18 Love Is Love

Love can be a powerful but often misguided motivator. A capture that we made in 1997 illustrates how the love between a man and a woman (or at least what people commonly call love) can drag down the innocent as well as the guilty.

A Philadelphia bail bondsman had hired us to find a man named Lamar Underhill, who had been charged with robbery and aggravated assault. He had pistol-whipped a clerk at a convenience store during a holdup because the man hadn't opened the cash register fast enough to suit him. Lamar was thirty-one years old at the time, and he'd had at least a dozen serious run-ins with the law, but he was clever and he was cautious. He had only one conviction, dating back to when he was a teenager, and for that he got a suspended sentence. He'd managed to keep himself out of prison for almost fifteen years, and he apparently intended to keep it that way.

But with the convenience-store charge, Lamar was looking at some serious time, so when he skipped out on his bail, he smartly severed all contact with former friends and family. According to the first bounty hunter who took the case, Lamar had just disappeared the day after his bail hearing, and no one but no one knew where he was. After working the case for a month, I had almost come to the same conclusion, but then I got a fresh lead from one of Lamar's cousins, who happened to mention to me that Lamar had an ex-girlfriend in Philly named Brianne Barnes. Lamar and Brianne had lived together for a while, and according to the cousin, they were engaged to be married until he broke it off. I asked if Lamar had left her for another woman, but the cousin didn't know.

I tracked down Brianne Barnes and found her apartment in West Philadelphia as well as the restaurant where she worked as a waitress. I went to the restaurant one night and ordered dinner from her, just to size her up. She was very attractive, but she was the tough, no-bullshit type. I had a feeling she'd just tell me to go to hell if I asked her directly about Lamar.

I trailed her for a couple of days and noticed that she ran with a different crowd from Lamar's other friends. What this said to me was that she had a different pool of information to draw from, so it was possible that she did know where Lamar had gone. I decided not to squander the opportunity with a direct approach. Instead I called on Jedidiah to do some undercover work.

Jedidiah has a unique talent for charming his way into a closed situation and becoming an insider very fast. I asked him if he'd be willing to try to get close to Brianne on a personal basis.

"You mean romance her?" he asked skeptically.

"A little bit if you have to. She's a tough woman. You're gonna have to soften her up a little to get anything out of her."

He was sitting in the passenger seat of my Land Cruiser sipping tea from a paper cup. "How much is a little bit?" he asked.

"I don't expect you to sleep with the woman. Just be nice to her and see what you can find out."

He thought about it for a while. "All right," he finally said. "I'll see what I can do."

Over the next two weeks, Jedidiah started hanging out at the restaurant where Brianne worked, chatting her up, flirting with her, pouring on the charm. She resisted him at first, but he knew how to keep the interest alive without coming on too strong. Some nights he'd go in and not even talk to her, just nod from across the room and spend all his time talking to the bartender. That piqued her interest, and

Jedidiah knew how to play it. Women want romance so badly it aches sometimes, and Jedidiah sensed that Brianne was no exception. By making himself a friendly but aloof presence, he let himself become her fantasy.

One night he stayed late at the restaurant and closed the place, timing his exit so that it coincided with Brianne's. He asked her if there was anyplace nearby where he could get a coffee that time of night. She told him there was an all-night diner within walking distance. He asked if she'd like to join him. At first she turned her nose up at the offer, but when he asked again, she agreed with a coy smile that transformed her face. It was the first time Jedidiah saw her let down her guard.

Well, one thing led to another, as they say, and pretty soon he was seeing quite a bit of Brianne. Fortunately, she worked nights, which helped to keep things under control. She probably would have slept with him on their second date, but he played the perfect gentleman, and when she started dropping heavy hints that she was more than willing to give it up for him, he suddenly had an "urgent business trip" that couldn't be put off.

Three days later, when he returned from his "trip," she invited him over to her apartment for a home-cooked dinner—smothered chicken, greens, and potato salad. He brought two bottles of wine, and they ate by candlelight in the kitchen. She asked about his past, wanting to know all about his former girlfriends. He made up a few stories, then turned the question back on her. By the time they were halfway through the second bottle, she had told him about the "no-good son of bitch" she used to live with, Lamar Underhill. She said he'd dumped her for a "ho" named Tiara.

Jedidiah feigned surprise. "You don't mean Tiara Johnson. From Forty-third Street?"

"No," she said, shaking her head. "Tiara Cummingham. She used to live on Arch Street near Fifty-fifth."

Jedidiah said that her name sounded familiar. "What's she look like?" he asked.

"A ho, that's what she looks like. A ho in a pink Buick Le Sabre."

"Pink? Buick doesn't make pink cars."

"OK, mauve maybe. A classy pink. But it's still pink."

Jedidiah then made an easy guess. "Did Lamar buy her that car?"

"Who do you think? Tiara may be a ho, but she ain't a good one. She could never afford a car like that."

"Did he marry her?"

"I don't know. Probably not."

"How come?"

"He wouldn't marry me—he won't marry nobody. He'll never settle down."

"So he broke up with her, too?"

Brianne shook her head sadly. "He ran off with her. They're shacking up someplace, I bet. But I know he won't stay with her."

Jedidiah had finally gotten some solid information out of Brianne, something we could work with, but he didn't want to hurt her feelings by just walking out on her. As tough as she was, she was still desperate for a man's attention. He eased off the topic of Lamar and Tiara and started talking about work, his supposed "job in sales." He tried to be as boring as he could possibly be because he knew he was going to have a hard time extricating himself from this situation. I didn't press Jedidiah for details on how the night ended, but he said he didn't take undue advantage of her. He also said that he didn't turn her off completely, just in case he had to go back for more information.

I checked the phone book and found a T. Cummingham listed on Arch Street on the block between Fifty-fifth and Fifty-sixth Streets. I gave Tiara's name, address, and the make of her car to Mr. Baines, my information analyst. Within twenty-four hours he'd uncovered a few interesting facts, including Tiara's driver's license number and her Social Security number. With these he was able to find out quite a bit more about her. For one thing she had traded the pink Buick in for a used white Oldsmobile Cutlass. Mr. Baines had gotten the Pennsylvania plate numbers for that car and an address in Nazareth, Pennsylvania, a town about forty miles north of Philadelphia. When Tiara had bought the car, she'd listed this as her permanent address. A cross-check with her Social Security number revealed that she'd also opened a bank account in Nazareth. If she was with Lamar, that's where they were most likely living. Unless they'd moved on, which was a definite possibility with someone as cautious as Lamar.

I took a ride out to Nazareth and found the address. It was a rental unit in an older garden apartment complex. There were lots of cars parked on the street, including Tiara's white Cutlass, so I parked the Land Cruiser and just watched the place for a while. It was about 8 P.M. when I arrived. There were lights on in the unit, and the glow of a television set lit the front room, but I didn't see anyone going in or coming out. The TV went off at around midnight. At about two in the morning, I left the apartment complex and checked into a motel on the outskirts of town.

At six forty-five the next morning I was back in position, sitting behind the wheel of the Land Cruiser watching Tiara's apartment. Over the next two hours, a variety of people emerged from other apartments, got into their cars, and headed for work. By nine o'clock things had quieted down. The sun was bright, the sky without a cloud. A small group of mothers with little kids in strollers congregated at a small playground in the middle of the complex. A brown UPS truck passed through, stopping here and there to make deliveries. A phone company truck parked a few doors down from Tiara's apartment, and a workman went up in the cherry picker to work on the lines.

At twenty after eleven the front door of Tiara's unit finally opened, and a woman came out. She was petite, with short hair, wearing black slacks, clunky black heels, and a waist-length black jacket. I had no idea what Tiara looked like, but the woman went over to Tiara's Cutlass, unlocked the door, and drove away.

I wondered if Lamar was in there alone or if he was there at all. I decided to wait it out to see if anything would happen. An hour and a half later the door opened again, and this time a man came out carrying a bag of garbage. He was wearing jeans, an olive-green fatigue jacket, and yellow Timberland boots. He crossed the road to a big gray Dumpster and heaved the plastic bag inside. I zeroed in on his face through the telephoto lens on my camera. It was definitely Lamar. He had grown a full beard, but it wasn't long enough to hide his very square jaw. He'd also grown his hair out a bit. In his mug shots his head was shaved clean.

I thought about taking him here and now, but two things bothered me: the presence of the little kids and their mothers and Lamar's loose-fitting fatigue jacket. Lamar could be carrying a weapon under that jacket. If he started a firefight, innocent bystanders could get hurt. I decided I would have to wait to make my move.

Forty minutes later Tiara returned and went back into the apartment. Ten minutes after that Lamar came out again, got into the Cutlass, and drove off.

I followed him to a local convenience store. He parked in the lot, got out of the car, and went inside. I pulled into the lot after him, waited thirty seconds, and followed him in. He was standing at the deli counter ordering a sandwich when I came through the door. He watched me as I went to the refrigerator case in the back where the milk was stored. I pretended to look for something as I watched his reflection in the glass door. I waited until he stopped looking at me and turned back to the deli counter. His back was to me now. No one else was in the store except the clerk, a young Asian man, who was behind the deli counter working the cold-cut slicer. I opened the refrigerator case and pulled out a half-gallon of whole milk as I simultaneously took out my .45. I walked toward the cash register with the gun down at my side.

As I came up closer to Lamar, I said, "Excuse me."

The clerk stopped slicing, thinking I was talking to him, and Lamar turned around as well. The muzzle of my gun was staring him in the face.

"Put your hands up, Lamar," I said.

He didn't move.

It wasn't a request, so I didn't repeat it. I moved in fast, grabbed a fistful of jacket behind one shoulder, and spun him around, but he kept spinning and tried to slug me backhanded. He was off balance, though, so I shoved him forward and slammed him against the deli case before he could touch me. I jammed my gun into the back of his neck where he could feel cold steel against his skin.

"Hands on the glass," I shouted in his ear as I grabbed his left wrist and kicked out his right leg so that he had to catch himself on the counter with his free hand.

Lamar didn't say a word as I started to pat him down. He was wearing a flak jacket under the fatigue jacket. I found a 9mm clipped to his belt and a short-barrel .22 in his inside pocket.

"Hey! Hey!" the clerk said nervously to me. "What do you want? Just tell me." His hands were high in the air, the cold-cut slicer whirring by itself.

"It's OK," I said. "This doesn't concern you. We'll be out of here in a minute."

I pressed the gun into Lamar's neck to keep him off balance while I got him cuffed. All the while he grumbled under his breath. "Shoulda popped you when I saw you coming in," he muttered. "Coulda put you down like a dog."

"Shoulda, woulda, coulda," I said as I grabbed him by the jacket and pulled him off the glass. I yanked up on the handcuffs chain to keep him bent over as I led him to the door.

"How'd you know, man?" he said. "How'd you know where to find me?"

When I didn't answer him, he tried to break away, but I just jerked up on the chain, which wrenched his arms and got him back under control. I got him squared away in the Land Cruiser and drove him back to Philadelphia. The whole way back he continued to grumble about how dangerous he was and what he would have done to me if I hadn't blindsided him. He bragged about all the guns he had and how he was prepared to use them if he had to. I put in a Keith Jarrett solo piano tape, turned up the volume, and tried to tune him out. He finally quieted down just as the Philadelphia skyline appeared on the horizon.

After turning Lamar over to the authorities in Philly, I made two phone calls. The first one was to Tiara.

"Hello?" she said after three rings.

"Tiara, you don't know me, but I want you to listen carefully. Lamar is in jail. You'll end up there, too, if you don't watch out."

"Who the hell are you—"

"Just listen to me. Get out of your house right now. Just take what you need and leave. Don't come back. And don't bother with Lamar anymore."

"What're you talking about, motherfu—"

"Just leave. Right now. You've been told." I hung up.

An hour later I put in a call to the Nazareth Police Department and asked to talk to the lieutenant on duty. After I explained who I was, I told the lieutenant that I'd just arrested a fugitive in their town who claimed to have a pretty large arsenal back at his apartment. I gave the lieutenant the address and suggested that he might want to check it out. I knew that if they found Tiara in the apartment with Lamar's guns, she'd be charged with possession of illegal firearms.

The lieutenant called me back later that evening to thank me for the tip. They'd found a sawed-off shotgun, an AK-47 assault rifle, a .357 magnum, a night-vision scope, and a kilo of cocaine at Lamar's place. He made no mention of finding Tiara there, and I didn't ask about her. I assumed that she'd taken my advice.

Lamar Underhill was a truly dangerous man. Not only did he have that stash of deadly weapons, he was physically dangerous as well, having studied martial arts from the age of five under the tutelage of his father, who was a professional martial arts instructor. That made me wonder about Lamar's upbringing. When properly taught, the martial arts promote discipline and self-control. They're about resolving conflict, not starting it. You would have thought that someone who'd been studying from that early an age and who had learned from his own father would have turned out a lot better than Lamar had. It really made me wonder.

Every capture I've made in my career has been unique in one way or another, but over the years I've noticed some common patterns of behavior and lifestyle in the vast majority of male fugitives I've brought back to justice. Obviously they have all failed to evolve. The particular reasons for this failure can vary, but basically it boils down to two problems: limited worldview and miseducation.

Too often young males take their ascendancy into manhood for granted. A young person reaches a certain age, and automatically he thinks he's a man. If he starts earning some money, he thinks he's a man. If he gets himself a gun, he thinks he's a man. If he has sex with a woman, he really thinks he's a man. But, in fact, none of these things make him a man.

To make matters worse, negative influences appear at every turn—from peers and parents alike—which only serve to reinforce the young male's miseducation. On top of that, if he never leaves the bounds of his own neighborhood, then he never meets other people, and never gets other points of view, thus his intellectual development is impaired. If he looks around at his environment and everyone he sees is living the same way he is, then naturally he thinks his lifestyle is normal, when in fact it's anything but.

In ancient societies, rituals and ceremonies marked a boy's passage into manhood. Whether he had to hunt a lion or endure a grueling ordeal at the hands of the elders, there was always some task that had to be accomplished in order for a boy to earn his manhood. It left him wiser and more mature. It showed him that his responsibilities went beyond his own selfish needs, and it gave him a role in society.

Without these educating rituals, young men today are left to wallow in their own immaturity. They become obsessed with their own needs. Add drugs to the mix—as many young men do—and the untrained and unschooled become even more vulnerable to disaster. The need to service their drug habits consumes them. They steal, they con, they subjugate others—they do anything to get what they crave. When drugs enter a young man's life, he not only fails to evolve, he *de*-evolves, becoming more animalistic in his behavior.

The young male's problem is often compounded by the females in his life. Unfortunately, women give their love away too readily. In the wrong-headed quest for romantic love, they make themselves vulnerable to a young man's wiles. Women offer men sex thinking it will cement the romance, but nothing is further from the truth. This kind of sex only enables the man's failure to evolve.

Love should not be a means to an end. Love is love. It's greater than sex. People try to dissect love and say that they have different kinds of love—one kind for a spouse, another kind for a child, yet another for a parent. But this is false reasoning. Love is love. If it's real love, there are no distinctions. This is why a person can never fall out of love. If you do, then you were never actually in love in the first place. Real love gets beyond physical attraction and petty games. *Love is love.*

What most women call love often drags them into their men's downward spiral. The woman de-evolves with the man. But what she doesn't realize is that she holds the key to raising him up. I know this will sound old-fashioned to many supposedly forward-thinking people, but if a woman wants a good man, she has to become a better woman. And if that means not giving him sexual pleasure whenever he wants it, then she must do that. Cut off the fruit, and the man will wake up.

A woman should make a man fill out an application before she agrees to be with him. Why not? You fill out applications to get a job or buy a car—aren't human relationships infinitely more important? A woman should find out what a man likes and dislikes, get references, talk to people who know him. Isn't it better to know if the man is a woman-beater *before* the relationship begins? If the man has to make an effort to earn the woman's company, she will certainly have his full attention, not just his meaningless affections for however long it takes to complete intercourse. And when a woman has a man's attention, they can then assess their love and make it real or not. If a couple can survive life without sex, then real love can begin. And where there is love, there can be evolution.

But Lamar Underhill, like so many others, was the product of his miseducation and limited worldview. He may have earned multiple black belts, but he never got the message. What should have been a rite of passage for him became a right to do whatever the hell he pleased. He mistook the ability to inflict pain and bully others as signs of personal development and acquired skills. The saddest part is that his father may have actually praised Lamar for his ability to hurt people.

The women in Lamar's life fell all over themselves to be with him. Brianne gave herself to him completely, and he still threw her away like an apple core after he'd had the fruit. Same thing with Tiara. I'm sure in time he would have abandoned her, too. These women gave him their love so readily that he just took it for granted. The love he received was totally unearned. So is it any wonder that Lamar failed to evolve?

Hopefully a day will come when bounty hunters won't be necessary. No bail bondsmen, no criminal attorneys, no judges, no police. Evolution will take us beyond crime and violence. That may sound idealistic, but it's a goal worth striving for, and if we want it to happen, it must start with the children. They are the ones we must concentrate on. Nurture them. Bring boys into manhood the right way. Teach girls that a woman's self-worth has nothing to do with a man's opinion. Teach them all that a man and a woman are each other's complement.

Also, read to your children. Teach them how to read. Teach them how to *think*. If a child has a book, he may never need a gun.

19 Crossing Borders

Some people who are free on bail figure that they can avoid apprehension by fleeing to a foreign country. Usually they'll go back to the place of their birth, seeking refuge on familiar ground. But national borders will not protect them from the Seekers. We have tracked down and returned fugitives from U.S. justice in Canada, Mexico, Puerto Rico, and the Dominican Republic, places where we have contacts who will help us when we're there. We don't give up just because a fugitive isn't in the United States. If the bond is big enough and the bondsman is willing to pay our price, we'll go wherever we have to in order to bring a fugitive back.

A case we worked in 1998 is particularly memorable, the hunt for Carlos Muñoz, a man who had shot a cop during a botched gas-station holdup in Edison, New Jersey. The cop had been wounded in the incident, and Muñoz escaped—but not for long. The police found him within twenty-four hours, but he claimed they had the wrong man. Because the gas-station attendant refused to positively identify Muñoz out of fear of retaliation, the grand jury wouldn't indict him on the most serious charge, attempted murder of a police officer. They did send back indictments for armed robbery and possession of an illegal weapon, because a search of his apartment had produced $1,328 in cash, which was almost the exact amount taken in the robbery, and an unregistered .38 revolver. The cop had been shot with a 9mm, however, and that gun was not found.

At Muñoz's bail hearing, bail was set at $150,000. Muñoz secured a bond from a bondsman in Perth Amboy by putting up $15,000 in cash and having his cousin put up her home as collateral. Why Muñoz's cousin would do that remains something of a mystery, given the fact that Muñoz was a repeat offender and a notoriously nasty son of a bitch to boot. Perhaps the cousin had extended her familial love to Muñoz in the hope that love could generate change, but as I could have predicted, Muñoz paid back that unselfish gesture by taking the first plane to Puerto Rico he could find.

The bondsman called me and asked if I wanted the case. He faxed Muñoz's file to me, and a couple of things piqued my interest. For one thing Muñoz was a bully. He had a long list of aggravated assaults on his record, quite a few of them against women. He was also a street fighter and, some say, a member of the Latin Kings. I checked his physical description—six feet even, 188 pounds. His photo was a little blurry because of the fax transmission, but the expression was clear enough. A thick face exuding pure arrogance. This could be interesting, I thought.

I called Eduardo, my contact in San Juan, and asked him to find out what he could about Carlos Muñoz. I faxed him all the information I had, which included his place of birth, a small village in the southern interior of the island.

Ten days later Eduardo called me back with a full report. According to Eduardo, Muñoz had gone back home to live with his mother. He had only been there a few months, but the police had already gotten quite a few complaints against him for harassing the locals and refusing to pay for goods and services. One young woman had even accused him of rape, but Muñoz hadn't been charged. A few days after the young woman lodged her complaint, she was beaten up badly, her legs sliced with a knife. After that she changed her mind and refused to cooperate with the investigation.

It sounded to me as if Muñoz was getting away with murder in his hometown, and I wondered why. Eduardo explained that Muñoz's village was in the jungle and fairly remote. They were served by a small regional police force that didn't always respond quickly. But the main reason for Muñoz's reign of terror, Eduardo felt, was that the village was the home of a boxing camp run by Muñoz's brother. Because Muñoz had lived in America, he was something of a hero to a bunch of wanna-be Latino Mike Tysons. Apparently no one, not even the cops, wanted to tangle with that crew.

I thanked Eduardo for his help and said I would be seeing him soon. After I hung up, I couldn't stop thinking about the woman who had been raped, imagining what her face looked like after taking a beating from a street fighter and maybe several trained boxers as well. I picked up the phone and called Jedidiah. "Pack your sweats," I said to him. "We're heading south."

Two days later we boarded a plane for San Juan from Newark International Airport, each of us traveling as light as we could. We brought only two handguns each, as well as two air tasers, all of which we had to stow in the baggage compartment after making prior arrangements with the airline. The captain himself checked our licenses before we took off, which is standard procedure for transporting firearms on a commercial flight. A captain has the right to stop a passenger from taking a weapon onto his plane, but it's not that uncommon for hunters and law enforcement personnel to take their guns with them, so we weren't denied.

When we arrived in San Juan, the sun was shining bright, glinting off the terminal windows as the plane taxied up to our gate. Eduardo was waiting for us at the end of the ramp.

"Welcome to Puerto Rico," he said facetiously as if he were our tour guide. We all shook hands. Eduardo is bald and somewhat round, but his appearance is deceptive. He's faster than he looks and strong as a tow truck. A couple of times in the past I'd entrusted prisoners to him for safekeeping while I was down there doing a sweep. Whenever I came back to pick them up, they usually seemed relieved to be back in my custody. I noticed that Eduardo had grown a goatee since the last time I'd seen him. It brought out the devil in his eyes.

"How have you been, my friends?" he asked. "It's been a long time."

"Too long," I said.

"Did you make all the arrangements?" Jedidiah asked. Jedidiah is by no means an unfriendly person, but he's not one for chitchat when there's business to be done.

"Your arrangements are all taken care of," Eduardo said. "We'll drive out tomorrow morning. I've rented you a good car as well."

"Fantastic," I said.

Jedidiah nodded, but his expression was serious. Every pickup has its own dynamic, but jobs like this one present additional demands. Jedidiah and I were going to pose as boxers so that we could infiltrate Muñoz's brother's camp. To be convincing, focus and concentration would be crucial, and Jedidiah was already getting into character.

After a dinner of beans, rice, and plantain stew, we checked into a quiet motel in Old San Juan that Eduardo had found for us and hit the sack. It was going to be a big day tomorrow. We needed to be rested and ready.

The next morning Eduardo came by at seven. We checked out, had a quick breakfast, and got on the road. He led the way in his maroon Toyota minivan. We followed behind in a rented khaki-colored Jeep. It took us over two hours to get there because even though on the map Muñoz's village looked like an easy ride from San Juan, the only road that went there was narrow and only partially paved. Once we got into the jungle, the road became muddy and rutted, and the vegetation overhead was so thick the sunlight was actually tinted green. I could see why the local police would have a hard time with 911 calls.

When we got to the village, I was surprised at what I saw. I had imagined a tiny backwater outpost, considering its remoteness, but it was much more civilized. On the main drag I noticed a grocery store, a hardware store, a fabric store, a gas station/repair shop, a cantina, and a small hotel. Eduardo pulled his van over to the side of the road and I pulled up alongside him.

"Is this the place?" I asked.

"Almost," he said. "The boxing camp is about a mile and a half from here."

Jedidiah pointed at the hotel. "Is that where we're staying?"

Eduardo flashed his devilish grin and shook his head. "You'll be staying out there. Don't worry. It's all been arranged."

Eduardo started up his engine and pulled out into the street. We followed him as he drove out of town on a paved road that ended as soon as the town was out of sight. It was back to the muddy ruts again. We came to a fork, and Eduardo took the road that branched off to the right. It wound through some spectacularly beautiful jungle, but the deeper we drove into it, the more concerned I became with the remoteness of this location. Strange things can happen in a wilderness where nobody sees anything.

As we came out of the thickest part of the jungle, the road evened out and became relatively smooth, and from here it only took about fifteen more minutes to get to Muñoz's brother's compound. As we rounded a bend, the compound suddenly appeared on our left. It consisted of four structures staggered on a terrace in a clearing: a long, low bunkhouse, the main house, a barn, and a tin-roofed open-air gym with screen walls. A boxing ring took up most of the space inside the gym. A heavy bag hung from the ceiling off to one side. In the ring, two men in boxing gloves and headgear were sparring, trading body blows. One was wearing a gray sweatshirt and blue nylon sweatpants. The other was wearing a white T-shirt with cut-off sleeves and red shorts.

We parked our cars near the barn and walked over to the gym. A small white Nissan pickup truck, an old two-tone blue Bronco, and a flashy black Pontiac Firebird with a gold firebird painted on the hood were parked near the main house. The ratta-tat-tat of a speed bag carried through the clearing and competed with the squawking complaints of unseen birds high in the trees. Eduardo opened the screen door in the screen wall and led the way in. A shirtless boxer was working the speed bag at the rear of the gym. An older man had his foot propped up on the side of the ring, one hand carelessly hanging on the lower rope, his eyes glued to the sparring match.

Eduardo called out to him, greeting him in Spanish. The man stood up to his full height and scrutinized the three of us. He was big, but he'd let his body go to seed. A protruding belly pushed out his loose-fitting short-sleeved shirt, and a hanging double chin encircled his fleshy face. Eduardo went up to him and they shook hands. This had to be Carlos Muñoz's brother, Hector, the man who ran the camp. I could see the family resemblance.

I understand a little Spanish, so I was able to get the gist of their conversation. Eduardo introduced himself and explained that he and Hector had spoken on the telephone. He pointed toward Jedidiah and me and said that we were the two American boxers who wanted to train at the camp because we had been very impressed with one of Hector's former students. Eduardo had done some research. The former student he mentioned was an up-and-coming middleweight who was now living in New York.

Hector said nothing, but it was clear that he was sizing us up. He came closer and circled around us. When he came back around, he pointed to Jedidiah. "You OK," he said in heavily accented English. "Heavyweight, good." Jedidiah weighs around 225.

He looked me over again, tilting his head from one side to the other. He slapped his belly. "How much you weigh?"

"One-ninety," I said.

He stuck out his bottom lip, and his brows slanted back. He seemed dubious about my prospects. "Light heavyweight," he finally pronounced. "You box. I see." He called to the man working the speed bag, then told the two men in the ring to get out.

Because of his size, Jedidiah had automatically been accepted, but apparently I was going to have to audition. Hector found a pair of gloves on the floor and tossed them to me. I was wearing sneakers and jeans, so I just took my shirt off, and Jedidiah helped me on with the gloves. Hector threw him a roll of tape to do my hands and wrists.

Meanwhile the man who'd been on the speed bag wandered over and checked me out, too. His nut-brown body was glistening with sweat. He rolled his head on his shoulders and shifted his weight from one foot to the other, maintaining continuous motion so that he wouldn't cool down. He had well-developed arms and washboard abs. He appeared to be a light heavyweight, but he had the kind of blank expression that was hard to read. Either he was dim-witted or, like Tyson, he was an emotionless punching machine—no feelings, just brute power.

Eduardo looked a bit concerned that Hector wanted me to fight right off the bat. He must have thought that we'd ease into it after a day or two and that by then we'd have Carlos in custody so we'd never have to actually get into the ring. But obviously that wasn't going to be the case.

Jedidiah and I exchanged looks as I stepped through the ropes into the ring. Fortunately, boxing is one of the martial arts that all the Seekers must study.

The other boxers clustered around Hector, waiting for the action to begin. My opponent was in the ring, bouncing on his toes, pounding his gloves together. I leaned on one of the posts and stretched my hamstrings, then rolled my head on my shoulders and rotated my arms a little to limber up.

"OK, OK," Hector said impatiently. "Box, box." He had trouble with his *x*'s. In his mouth *box* sounded like *bosh*.

I put up my gloves and got into a stance. My opponent did the same, and we started circling each other. I caught a glimpse of Eduardo's face. He looked worried.

My opponent threw a few left-handed jabs, testing the waters. I backed away from them. We circled some more, and he flicked out a few more jabs, then tried to surprise me with a right cross. I ducked, and it just grazed the top of my head, but while I was down there, I threw a right uppercut to the body. It didn't seem to have much effect on him, though. Those washboard abs were pretty solid.

"Break! Break!" Hector shouted, and we each took a step back before we continued.

My opponent started circling again. I stayed on my toes and kept just enough distance between us to be out of his range. Boxing, as opposed to brawling, is a game of patience, waiting for your moment, waiting for an opening. After all my years as a bounty hunter, I'd gotten pretty good at waiting. The question was, how good was he?

"Come on, come on," Hector shouted from the edge of the ring.

"Take your time, Joshua," Jedidiah coached.

That's exactly what I intended to do. I wanted my opponent to come after *me*. Let *him* overcommit and make the mistake so that I could take advantage of it.

He threw a few more jabs. I countered with a left hook that caught his shoulder. He returned with a quick left hook of his own that turned my head around. I backed off. The side of my face stung. Neither of us was wearing headgear. I pulled in tight and moved back in, landing two hard blows to his midsection. He threw his arm around my neck, and we ended up in a clinch. Hector had to yell for us to separate again.

I tried to make eye contact with my opponent, hoping to get a clue to what he was thinking, but his eyes were blank. He was definitely a punching machine. I got the impression that this fighter didn't make a distinction between light sparring and real bouts. It was all the same to him.

My face was beaded with sweat. I took a deep breath through my nose and blew it out my mouth. I nodded to him that I was ready and he nodded back. Immediately he lunged at me, leading with a straight right. I deflected it with my left glove and simultaneously countered with my own straight right. I tagged him good this time, catching him flush on the face. He winced and staggered back to regroup, but I stayed with him, throwing a left uppercut that caught him in the ribs. He threw a weak right while I tagged him in the ribs a second time. He bent over at the waist, covered up, and twisted out of my range, but I don't think he realized how far into the corner he was. I moved in on him, aiming to trap him in the corner—

"E-stop! E-stop!" Hector yelled. "Is good. Need headgear for more."

My opponent and I both straightened up and dropped our gloves. He nodded and smiled at me through his mouthpiece. He seemed to be a good sport after all. Just a hard puncher, that's all.

As I climbed out of the ring, Eduardo looked surprised and relieved. I guess he didn't know that the Seekers could box, too.

Hector and Eduardo started talking in rapid-fire Spanish. Eduardo was smiling and so was Hector, so I assumed I had made the cut. The two middleweights who had been sparring when we arrived climbed back into the ring and picked up where they'd left off.

Jedidiah was helping me take off the gloves when we heard a door slam. Through the screen wall, I saw a man coming out of the main house, clomping down the wooden front steps in cowboy boots. He was wearing jeans and a short-sleeved khaki shirt unbuttoned to the middle of his chest. The man jumped into the Firebird, revved the engine, and took off, kicking up gravel in his wake. He tooted the horn as he passed the gym, and Hector gave him a lazy wave.

"That's him," I whispered to Jedidiah as he unlaced my gloves. "That's Carlos."

Now we knew what kind of car he drove. A vehicle like that wouldn't be hard to spot, especially out here in the boonies. The roar of

Carlos's engine rumbled back through the jungle as he drove away.

Eduardo stood between us and put his hands on our shoulders. "It's all set. Hector says he will train you for two weeks. I have paid him for one week, which of course I am certain you will reimburse me for. I told him I'd pay him the rest after the first week." He lowered his voice. "Do you think you'll need longer than that?"

I raised an eyebrow and looked at Jedidiah. "I hope not," I said.

That afternoon Eduardo left for San Juan. After he left, Hector took us to the bunkhouse and got us set up with bed sheets and towels. In contrast to his hulking appearance, he was quite motherly, going out of his way to make sure we were comfortable, then preparing a chicken and rice dinner for all of us at the main house. We all ate together at a long table on the back porch—Hector, Jedidiah and I, and the four other boxers who were training at the camp. Baltazar, the camp heavyweight, had been in the village doing the shopping when we arrived. He was very happy to see Jedidiah because finally he had someone in his weight class to spar with. We were happy to see him, too, because he spoke a little more English than the others and could act as our translator.

Hector kept a plastic cooler on the porch filled with bottles of the local beer, and he made sure everyone had one. By the time we were into our second round, Hector had become quite a convivial host, laughing and smiling, urging us through Baltazar to have as much to eat and drink as we liked.

"So what's the drill around here?" I asked Hector, indicating that I wanted Baltazar to translate.

Baltazar looked puzzled. "Drill?"

"The routine, the schedule," I clarified. "What do you do for training here?"

"Ah." Baltazar finally understood, and he translated it for me.

Hector laughed. His response was very short.

"We box," Baltazar translated. "That's what we do."

"Tell Hector we always like to run first thing in the morning," I said. "Jog." I looked at Hector and pantomimed jogging.

Hector's brow was furrowed until Baltazar finished translating. His face relaxed as he responded. "Sure, fine," Baltazar translated. "Just stay on the road. There are bad snakes in the jungle. Some especial kind of snake. I don't know the name." He cramped his hands and mimicked strangling someone around the neck.

"Boa constrictors?" Jedidiah ventured.

"Yes, yes, constrictor," Baltazar said excitedly. "That's the word." His eyes widened. "Some big ones, too."

"Then we definitely won't be going into the jungle," I said, laughing. "We won't even go *near* the jungle."

"Good idea," Baltazar said, laughing with me.

Hector picked up on what I was saying, and he started to laugh, too. He hoisted his beer bottle and clinked it against ours, and we all took a drink. Of course, Jedidiah and I had no intention of going into the jungle. We had something else in mind for our morning jog.

At sunrise Jedidiah and I got up and threw on our sweats. The air was cool and moist, the ever-present sound of birds in the trees more noticeable in the early morning stillness. We both wore hooded sweatshirts with front pouches, and we both carried our Glock 9s inside them, just in case. We jogged down to the dirt road and headed toward the village. To all the world what we were doing was just roadwork, but in fact it was a reconnaissance mission. We were out looking for Carlos's black Firebird.

Again, thanks to the Seekers' mandatory training regimen, the jog into town was a piece of cake. We were just breaking a sweat when we emerged from the overhanging foliage and reached the village. The aroma of freshly baked bread wafted through the air as we passed the row of stores. An old woman was sweeping the front steps of the hotel. She glanced up at us but paid us no mind. Jogging boxers must have been a common sight around there. The mechanic at the gas station was just lifting his garage door. We kept our eyes peeled for the black Firebird, but there wasn't a vehicle that slick anywhere in sight. Most of the vehicles were older economy models that showed a lot of wear and tear.

"Which way?" Jedidiah asked as we came to the end of town.

The road ahead was the road we'd come in on from San Juan, and I hadn't seen anything but jungle when we'd driven in the day before.

"Let's circle back around the hotel and look for another road. There must be a residential section somewhere around here."

We took a right and then another right, cutting through a narrow street of squat two-story adjoining stucco houses. Cars were parked every which way. We saw a few people, all of them women, but no men and no Firebirds.

At the end of that street, another road branched off to the left and went up a hill. I pointed for Jedidiah to go that way. It was steeper than it looked, with thick, hanging vegetation on both sides. We were sweating through our shirts by the time we reached the top, which was a clearing that overlooked the village. A small church had been built at the summit, the clearing graded with cinders to form a parking lot. The church was smaller than Hector's gym, and it didn't have a spire, just a wooden cross mounted on top, which was why we hadn't noticed it before. We jogged around the perimeter. Rooftops were visible on the terraced slope on the other side of the hill. These houses looked a little nicer than the ones we'd seen so far, bigger, some with terra-cotta roofs.

"Must be where the rich people live," Jedidiah said.

"Looks that way," I said. "Let's go check it out."

We jogged back down the hill and found another road that led to the residential section. The houses there weren't exactly mansions, but they were built on fairly big lots so that each house had some privacy. As we jogged along, signs of middle-class prosperity became evident—barking dogs in fenced-in backyards, hanging pots of flowering plants on the porches, storm windows, newer cars in the driveways. We followed the road out as far as it went, then circled back toward the village on yet another, smaller road.

"Nice ride," Jedidiah suddenly said as we approached a ranch-style house set back on a large lot. A small well-tended lawn surrounded the front porch like an island in a sea of wild jungle scrub.

I saw what he was referring to. Parked in the driveway was the black Firebird. An older woman was on the porch watering her hanging plants. I wondered if this was Hector and Carlos's mother. She was too far away to get a good look at her face. There were two other cars in the driveway, a small white pickup and a blue Toyota Corolla.

We kept jogging and passed on by. It was way too soon to make a move on Carlos—too many question marks as to his habits and living arrangements—so we headed back to Hector's compound. We had more recon work to do.

That afternoon Jedidiah and I were in the gym, working out and maintaining our covers. Jedidiah was in the ring with Baltazar. I was working on the heavy bag, Hector holding it from behind and giving me instructions half in English, half in Spanish. I kept an eye out for the black Firebird. I was hoping that Carlos would come back to the compound so I could get a better look at him.

"You spar next," Hector said to me over the pounding of my gloves against the bag.

"Who?" I asked, expecting him to pair me up with Roberto again, the light heavyweight I'd fought when I first arrived.

"You fight Baltazar," Hector said. He couldn't help but notice the dubious look on my face. "Is good for you," he said with great conviction. "Baltazar, too. He big, you fast. Good match."

I stopped whamming the heavy bag and took a closer look at Baltazar. He wasn't a great fighter, but he had some skill, and he was a lot fiercer in the ring than I would have expected given his easygoing personality. He was certainly giving Jedidiah a good workout. Baltazar's best attributes were his long arms and his hard punch. He must have connected at least once with Jedidiah because I noticed that Jed was being very careful to deflect Baltazar's blows, which threw his timing off and kept him from landing any decent blows of his own. As Hector had said, Baltazar wasn't fast, but he punched hard enough to give his opponent something to think about.

Hector and I had wandered over toward the ring to watch when suddenly I heard the throaty *vroom* of a car engine. I turned around and through the screen saw the black Firebird kicking up gravel in the driveway. It circled around so that the driver's side was facing the gym. The automatic window rolled down, and there was Carlos behind the wheel. He called out to Hector, who went outside to greet him. Hector leaned on the roof of the car and talked to his brother for a while. The engine was idling, so I assumed Carlos wasn't going to be staying.

Roberto, who had been skipping rope off to the side, noticed me looking at Carlos, and he came up beside me. He frowned and shook his head. "Bad man," he said. "No good."

"Why is he bad?" I asked, but Roberto didn't understand the question. He only had a few words of English.

"Bad man," he said again. "No good for woman." He went back to where he'd been and started skipping rope again.

It was a pretty rudimentary indictment, but the gravity in Roberto's face was enough to convince me that Carlos had raped the woman Eduardo had talked about. I caught Jedidiah's eye when he and Baltazar stopped to take a breather. He had noticed Carlos, too. I went back to pounding the heavy bag. Five minutes later Carlos drove off, and Hector came back inside. The Firebird's exhaust fumes seeped through the screen and into the gym.

I sparred with Baltazar that afternoon. All the other boxers gathered round to watch the spectacle of a light heavyweight taking on a boxer who was thirty-five pounds heavier and had a significantly longer reach. Hector kept assuring me in his broken English that everything would be all right, not to worry. But I wasn't worrying. At least I hadn't said I was worried. I had gotten quiet and introspective, though, as I tried to figure out how I was going to handle this.

When we got into the ring, both Baltazar and I were wearing headgear. I was wearing a sleeveless muscle shirt; he was bare-chested. As soon as Hector yelled for us to begin, Baltazar went into a tight protective crouch. I put up my gloves to protect my face and moved to my right. He pursued me, but I noticed that he had an odd lumbering shuffle. Like many heavyweights, he was lead below the waist. I hadn't noticed this when he fought Jedidiah, but the man's footwork was atrocious. Speed was definitely on my side.

We circled like that for a while as everyone down on the ground shouted for us to mix it up. Baltazar finally responded to this and lunged at me, leading with a right. I slipped past it and countered with a hook to his ear, but apparently my blow did no damage because he kept coming, throwing straight punches at my head. I was able to duck a few of them, but one caught me on the side of my neck and almost knocked me off balance. I retreated, having felt his power. I had a feeling that wasn't even close to his best shot.

I stayed out of his range, but Hector wanted to see some more action. "Inside, Joshua," he yelled. "Inside."

Well, that had already crossed my mind. If I could get in close, Baltazar's arms would be cramped and he wouldn't be able to throw any bombs. I could work his body and hopefully take some of the wind out of his sails. The problem was getting in there. I'd have to move into his range to get in close.

I tried to sucker him into overcommitting on a punch so that I could safely get in his face, but Baltazar knew what I was trying to do, and he wasn't falling for it. The other boxers hooted and made catcalls whenever I tried something and Baltazar didn't take the bait.

We were both dripping with sweat, but the bout was young. We were supposed to go three rounds, which wasn't nearly enough to tire Baltazar out. I was going to have to box him.

But it was better that way, I thought to myself. Why duck a challenge? I saw this as an opportunity to learn something.

I stopped evading him and stood my ground, resigned to taking a blow or two to get an inside position. So be it, I thought. If I told myself I could take a punch, then I could.

Baltazar threw a series of left jabs, setting me up for the hard right, but he broadcast his intentions with too many jabs, so when the straight right came, I was prepared to deflect it. What I wasn't prepared for was the left cross that came right after it. He caught me on the chin and turned my head around. I definitely felt that one, but it wasn't the hardest hit I'd ever taken. He threw another right, but I bent at the waist and swung my body under his arm, and as I came up, I threw an uppercut into his ribs that knocked him up onto his toes. I threw more uppercuts into his ribs and midsection. He tried to move away from me, but I stayed with him and kept punching. Unable to land the kind of punch that would dissuade me, he finally threw his arms around me and hugged me to stop the action. Hector yelled for us to break up.

We retreated to opposite corners. I bounced on my toes to stay loose. Jedidiah threw me a towel to wipe my face.

"You call that a fight?" someone shouted.

I looked across the gym, and there was Carlos Muñoz coming through the screen door, heading toward the ring. He had a cocky smirk on his face, and he was looking right at Baltazar. "How can you let a smaller man beat you like that? What are you, a pussy?" Carlos had lived in America for many years so his English was very good.

I don't think Baltazar realized that Carlos was talking to him until Carlos hauled himself up into the ring and got in his face. Carlos started throwing bare-fisted shadow punches that came uncomfortably close to Baltazar's face. Baltazar raised his gloves to protect himself, and Carlos just doubled his speed, throwing piston uppercuts, some of which connected. Baltazar took at least one to the gut that made him wince.

"You got to fight like a *man,*" Carlos grunted through clenched teeth as he punched. "Not like a pussy."

Baltazar pushed him away with his gloves, refusing to retaliate. I knew he was holding back, because he was capable of doing some real damage if he wanted to. But I wondered why he was being so restrained. Because this was Hector's brother? Or because Carlos Muñoz had a reputation for hurting people?

The armpits of Carlos's shirt were quickly soaked through with sweat, and he soon stopped the barrage of punches. He was breathing hard, having burned himself out, but he was also laughing. Hector laughed with him, and the two middleweights at the edge of the ring joined in halfheartedly. Carlos leaped over the ropes and landed on his feet, still laughing his head off. He clapped Hector on the back and led him out of the gym and on to the porch of the main house. If I understood his Spanish correctly, he was telling Hector he had some good news for him.

Hector called back over his shoulder that we should all work out by ourselves until he came back. Baltazar looked a little shaky. I asked him if he was OK, but he didn't answer me. I had a feeling that Carlos might have cracked one of Baltazar's ribs or maybe done something worse. All the boxers dispersed, each one doing something different—heavy bag, speed bag, free weights, shadow boxing. The day passed, but Baltazar and I never got around to finishing our bout.

For the next two days Jedidiah and I tried our best to find out more about Carlos Muñoz's habits, but the man remained frustratingly elusive. He'd stop by the gym for short visits, and one morning when we went out jogging, we saw his car at his mother's house again. But whenever we drove into the village in the evening to have a beer at the cantina, he was never at his mother's place. Same thing when we checked after dark on our way back to the camp. Obviously if we couldn't pinpoint him, we wouldn't be able to get him alone or take him by surprise.

But then a possibility presented itself. On the morning of our fourth day at the camp, all the boxers were in the gym working out. I was in the corner where the free weights were set up, spotting Jedidiah as he worked on his bench presses. Hector breezed in with a big grin on his face and clapped his hands loudly to get our attention. Jedidiah hung up the heavy barbell and sat up.

Hector started speaking in Spanish, then repeated himself in English. "Tomorrow big party," he said, looking toward Jedidiah and me. "At my mother's house. Food, girls, beer. Everybody come."

I caught Jedidiah's eye. An invitation to the mother's house—what could be better? With girls and beer on the menu, there was a good chance Carlos would be there, too.

"*Gracias,*" I called out to Hector. "We'll be there. What time?"

"One o'clock," Hector said, holding up a finger. "Big party. All day, all night."

I nodded and grinned, feigning enthusiasm. "All right!"

"You bring your dancing shoes?" Jedidiah muttered to me.

"Hell, yes," I said. "I'm a party guy. I thought you knew that."

"Oh, yeah. I *always* knew that," he said with a sly grin.

Roberto was working on the speed bag nearby. I noticed that as soon as Hector turned around and went back outside, Roberto put on a sour face.

I went over to him. "Something wrong?" I asked.

He wouldn't look at me. "Bad people," he grumbled as he pummeled the speed bag. "Very bad. Tomorrow I stay here."

I wished I spoke better Spanish or he understood more English so that I could find out more about these "bad people."

The next morning Jedidiah and I got up early to do our roadwork. We jogged into town and took the road up into the hills that overlooked the residential section where Carlos's mother lived. We found a path off the road that led to a shaded clearing where the morning light filtered through the overhanging branches and vines. It was enclosed, tranquil, and secluded. Looking out across the hilltops, we got a different perspective on the landscape. It was the perfect spot for our spiritual prep.

I had brought along two crystals and a few sticks of incense, which I lit and stuck into the moist soil. I handed Jedidiah one of the crystals, and we sat down on a log in the shade. We stared out at the view in silence for a while, tracing the facets of the crystals with our fingers, absorbing their power. We said nothing. Jedidiah and I are sufficiently evolved not to need words to put us in sync. Our spirits can harmonize without the distraction and confusion of talk.

Time became meaningless. After a while we began to feel recharged and renewed. Gradually we came out of our silence and started to discuss a strategy, planning out how we would take Carlos and how we would escape afterward. After we'd covered all the necessities, we became quiet again, releasing ourselves back into the meditative state.

As midmorning approached, the day began to heat up and the humidity in the jungle rose. I focused my eyes on my crystal, studying the light beaming through it. We meditated like this until the incense sticks burned themselves out. Without a word Jedidiah handed his crystal back to me, and I put them both in my pocket. We stood up and headed back for the camp. We were now ready for what had to be done.

Back at the camp, we showered and put on our tropical Sunday best—khaki pants and Hawaiian shirts. The loose-fitting shirts with their distracting floral patterns hid the guns we were carrying in our waistbands—Glock 9s. In a knapsack I would be carrying two .45s and extra clips for all the weapons.

We packed the rest of our essentials into one plastic garbage bag and stowed it under the seat in the Jeep. It would look too suspicious if we packed our duffels and left them in our vehicle. We were just going to have to sacrifice the rest of our clothes and our shaving kits.

We arrived at Carlos's mother's house at around one-thirty. Eight cars were parked in the long driveway. The black Firebird was the first one in, penned in by all the other cars. I parked the Jeep in the driveway but on the lawn side so that I could cut across if other cars parked behind us.

We followed the music and walked around to the back of the house. Tables and chairs had been set up in the backyard, but no one was out there because of the midday sun. A boom box on one of the tables blared salsa music. Everyone was inside on the screened-in back porch.

We mounted the steps, and I opened the screen door, smiling awkwardly at all the strange faces. It was a mixed crowd, six women and four men. They seemed friendly, but I didn't recognize any of them except Baltazar, who was sitting on a wicker sofa with a plate of food balanced on his lap as he gnawed on a pork rib.

"Come in, come in," he said, licking his greasy fingers. He nodded at a long table loaded down with food. "Help yourselves," he said.

A stout woman in her seventies with a deeply lined face and blue-black dyed hair emerged from the doorway that led into the house. This had to be Carlos and Hector's mother—she had Hector's sleepy eyes and egg-shaped face. Mrs. Muñoz spoke to Jedidiah and me in raspy Spanish, snatching up paper plates and handing them to us. I didn't have to understand the words to know that she was encouraging us to eat, eat.

"The beer is inside," Baltazar said with his mouth full. "In the kitchen."

I gestured to Mrs. Muñoz that we'd like to get a drink first, and she eagerly showed us the way. We had to pass through the living room to get to the kitchen, and there was our man, splayed out on the sofa. Carlos was surrounded by an entourage that hung on his every word. The group included Hector, the two middleweights from the camp, and two rough-looking men I hadn't seen before. Four women were cuddling up to Carlos and his friends, very young women. Carlos had his arm around a peroxide blonde who barely looked legal. Brown beer bottles and Coke cans littered the floor, and a half-gallon of dark rum sat on the coffee table. The unmistakable aroma of marijuana was in the air. A colorful ceramic bowl full of it was sitting on the coffee table next to the rum bottle, there for the taking.

Jedidiah and I waved our greetings to the living-room party and headed off to the kitchen to fetch some beer. We exchanged glances as

Mrs. Muñoz opened the refrigerator and handed us two bottles. As we passed through the living room on our way out to the porch, I flashed my awkward party smile again and caught a glimpse of Carlos's face as he tracked us with his eyes. His expression was bleary.

When we got back to the porch, we filled two plates to make Mrs. Muñoz happy. The food was very enticing, but I had no intention of eating or drinking much. I had to stay sharp. Since it was pretty crowded on the porch, and it was clear that not everyone was welcome in the living room, we took our plates outside and found a table in the shade.

"So what do you think?" I said to Jedidiah as I tried the black beans and rice.

"One of those two ugly characters in the living room is carrying," he said.

"I didn't see that."

"It's an automatic. He's got it in a belt clip on his right side."

"How about the other one?"

"I didn't see anything on him, but I didn't really get a good look."

"I don't think Carlos is carrying," I said. "But he's got a lot of muscle in there."

"You think they'd get in the way?"

"They look pretty loyal."

"Yeah, I guess you're right," Jedidiah said.

"Why don't we just wait awhile and let the weed do its job? They're pretty fucked up right now. Give 'em a couple of hours and they'll be on the floor."

"On top of those young girls?"

"Not if we time it right."

"We should try," Jedidiah said. "We should definitely try."

I agreed wholeheartedly.

By two-thirty more people had arrived and the party was cooking. As the sun started to set, the tall trees provided a little more shade, and the party moved outside where there was room to dance. All except Carlos's private party, that is. They stayed in the living room. Jedidiah and I worked it out so that one of us went into the kitchen for a fresh beer every half-hour or so. We didn't drink them, of course; we just wanted to keep tabs on Carlos and his buddies.

I was sitting at a folding table, watching Baltazar do some wild gyrations with a hot little brunette who was about a third of his size, when Jedidiah came out with his third beer. "Anything new in there?" I asked.

He sat down next to me and pretended to take a sip from the bottle. "Some of them are nodding off—the boxers and one of the two ugly guys. The one with the gun is still hanging in there, though, and Hector looks wide awake. I don't think he's been smoking."

"What about Carlos?"

Jedidiah frowned. "He's practically on top of that little blonde now. Her dress is on the floor, and she's sitting there in her slip."

I let out a slow breath as I thought about it for a few seconds. The bulk of the party was out here, away from the living room. Even Mrs. Muñoz was out here. I had a feeling she'd definitely get in the way if she saw us trying to arrest her son.

I thought about waiting a little longer in the hope that they'd all pass out and we could just carry Carlos unconscious to the Jeep. But what if they stopped smoking and started to sober up? That was always a possibility.

And what if they moved out of the living room? Strategically, that was a better place for us to make our move. We could whisk him out the front door and across the lawn to the Jeep. If he moved outside, we'd have to get him through the crowd, which could present all kinds of problems, and I didn't want to see any innocent bystanders getting hurt.

"Let's do it now," I said to Jedidiah. "You keep your eye on the two ugly ones. Soon as I get Carlos in cuffs, we'll take him out the front door."

Jedidiah nodded and started to stand up. He went back inside and pretended to be perusing the food table. Two minutes later I went in and joined him. We were the only ones on the porch. Outside, the music was hot, more than half the people dancing. I went down on one knee as if I were tying my shoe and pulled out my Glock. Jedidiah did the same, but he also went into my backpack, which I'd kept with me, and pulled out one of the .45s.

"Joshua! Jedidiah! Come and dance." Baltazar was calling to us from outside.

I raised a finger, holding my gun behind my leg. "One minute. Gotta find the little boy's room."

"OK, hurry up," he called back.

"Be right with you," I said, then turned toward the living-room doorway. I looked at Jedidiah, and he gave me a nod. The time had come.

We stepped into the living room. The scene looked like a Chinatown opium den, limp bodies sprawled out everywhere. Even Hector, who I'd thought didn't smoke dope, looked pretty spacey. Maybe he'd gotten a contact high, or maybe it was the rum.

One of the rough-looking dudes was in dreamland with his head tipped back and his eyes closed. The one with the gun was awake but just barely. He was hunched over with his elbows on his knees, watching Carlos as he tried to maul the blonde. Fortunately, Carlos was so impaired he couldn't do much harm. He had his big paw on the girl's breast, but he was more like a groggy old lion holding his prey down so that she wouldn't get away than some young stud who could do anything about it. The girl didn't look comfortable with this arrangement, but she was too high to do anything for herself.

None of them paid much attention to us when we came in, because people had been going in and out of the kitchen all afternoon. I moved directly to the man with the gun and pulled his weapon out of the holster. At the same time Jedidiah showed his weapons. He stood in the center of the room where he could cover everyone. The man in front of me didn't realize right away that I had his gun. When he did, he slapped his empty holster and sat up straight. It was only then that I noticed the badge pinned to his khaki shirt. He was the local sheriff or whatever they called them out there.

A flash of anger ran through me. This guy was a law enforcement officer and here he was smoking weed with the bad guys. No wonder that rape charge against Carlos had gone nowhere.

"Wake up, Carlos," I said, raising my voice. "Sit up."

He turned his head and blinked at me. The blonde curled her lip and made a face at me.

"Get up, Carlos. You're under arrest."

"No, no, no," Andy of Mayberry slurred. "I make arrest here." He started to stand up, but I pushed him back down into his seat.

I made sure he saw my Glock. "Don't talk. This is none of your business."

His eyes popped out of his head. He sat up very straight and pursed his lips into a frown.

"Up, Carlos." I reached over, grabbed a fistful of his shirt, and hauled him off the couch. He toppled onto the floor, knocking over bottles and cans. The fall woke him up. He started cursing in Spanish, flailing his arms and legs violently. I pulled out my taser, put it to his shoulder, and zapped him. Instantly his body stiffened with pain and he was unable to fight.

I rolled him over and patted him down. He had a butterfly knife in his back pocket, which I removed and put in my own pocket. He was growling and moaning, but he didn't have enough energy to resist. I pulled out a pair of handcuffs and cuffed him behind his back, then tried to get him to stand up. This was the hard part. He could barely get to his knees.

"No! No!" Hector was reaching out to his brother from where he sat. "What you do with my brother?"

Jedidiah aimed one of his guns directly in Hector's face to settle him down. We didn't want any trouble from him. He'd been decent to us, and we appreciated that. It would be a shame if we had to humiliate him with restraints so that we could finish our job.

Carlos's young blonde was draped over the couch like a rag doll, marking the spot where he'd been. She was too wasted to move. The three other girls in the room didn't look much better. I wanted to tell them to get the hell out of there, but I knew it wouldn't do any good. Even if we carried them out, I had a feeling they'd come right back. Over the years I've found that you really can't take care of another person. The only person you can take care is you. These girls had to figure that out for themselves.

Hector kept pleading with us to leave his brother alone, but he wasn't moving off his chair. The rest of the people in the room didn't seem to understand what was going on. Carlos was flat on the floor, unable to move. I shoved the coffee table aside and quickly rolled him up in the rug. I took the head end and Jedidiah grabbed a fistful of rug on the other end, keeping his gun hand free. Together we whisked Carlos out the door and carried him to the Jeep. He tried to fight us, but he was in no shape to do anything. I opened up the back of the Jeep and forced him in. It was a tight fit, and I had to use the back door to encourage him to find a comfortable position.

I got behind the wheel then, and Jedidiah hopped in on the passenger side. Carlos's mother poked her head out the front door and shook her fist at us as I made a U-turn across her lawn. I headed directly for the village and the road that would take us back to San Juan. I was all set to make this a cross-country road rally if I had to, but surprisingly, no one chased after us. Either they were too high to get it together or Carlos was such a bastard, nobody cared.

Carlos sobered up quite a bit on the bumpy ride back to San Juan and managed to wiggle his head out of the rug. At one point he got huffy and started yelling and kicking, demanding that we set him loose or else he'd kill us. We didn't yell back at him since that isn't the Seeker way. We didn't have to. I simply pulled out his butterfly knife and explained that if he made any more trouble, I would hand the knife over to the national police and tell them that it had been used in the commission of a rape in his village. Carlos got very quiet after that.

Eduardo met us in a parking lot at the airport, where I gave him the butterfly knife and the keys to the Jeep so he could return it. "Hold on to the knife," I told him, "just in case we need leverage." I didn't have to explain any more than that. Eduardo knew exactly what I meant. I thanked him for his help and promised to wire him his share of our fee as soon as I got paid.

"Fine," he said. "Whenever." I'd worked with Eduardo many times before, so he knew I was good for it.

Before we went into the terminal, we freed Carlos from the rug. I switched his handcuffs to the front and let him hold my jacket to hide them. When I bought our tickets back to Newark International, I asked to speak to the pilot about a "special circumstance" and informed him that Jedidiah and I would be escorting a fugitive from justice back to the United States. He asked about our guns, and I showed him that we had locked cases for them, which we would stow in the baggage compartment. I assured him that we would not disturb the other passengers. The pilot asked that Carlos keep the jacket over the cuffs until we were off the plane in Newark, which is standard procedure for transporting prisoners on commercial flights.

When the pilot was satisfied that we had everything under control, he told me that he'd put us in the last row at the back of the plane. We would board first, before any of the other passengers were allowed on board. This is also standard procedure. Federal agents transport prisoners this way all the time. (Next time you're on a plane, particularly on a long-distance flight, check the back row and see who's sitting there. If one of the passengers has an article of clothing in his lap covering his hands, it's a good bet that he's a prisoner in transit.)

We touched down in Newark just before 10 P.M. During the flight, Carlos was so depressed he was almost catatonic, but as soon as we got into the terminal he started getting mouthy again, so we whisked him out of there as fast as we could. While Jedidiah went to get his car out of the long-term parking lot, I baby-sat Carlos at the curb. Ten minutes later Jedidiah picked us up, and we took Carlos directly to the Middlesex County lockup in New Brunswick. By eleven-thirty, Carlos Muñoz was out of our custody and back in the system. Four months later he was tried and convicted for the attempted murder of a police officer. He was sentenced to fifteen years minimum before he could be eligible for parole.

International bounty hunting involves crossing borders—physical, legal, sometimes moral. Extradition laws are often ineffective when fugitives move into foreign jurisdictions. There are always complications: formal requests have to be made, paperwork has to be filed, fugitives don't always stay in one place, and local law enforcement doesn't always make apprehending another country's felons its top priority. For these reasons it's often more practical to call the Seekers, who can cut through red tape with minimal disruption. Police agencies are often rendered useless by their own rules and bureaucracies, but the Seekers have no such restrictions. When a border must be crossed to catch a fugitive, we will cross it.

Epilogue

The Seekers currently concentrate on cases that carry higher bonds, typically in the $100,000 to $250,000 range. These are fugitives who have been charged with serious crimes, like armed robbery, kidnapping, high-level drug dealing, and murder. Tracking down this kind of individual is often more difficult and takes more time, but the monetary reward is greater. However, a low bond will not prevent us from taking on cases that we deem worthy of our attention, such as fugitives who have been charged with rape or child molestation. Even though our expertise now enables us to take on more lucrative cases, we will never overlook cases that cannot be ignored.

My personal evolution continues. I look back on the stages of my growth to assess where I am now and where I must go. I was brought up in Elizabeth, New Jersey, and left at the age of eighteen and a half. I went out West to seek my fortune and found unexpected lessons along the way. My time on the Bering Sea seasoned me. After working on the fishing fleet, I lived for a time in Seattle and settled into the good life. I was young, single, and I had money in my pocket. I considered staying there, but something drew me back home to New Jersey. Through my reading and my observations about life, I felt that something else was steering my ship, something greater than me, and it was taking me beyond the madness of the mundane.

When I moved back to Elizabeth, I didn't recognize my neighborhood. It was drastically different. New ethnic groups had moved in, and the vibe had changed. Crime was no longer committed behind closed doors and under cover of darkness. Drug dealers worked their corners in broad daylight. Murder had become all too common. Nine of my friends had died in violent circumstances during the time I was away. I knew that something had to be done.

I formed the Seekers, and we strove to evolve as fast as we could. I found a good woman and gave her my love, then expanded that love when my two sons were born. We are all doing well, and I'm happy, but just hanging on and being content is not enough. My evolution must continue. If I ever hope to become a true stellar man, I cannot rest. For civilization to survive, people must have examples to show them how to live. I must now concentrate on being an example to others.

The Seekers were once hired to find a young man who had been charged with running a drug ring in the New York City area. He'd skipped out on a sizable bail bond and was on the run. The young man happened to be the son of a prominent minister who had a large congregation in northern New Jersey. I decided to pay a visit to the minister to see if he knew anything about his son's whereabouts.

The minister's church was a massive structure with high vaulted ceilings and a huge carved oak pulpit. When I knocked on the office door, I was greeted by one of the minister's assistants, a friendly woman who was clearly devoted to the minister. As she led me down a hallway to his inner office, she told me about the Mercedes-Benz the congregation had just purchased for him. She confided that it was bigger and much more expensive than the Mercedes that the congregation of the rival church across town had bought for their minister.

The minister was on the phone when I was shown into his office. He was in his early sixties, round-faced and gray-haired with the self-satisfied calm of a man who truly believes that he walks in the Lord's light. A mail-order clothing catalog was open on his desk; he was apparently ordering something over the phone. The dark blue suit he was wearing was well tailored and looked expensive. His shirt was pure white and starched to perfection; his tie was a muted gold color. Nearly two dozen framed degrees, diplomas, and certificates decorated his walls in addition to photographs of him posed with politicians and civil rights leaders. I thought it was odd, though, that the bookcase contained more framed photographs and knickknacks than books.

When the minister finally got off the phone, he leaned back in his leather chair and pressed his palms together. "Have a seat, Mr. Armstrong," he said with a smile. "I understand that you're looking for my son."

I explained that I had been hired by the bondsmen who had put up the money for his son's release on bail. "Do you have any idea where your son might be?" I asked.

The minister's benevolent smile didn't waver. "You know, Mr. Armstrong, I have a very strong feeling that this whole business with my son is a great misunderstanding. I fear that the police may have grossly exaggerated my son's participation in the alleged criminal activities. I'm not saying that my son isn't acquainted with people of that ilk, but I sincerely do not believe that he is a criminal himself."

"That's for a jury to decide," I said. "The fact remains that he skipped out on a bail bond. He reneged on a contract."

"The courts of man are subservient to He who judges us all, and ultimately my son need only face the judgment of our Lord Jesus." The minister lifted his eyes toward the heavens.

"Maybe so," I said, "but—"

The minister interrupted me. "I was led to believe that you were a spiritual man, Mr. Armstrong. A truly spiritual man would understand what I'm talking about. Perhaps you need further guidance in the matters of your own soul."

"I prefer to do my own research in the matters of my soul," I said. He was trying to steer me off the topic of his son.

"Your *own* research?" he said skeptically. "I don't understand." His patronizing tone was insulting. His attitude was clear as day: How could a lowdown street thug who calls himself a bounty hunter dare to discuss spirituality with a respected minister of the church?

"Reverend, when was the last time you saw your son—"

"No, no, no," he blurted out. "I can't let this lie. I want to know about your so-called research. Is this research done under the auspices of your church?"

I could see where this was going. "I don't belong to a church," I said. "I don't believe in organized religion."

"Is that a fact?" The minister leaned forward and looked me in the eye. "Without guidance, how can you know if you're walking the correct path? What *kind* of research can you possibly be conducting? How would a person without a shepherd know where to begin?"

I happened to have my laptop computer with me. Instead of answering the minister, I took it out of my backpack and set it down on his desk. Opening up a directory, I turned it around so that the minister could see the screen.

"This is a list of books, chapters of books, articles, and scholarly papers that I've downloaded onto the hard drive. They cover religion, spirituality, history, and the mind sciences. This is just some of my research." I held my finger on the arrow key and scrolled down through the whole list. There were more than 300 items on it, considerably more literature than he had on his bookshelves.

The minister puffed out his cheeks and leaned back in his chair as if to get out of the tainted glow of my computer. "This is all very impressive on the surface, but—"

I interrupted him. "May I ask *you* a question?" I said. "With all due respect, sir, what makes *you* qualified to lead a congregation? What makes any man qualified to lead other men?"

The minister's eyes bulged out. His benevolent smile was gone; his mouth had turned into a gruesome fish pout. He reached over to his intercom and pressed the buzzer, his hand shaking with anger. The woman who had showed me in instantly appeared at the door.

"Please show Mr. Armstrong out," the minister said to her.

"I don't think we're through yet," I said to him. "There's a lot more we can discuss if you're interested."

"We're through," he said emphatically. "And don't come back."

I didn't argue. Instead I just packed up my laptop and left. The Seekers eventually found the minister's son through our own network of sources, but my little chat with the minister dramatically reinforced something that I already knew to be true. Church doors are always open to whoever wants to enter, but they're only open to those who are willing to be sheep. The service of God is really service to those self-proclaimed holy men who hold the franchise. Accumulating material grandeur is the goal, not the improvement of the people's lives. Independent thought is discouraged. Raising the individual up is not part of the plan; keeping the flock docile, distracted, and deluded is what it's all about.

I will never forget that meeting with the minister because for me it symbolized all that's wrong with organized religion. The Seekers have studied this problem for many years, and we are now in the process of establishing Earth Church. Before you get the wrong impression, I have no intention of becoming a preacher myself or building a lavish house of worship similar to that minister's. Earth Church will simply be a place where mental, physical, and spiritual progress is nourished and encouraged. It will have a main hall, not unlike a town hall, where lectures and discussion groups will take place, where ideas will be presented and debated, where people will learn how to think and reason. All kinds of topics will be aired in the hall, be they intellectual quandaries, questions of spiritual development, or the practical matters of everyday life like health, nutrition, and personal finances. The Earth Church will be a center for knowledge, well-being, and self-improvement. My hope is that the Earth Church will give people everything they need to survive, prosper, and evolve.

The Seekers will continue to hunt for fugitives but only as a means to fund our research. The real hunt is for wisdom, knowledge, and understanding. I constantly explore the raw vibe of reality, always pondering my next evolutionary process. Evolution eludes 90 percent of the population, but those who do evolve continually evolve and progress. I am where I am today because I have striven to evolve. I explore my past so that I may establish a future. My Black (African) Phoenix is burning bright now, about to burn out and become ashes. But the Phoenix always rises again from its own destruction. What form mine will take in the future is yet to be seen. Until I find my oasis, the hunt for both fugitives and knowledge will continue. I can only wait and see where the journey takes me. For as it says in the "Desiderata," "All things unfold as they should."